D0872050

SAINTSBURY

Before we had a name, we had a friendship (we met in a class on the science of brewing at UC Davis, where we studied winemaking) and a dream (a winery devoted to Pinot Noir and Chardonnay). In 1982, our first vintage was in barrel and soon needed to be bottled and labeled. We still needed a name but were consumed with finding vineyards to supply the next vintage, finding a winemaking home, working on a sales and marketing strategy, and raising money to finance our venture. Out of the blue, a friend suggested that we name the winery in honor of George Saintsbury.

We had both read *Notes on a Cellar-Book* and enjoyed the quirky, personal journey with George (as we like to refer to him). After about an afternoon of consideration (no focus groups for us!), we set our designer to work on a label. And Saintsbury (the winery) was born. Since then we have had the good fortune to meet some of George's English and Canadian descendants and to have collected most of the many editions of *Notes* and other volumes of George's prodigious scholarship. We have helped underwrite several symposia at the University of Edinburgh, where Saintsbury was Regius Professsor of English Literature. We have even been very kindly received by members of the Saintsbury Club in London, keepers of the flame since 1932.

We were very pleased to learn that leading wine scholar Thomas Pinney, emeritus professor of English at Pomona College and author of *A History of Wine in America*, had embarked on a long-overdue annotation of *Notes*, and were determined to support this worthy effort. Now that the University of California Press has published *Notes on a Cellar-Book* with Professor Pinney's own illuminating notes, no more must the casual reader despair at a quote in Attic Greek or an obscure (to the unwashed) reference to a long-forgotten English novel. Read on, and please heed George's admonition in the frontispiece of the first edition and every subsequent one—"*Trinc!*"

—David Graves and Richard Ward

The publisher gratefully acknowledges the generous contribution to this book provided by the owners and founders of Saintsbury, a California winery named in honor of George Saintsbury.

NOTES ON A CELLAR-BOOK

George Saintsbury, 1923, by Sir William Nicholson. Courtesy the Warden and Fellows of Merton College, Oxford.

NOTES ON A CELLAR-BOOK

GEORGE SAINTSBURY
EDITED AND ANNOTATED BY THOMAS PINNEY

UNIVERSITY OF CALIFORNIA PRESS
BERKELEY LOS ANGELES LONDON

University of California Press, one of the most distinguished
university presses in the United States, enriches lives around
the world by advancing scholarship in the humanities, social
sciences, and natural sciences. Its activities are supported by
the UC Press Foundation and by philanthropic contributions
from individuals and institutions. For more information, visit
www.ucpress.edu.

University of California Press
Berkeley and Los Angeles, California

University of California Press, Ltd.
London, England

Library of Congress Cataloging-in-Publication Data

Saintsbury, George, 1845–1933.
    Notes on a cellar-book / George Saintsbury ; edited
and annotated by Thomas Pinney.
      p. cm.
    Includes bibliographical references and index.
    ISBN: 978-0-520-25352-0 (cloth : alk. paper)
    1. Wine and wine making. 2. Liquors.
3.   Menus. I. Pinney, Thomas. II. Title.
PN6237.S25 2008
641.2'1—dc22   2007046969

Manufactured in the United States of America

17 16 15 14 13 12 11 10 09 08
10 9 8 7 6 5 4 3 2 1

The paper used in this publication meets the minimum
requirements of ANSI/NISO Z39.48–1992 (R 1997)
(Permanence of Paper).

CONTENTS

ILLUSTRATIONS

INTRODUCTION

George Saintsbury and Notes on a Cellar-Book

George Edward Bateman Saintsbury (1845–1933), to give him his resonant full name, wrote only one book devoted to wine (or, more accurately, to drink). That book, however, the celebrated *Notes on a Cellar-Book*, published in 1920, puts him at the head of the long list of those who, in the near-century since then, have written about wine not as technicians or professionals but as *amateurs*, in the proper sense of that word.

A BRIEF SKETCH OF SAINTSBURY'S CAREER

Saintsbury's extraordinarily productive life was divided between teaching and journalism. He was born in Southampton, England, but the family soon moved to London, where his father was secretary of the East India and China Association. George's father died when George was only fourteen, but not before imparting to his son "some knowledge of good wine and an unlimited horror of bad." Saintsbury went up to Merton College, Oxford, in 1863, and thoroughly enjoyed his stay there. He had already, as a schoolboy, showed a passionate love of literature, and Oxford suited his scholarly and literary tastes. Saintsbury's appetite for books was as powerful as his thirst for drink, and it is difficult even to suggest what quantities of reading he achieved in his lifetime. Edmund Wilson thought Saintsbury probably came as near as anyone ever has to reading the whole of English literature, and of course that says nothing about his reading in classic and continental literatures.

To his great disappointment, Saintsbury failed to win an Oxford fellowship; it was a deep satisfaction to him in his later years when he was, on account of his many accomplishments, made an honorary fellow of Merton. At the time of his graduation, however, he was compelled to look for work. After a brief episode of teaching in Manchester, he went on to Elizabeth College on the Isle of Guernsey and spent the next six years there as a classics master. Guernsey, as Saintsbury remembered it, was a propitious place for a lover of wine and good drink. Wine was cheap and in good supply, the society was attractive, and Saintsbury was therefore able to advance his education in drink begun by his father and continued to good effect during his Oxford years. In 1874 Saintsbury left Guernsey to be headmaster of a new, and short-lived, boarding school in Elgin, Scotland. Saintsbury seems to have prospered as a student of wine wherever he went. Though the new school did not work out, and though he found himself at the end of two years financially worse off than he had been to begin with, he always fondly remembered Elgin as the place where he "laid the foundation of a real cellar."

At the end of the Elgin venture, in 1876, Saintsbury determined to make his living by his pen and went off to London. There followed twenty years of strenuous, unremitting work as a journalist. For most of that time, he was assistant editor of the *Saturday Review*, a respected weekly, but that bald statement hardly begins to suggest the scope and variety of his work. The Victorian age, whatever else it might have been, was certainly an age of giants, so far as the capacity for productive work was concerned. Besides his editorial work, Saintsbury wrote regularly for the *Saturday Review* on politics, literature, economics, crime, and other topics of the day; he contributed to many other periodicals as well—the *Pall Mall Gazette*, the *St. James's Gazette*, the *Athenaeum*, the *Examiner*, and so on—and he continued the critical and historical work that had given him his entrée into London journalism in the first place. He produced a *Primer of French Literature* in 1880, a *Short History of French Literature* in 1882, a *History of Elizabethan Literature* in 1887, a life of Dryden in 1881, a life of Marlborough in 1885, and a thicket of articles for the *Encyclopaedia Britannica*. All this was, of course, only the tip of an iceberg whose great mass lay concealed beneath the surface of the sea of anonymous journalism that flooded over the Victorian era. Saintsbury later estimated that his anonymous articles from this period would have filled a hundred volumes, and this is probably a modest estimate.

Saintsbury already had a wife and children by 1876, when he began his work as a London journalist, and for the first decade of that career he lived with his family in Kensington. In 1882 he bought a new house in Kensington, and this was the place where he created his first proper cellar and where he began to keep the cellar book that forms the ostensible basis of *Notes on a Cellar-Book*. That book, by the way, is still extant, though not, at the moment, accessible. It was sold at auction at Christie's in the 1950s for £300 and then auctioned again in 1977, when it went for £1,550.

In 1895 Saintsbury, who had by now acquired a formidable reputation as reviewer, critic, editor, and scholar, was the successful candidate for appointment as the Regius Professor of English Literature at the University of Edinburgh. For the next twenty years, until his retirement in 1915, he carried out the duties of his professorship and continued his literary work. During these years he added such trifling items to the list of his publications as the two volumes of *A History of Criticism and Literary Taste in Europe*, the three volumes of *A History of English Prosody*, a *History of English Criticism*, a *History of English Prose Rhythm*, and *The English Novel*. These are titles selected from among those books that Saintsbury wrote himself during the years of his professorship; according to one reckoning, there are another 450 volumes in which Saintsbury "had a hand as editor, anthologist, introducer, or contributor."

With this vast accumulation of reading and writing behind him, Saintsbury, at the age of seventy, retired and took up residence in an apartment in the Royal Crescent, Bath, where he lived to the end of his days, without a cellar but not without drink in steady and various supply. He was not quite done with his scholarly tasks. He published *The Peace of the Augustans*, a study of eighteenth-century English literature, in 1916, and *A History of the French Novel* in two volumes, 1917–19. That was his last work of original scholarship, but the habit of publication was too strong upon Saintsbury for him ever to subside into complete silence. He published a series of *Scrap Books*—detached notes and remarks on whatever caught his interest—in the 1920s, and, of course, he wrote the *Notes on a Cellar-Book*.

One may put down a few remarks on Saintsbury's character and reputation here. He was, in politics, an unreconstructed Tory, unsympathetic to democratic ideas and hostile to almost every one of the many reforms that marked the age he lived in. He would not move in the direction in which everyone else was headed, and as his aversion to the tendencies of the time became more and more pronounced he began to exaggerate, with no doubt some pleasure in the exaggeration, his pose as the archetypal Tory. This made him unattractive to some people. That excellent writer Cyril Ray, for example, whose socialist politics put him at the opposite pole from Saintsbury's, thoroughly disliked him—he was, to Ray, a "bully," and a bully who did not really know what he was talking about.

People have shown mixed responses to another of Saintsbury's most striking characteristics, his gourmandise in literature as well as in matters of the table. He had read *so much*, and he had written *so much:* how could there be any genuine element of discrimination, any true refinement of understanding and judgment, in one who dealt in such quantities? And so, too, regarding Saintsbury's pleasure in food and drink. Look at the menus appended to *Notes on a Cellar-Book:* how heavy, not to say gargantuan, they are! Dinners of eight courses and more, accompanied by an equal number of wines white and red, still and sparkling, sweet and dry. Of course the Victorians liked abundance, even profusion, in all material things, but there is a point beyond which profusion becomes mere coarse excess. What can one say of a man who consumed a new French novel every day before breakfast, as Saintsbury is alleged to have done? And what can one say of a man who says, as Saintsbury certainly did say, that "a bottle of hock at dinner and a bottle of claret after it [is] a decent and moderate allowance"? The only thing that occurs to me to say is that for Saintsbury such quantities were not excessive. He had a powerful appetite for the things he loved, and that appetite was never dulled. To delicate and fastidious tastes, such an appetite may seem coarse and undiscriminating; but there are others who may find it splendid, even heroic. The capacity to enjoy is, after all, a virtue. Saintsbury certainly had it, and in superlative measure.

A final remarkable thing about Saintsbury should be noted. He must have written literally tens of thousands of manuscript pages, containing millions of words, all of which had to be translated by a typesetter (and for much of Saintsbury's career, all typesetting was done by hand) into print—and yet his handwriting was practically unreadable, as the accompanying illustration from one of his letters shows. It staggers the imagination to think of all those wretched compositors straining to make sense of page after illegible page of Saintsbury's unending stream of manuscript. It is said, in at least a partial excuse of this terrible practice, that the thumb on Saintsbury's writing hand had been somehow damaged by an early illness.

THE HISTORY OF *NOTES ON A CELLAR-BOOK*

Saintsbury had long intended to write a substantial history of wine, but had postponed doing so while he held his professorship, and then had decided against attempting so ambitious a work in his retirement—"I was," he says simply, "getting too old for such a work." However, when the editor of a new journal called the *Piccadilly Review* asked Saintsbury for a series of articles on drink, he accepted the commission, since what was called for was not a formal history but only "certain notes and reminiscences on the subject." But the wish to rescue something from the unpublished history probably had an effect on Saintsbury's decision. The first installment of a series called "Notes on a Cellar Book" (without the hyphen) duly appeared in the *Piccadilly Review* on 23 October 1919; the second appeared on 13 November, and then the magazine expired.

Saintsbury, however, had already decided that his "Notes" were the stuff of a book and did not depend on magazine publication. On 15 November 1919, only two days after the second and last of his contributions had appeared in the *Piccadilly Review*, Saintsbury wrote to Sir Frederick Macmillan, the publisher, telling him

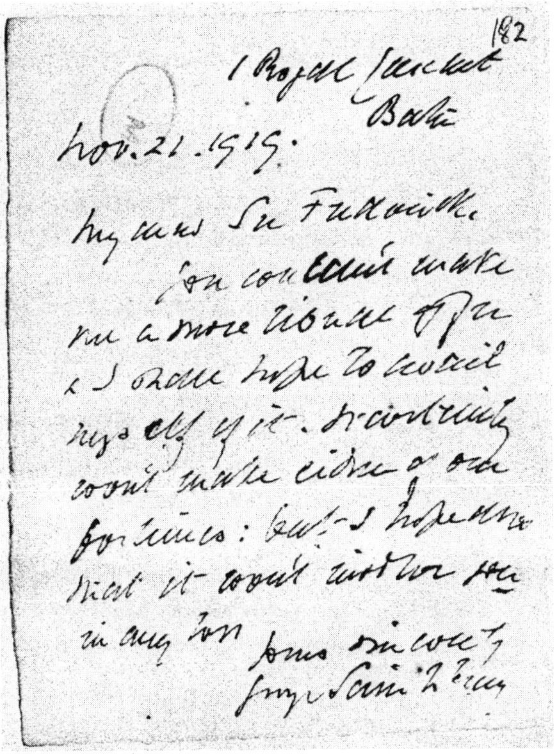

FIGURE I. Letter from Saintsbury to Sir Frederick Macmillan, 21 November 1919, accepting Macmillan's terms for publishing *Notes on a Cellar-Book*: compositors dreaded to work from his manuscript (Macmillan Papers, British Library).

that he, Saintsbury, had a "small" book on wine that was meant to "entertain people." "Would you care for the refusal of it?" he asked. Macmillan replied at once that

> we shall be very pleased to re-publish your articles *Notes on a Cellar-Book* in a little volume when they are completed. I am afraid that I cannot promise any likelihood of profit

from such a publication in view of the present cost of production, but you shall have half the profit that is earned if
there ever is any.

Saintsbury, for his part, thought this a "liberal offer" and went
on with the work. On 10 January 1920, he wrote to Sir Frederick to say that the manuscript was ready: "I reworked the unpublished articles from the liquidation of the *Piccadilly Review*, altered
them a little and compacted them a great deal. The thing is
crammed with stories and reminiscences, and may amuse people,
I think." With the swiftness that seems to have marked those pre-
electronic days, the manuscript was sent to the printers at the end
of January; by June a publication date was fixed, and the book
duly appeared in an edition of fifteen hundred copies at 7/6 on
2 July 1920.

Among those who might be expected to have taken an interest in such a thing, the book made an immediate hit. "A delightful book. . . . A little masterpiece"; "a book that will delight all
who love good wine and all who love good literature"; "rich in
flavour and bouquet"—such was the style of the reviews. A second printing followed in August, a third in November. Before
Saintsbury's death in 1933, *Notes on a Cellar-Book* had reached its
eighth printing.

Contemporary readers had no trouble estimating the book:
they saw it as Saintsbury did, as an agreeable mélange of notes
and comments from one man's (admittedly extensive) experience
of drink, intended to amuse rather than to instruct. As Saintsbury
had written to his publisher on offering the book, it was not to be
a thorough history but rather a "small" book, written to "entertain." In the years since its publication, however, a habit has grown
up of referring to the book as a depository of magisterial wisdom,

demanding reverence and obedience. Probably Saintsbury's formidable reputation as a scholar has infected notions about his book; and as with all books that last long enough, many people will have formed their ideas about it without actually reading it. If they *do* then get around to reading it, they are likely to be disappointed. Something like that seems to have happened in the case of Pamela Vandyke Price, for example, who writes:

> Many have ascribed an exaggerated importance to the *Cellar-Book* but it is only some personal jottings by an amiable, pompous don, useful as a source of anecdotes and opinions, but for nothing serious about wine.

Apart from the hostile phrase about "pompous don," Saintsbury himself would have found nothing to object to in this description. But to talk of "personal jottings" does not necessarily tell us much. It depends on who is doing the jotting.

WHAT, THEN, IS *NOTES ON A CELLAR-BOOK?*

In the first place, it is a very topical book. The Eighteenth Amendment to the U.S. Constitution had been ratified early in 1919, not long before Saintsbury began work on *Notes on a Cellar-Book;* a year later, the dark night of constitutional Prohibition descended upon the United States, just a week after Saintsbury finished his manuscript. If one keeps this in mind, the antiprohibitionist theme of the book comes out strongly, beginning with the very motto of the book—a loud and imperative *"Trinc!"* asserted on the title page in contradiction of the Dry Spirit's "thou shalt not drink." The archvillain of the book is the mean-spirited "Pussyfoot," the embodiment of the prohibitionist, without culture, without generosity, without the capacity for pleasure. Other obstacles to the enjoyment of sound, inexpensive drink come in for abuse—the restrictions of the Defense of the Realm Acts, the soaring taxes applied to drink—but none so violent as that directed to the hateful dishonesties of Pussyfoot, as Saintsbury held them to be.

Notes on a Cellar-Book is, as the title affirms, only a set of notes: it does not pretend to exhaust any one subject or to cover a prescribed range of territory. One should observe too, that Saintsbury kept to the magazine format that belonged to the original scheme of publication. Each short chapter, no matter what the subject, is more or less of the same length, an artificial disposition of things. The subject of liqueurs, in this arrangement, gets as much space as the subject of claret and burgundy combined, though Saintsbury can hardly have drunk equal quantities of them or have supposed that they were of equal importance in the traditions of drink.

Within these narrow limits Saintsbury nevertheless manages to touch on a great number and a great variety of things: a glance at the index (there was none in the original) shows a range from Ampurdam and Bucellas through Lagavulin and Picardan to Vöslauer, Walporzheimer, and Wedderburn. The book is sometimes described as though it were devoted to wine, but in fact it takes the whole world of alcoholic drink as its province, from small beer to absinthe and every point in between. The number of omissions, measured against what an encyclopedia of drink might contain, is no doubt large (there is, for example, no reference to Australian wine, though it had long been available in England, nor to Calvados). But measured against the conventions of nineteenth-century drinking in England, it is extraordinarily inclusive. Saintsbury liked to think of himself in this matter as a "minor Ulysses," eager to try everything that experience might offer.

This openness to variety and novelty is surely one of the most attractive things in the book. What he drank, he says, "pleased my senses, cheered my spirits, improved my moral and intellectual powers, besides enabling me to confer the same benefits on other people."

Saintsbury was always prepared to approve if he could, and in this he differs strikingly from the narrow conventionality that seems to have marked the cultivated English drinker of his day, who stayed tamely within an approved circle of port, sherry, claret, burgundy, and hock. Even when it was a question of a "safe" wine, such as port, Saintsbury was eager for variety and experimentation. Instead of laying down a large supply of only a few vintages, he bought small parcels of many different wines from many different shippers. "The permutations and combinations of experiment were practically infinite, and always interesting in the trial, even if disappointing in the result." The wine merchant Ian Maxwell Campbell wrote that "more than once I have heard George Saintsbury criticized, with no little scorn, for the extensive, quasi-indiscriminate universality of his taste in the matter of drinks." This is a predictable but not necessarily correct judgment. Real discrimination need not mean that enjoyment is strictly confined to the few superlative instances of a thing: one may enjoy a wide variety of different things, as Saintsbury clearly did both in literature and in drink. But the purists, Saintsbury must often have found, did not understand. As he wrote with some feeling, in all criticism "not only the hardest thing to attain but also the hardest thing to get recognized when attained, is the appreciation of difference without insisting on superiority." And it can hardly be the case that a man who enjoyed Lafite, Latour, and Margaux but not Cheval Blanc, and who found Chambertin "coarse," was "indiscriminate."

All this is presented in directly personal terms, the account being of what actually lay in Saintsbury's cellar or of what he had enjoyed at some time or another in the course of his long life. It was his boast that he had never given "a second-hand opinion of any thing, or book, or person." Since the *Notes* grew directly from Saintsbury's own experience, they also show us many remembered moments from his private life. He had, as he said, "crammed" *Notes on a Cellar-Book* with "stories and reminiscences," and they are certainly among the attractions of the book. It is distinctly interesting to learn, for example, how the future Bishop of London was accustomed to drink absinthe in his Oxford lodgings, or how Father Stanton compounded a sherry cobbler.

A special interest of the book is in the many separate glimpses of Saintsbury himself, at all ages, that are scattered through the book in association with remembered drink. It was from his father that he had his first knowledge of wine, and though the elder Saintsbury died when his son was but fourteen, he left at least a cellar book with "quite respectable entries" and a memory of the "modest Marsala which used to suffice professional and city men." Or there is the anecdote about an aunt, his father's sister, who, being advised to take a little wine for her health's sake, and having to choose between a costly Richebourg and a "sound Pommard," chose the Richebourg, observing that "the best always *is* the best." Saintsbury records his pleasure in finding that one of his children had adopted an empty set of Champagne bottles in varied sizes as a plaything. "Beeswing" reminds him that he once "sought in vain for silk or samite of its colour to form part of a vesture for the lady of my house." Sparkling Moselle is associated with "Oxford in the time of fritillaries," and his remembered pleasure in wine reminds him of other good things, such as having "walked by oneself five hundred miles in twenty days" or having read *The Earthly Paradise* twenty times. There are many such moments, taking us by isolated flashes of recall through Oxford, the years in Guernsey, the life of a journalist in London, and his professorial life in Edinburgh.

One of the more recent episodes in Saintsbury's life is enshrined in the dedication of the book to "R. K.," that is, Rudyard Kipling. The two men had known each other briefly in London in the early 1890s but had then gone their separate ways. After the First World War, Kipling was frequently in Bath, to which Saintsbury had retired, and their renewed acquaintance soon turned into friendship. The failure that Saintsbury regrets in the dedication, that by some "cantrip of fortune" he had never been able to offer Kipling even a single bottle of wine, was redeemed later. In his autobiography Kipling says that, on one of his visits to Bath, Saintsbury produced for him a bottle of "real Tokay." Kipling tasted it and incautiously said that it reminded him of medicinal wine: Saintsbury "merely called me a blasphemer of the worst, but what he thought I do not care to think!" This, however, lies outside of *Notes on a Cellar-Book*.

Most readers can respond to the elements of variety and personal experience in the book. There are two much more problematic elements to be faced, however. The first is the dense literariness of the book. Saintsbury's reading is always obtruding itself, and since it may be safely said that none of his readers ever read as much as Saintsbury did, it is often hard to keep up with him. Take the first page of the first chapter, which bristles with references to Planché (contemporary and minor), Dante (medieval and major), Tennyson (contemporary and major), Horace (classical), and Dryden (seventeenth century and important if not major), a sequence developed by five quotations expressing contrasted views on the relation of past and present, the whole packed into two complex sentences. Nothing quite so formidable as this opening occurs again in the book, but the reader has been warned: books are as important as personal experience in what follows.

Indeed, for Saintsbury books were indistinguishable from personal experience.

As one who explored the world of words so extensively, Saintsbury exhibits a diction sometimes out of the ordinary; it is mannered, no doubt, but not at all surprising. He likes nonce words ("*bo*bolitionist") and, especially, words whose meanings are still half-hidden from most of us behind their learned origins: "supernacular," "compurgator," "morigerant," "subdolous," and the *Apeiron* that violates the law of the *Peras*.

Another consequence of Saintsbury's prodigious reading is his habit of isolating as quotations small phrases and turns of expression that I, for one, do not perceive as having any very distinct identity: "small quantity, many kinds," "the farmers of Aylesbury," "before the dear years," and "like a torch-light procession"—these, and many like them, were evidently in Saintsbury's eyes other men's property, and so they stand as quotations in the text. But where did they come from?

The other difficult element grows out of his bookishness. Saintsbury could not resist the ornamental device called allusion, that is, not naming a thing directly but evoking it by something associated with it or by some circumlocution—a way of identifying and yet concealing what is meant. Who was the "tenant of Amerongen"? What was "Freytag's best novel"? What were the "sacrilegious hands of Dr. Richardson"? What was that beach that "afforded neither golden cricket-ball nor coin-filled casket from the wreck of the *Carmilhan*"? Who was "poor Rosa Timmins's volunteer assistant"? And so on and on. Saintsbury was aware of his practice. "I have," he wrote, "received complaints, mild and other, of the frequency of my unexplained allusions. . . . I can only plead that I follow the Golden Rule. Nothing pleases *me* so much as an allusion that I understand—except one that I don't and have to hunt up." But what was pleasure to Saintsbury may be pain to those who toil after him. How many of us can construe, without help, such a passage as this?

> And Martinique can hold its own with Zara; though Noyau condescends sometimes to rouge itself, while the wares of Luxardo and Drioli remain stainless.

Or this:

> However, I will not close this short chapter without saying something of the supposed wickedest of all the tribe—the "Green Muse"—the Water of the Star Wormwood, whereof many men have died—the *absinthia tetra*, which are deemed to deserve the adjective in a worse sense than that which the greatest of Roman poets meant.

I have yet to meet the man or woman who, unaided, could identify such a string of allusions. No wonder that Kipling, himself a master of allusion, wrote in his copy of *Notes on a Cellar-Book* (now in the library of his home, Bateman's, in Sussex), after having marked passage after passage in the book, that Saintsbury is "the most allusive writer I know."

The consequence of the bookishness combined with an unremitting allusiveness is, I am convinced, that there are large tracts of *Notes on a Cellar-Book* that readers today (emphatically including me) *simply do not understand*—we do not know what he is talking about. Like any work of a certain age, the book can use some editorial help: the great vintages of the nineteenth century that Saintsbury writes about have now become legend, and the mere citation of a date can convey nothing to an audience that has had no chance to know the wine of that year. An editor can at least report on what was said about them by those who did know. Other things that figure in the book have simply become old-fashioned and have dropped out of our view: mum, flip, purl, and the like.

We might have them again if we chose to, but meantime we have to be told what they were. But any history must deal with things that have gone out of mind. What is special, and specially difficult, about Saintsbury's book is its style of statement, and I have tried to elucidate the obscurities that come from this style.

Another point that an editor can help with arises from the mere brevity of Saintsbury's account—the fact that he has written "notes" rather than a history. On receiving his copy from Saintsbury, Kipling wrote to him that "what I should like to do would be to come to Bath and have you go through the Book, *viva voce*, with amplifications and memories." I cannot supply the memories, but in some places, at least, I have tried to give the "amplifications"—and in doing so I have not hesitated to appear pedantic. Most readers who can be imagined as taking an interest in the book will already know a good deal about wine, beer, and spirits, so it is certain that much of what I have put in the notes will be familiar to them already. But in this matter it is surely better to err on the side of excess. No one is compelled to look at the notes, and those who might want information would be annoyed at not finding it. Even the most sophisticated and informed of readers will not, I am confident, be able to meet Saintsbury at all points but will, sometimes, require a little quiet assistance. That is what I try to provide in the notes. On one subject only have I declined to provide any information: the classed growths of the Médoc. Information about them is so well known and so readily available that it seemed to me otiose to identify, for example, "Château Margaux" as a "first great growth."

Sometimes—or, rather, many times—I had to admit defeat. Who made "Old Rose" Champagne? Who said "a facetious and rejoicing ignorance"? What is a hen-master? These and other questions no doubt have their answers, but I have not found them.

To conclude, no one, so far as I know, has yet written anything remotely like *Notes on a Cellar-Book;* nor do I think that anyone ever will. Saintsbury's qualities as journalist, scholar, critic, teacher, gourmand, and *grand buveur* were all remarkable. That anyone will ever again combine them seems most unlikely.

EDITORIAL NOTE

For the text of this edition I have used the so-called third edition. Saintsbury sent typographical corrections and a few revisions of statements to Macmillan for this edition (really the third printing) and added a prefatory note. The book was unaltered in subsequent reprintings. Saintsbury was not careful about certain details of punctuation—capitals, hyphens, italics—but I have not imposed consistency upon his practice. I have kept Saintsbury's footnotes in their original position and added my comments at the end of each of his notes. The annotation at the end of the text is all editorial.

As an appendix I have reprinted, in the order of their original publication, nine brief items on wines and spirits written by Saintsbury between 1894 and 1924. They seem to me to fit readily into the spirit and manner of *Notes on a Cellar-Book.*

The illustrations chosen for this edition of the book are intended to refer as directly as possible to Saintsbury's text, and I hope they will contribute to the period flavor of the work as well.

I owe thanks to Gail Unzelman, editor of the *Wayward Tendrils Quarterly,* in which an earlier form of this introduction appeared, for permission to reprint.

BIBLIOGRAPHICAL NOTE

Most of the information in this note is drawn from the Macmillan Papers in the British Library and from the printing histories given in the successive printings of *Notes on a Cellar-Book*. It is a publication history rather than a proper bibliographical description.

1920: *Notes on a Cellar-Book*, London: Macmillan and Co., Ltd., xxi + 228 pp. The first edition was published on 2 July as a super royal 16mo. in an edition of 1,500 copies, price 7/6. It was reprinted in August 1920.

1920 (Third edition): *Notes on a Cellar-Book*, London: Macmillan and Co., Ltd., xxxi + 228 pp. This "third edition," as Saintsbury calls it in his prefatory note, is more properly a third printing. On 1 September 1920 Saintsbury sent some corrections to Macmillan, and not long after that he sent some "new matter," dated 23 October 1920, which appears as the "Note to Third Edition" following the "Preliminary" to the first edition. The "third edition" is in all other respects unaltered from the first and has served as the text from which subsequent printings have been made. The date of the third edition is given as November in the printing history in the preliminaries of the volume, but it probably came out in December. Sir Frederick Macmillan, writing to Saintsbury on 25 November 1920, says that the book will be on the market "before Christmas."

The trade edition of the third edition was reprinted in May 1921, January 1923, October 1924, March 1927, and June 1931, all during the life of the author; further reprintings were made in 1939, 1951, and 1953.

1921: *Notes on a Cellar-Book*, London: Macmillan and Co., Ltd., Fcap 4to, xxxi + 228 pp. Printed by University Press, Robert Maclehose and Co., Ltd., Glasgow. Edition de luxe. Five hundred copies on handmade paper watermarked "Holbein" and "London Assurance"; signed by the author: 25 shillings. A large-paper reprint of the third edition.

1933: *Notes on a Cellar-Book*, New York: Macmillan Co. With a preface by Owen Wister.

1963: *Notes on a Cellar-Book*, London: Macmillan and Co., Ltd. A "reissue" with a preface by Andrew Graham and frontispiece portrait by Sir William Nicholson. A reprint of the third edition.

1978: *Notes on a Cellar-Book*, London: Macmillan and Co.; New York: Mayflower Books, 1978. "Second reissue" with a new preface by H. W. Yoxall. A reprint of the third edition. It includes Graham's preface of 1963

and, as an epilogue, *The Times'* leader on the death
of Saintsbury, 30 January 1933. The English edition
is described as a "Special edition by Christie's Wine
Publications. Limited to 500 numbered copies" (James
M. Gabler, *Wine into Words: A History and Bibliography
of Wine Books in the English Language*, 2nd ed. [Baltimore:
Bacchus Press, Ltd., 2004], p. 317).

NOTES ON A CELLAR-BOOK

GEORGE SAINTSBURY

Trinc!

TO

R.K.

ONE OF THE BEST OF FELLOWS

THE BEST POET AND TALETELLER OF HIS GENERATION

AND ONE THAN WHOM

NO LIVING ENGLISHMAN

HAS DONE MORE TO FOSTER THE SPIRIT

THAT WON IN 1914–18

I OFFER

THIS MY FIRST AND LAST DEDICATION

IN PLACE OF

THE MANY REVIEWS AND THE MANY BOTTLES

OF WHICH

BY SOME CANTRIP OF FORTUNE

IT HAS NEVER BEEN MY LOT OR LUCK

DURING SOME THIRTY YEARS ACQUAINTANCE

TO OFFER HIM

ONE

G.S.

(Bath, Easter, *1920)*

PRELIMINARY

The old joke "Who has tied my son to this sword?" may occur to some in respect of any prefatory matter to so very little a book as this is likely to be; but perhaps it may be possible to make it a not quite superfluous part of the book itself. Not improbable and welcome readers of it may know that, in a larger and more serious work* some time ago, while disclaiming the intention of trespassing further on shelf-room and public time, I mentioned that I had been asked for, and had actually begun, a *History of Wine*, and that, if circumstances had been more favourable, I should have liked to resume it. Rather to my surprise the hint was jumped at, and not only private but public, and (if I may coin a word in the manner in which I have often of old shocked purist ears) even "publisherial" requests reached me. I felt the compliment, but could not fully entertain the idea. There would have been a considerable literature to look up; and while I was not favourably situated in respect of access to it, my original farewell

* *History of the French Novel*, vol. ii. Preface.

had been no trick, but the result of a genuine sense that I was getting too old for such a work. It would need infinite research to satisfy my own ideas of thoroughness: for I have never yet given a second-hand opinion of any thing, or book, or person. Also, I should have had to drink more good wine than would now be good for my pocket or perhaps even my health, and more bad than I could contemplate without dismay in my advancing years. So I resisted, not indeed the devil (who for the best of reasons hates wine), but these too amiable angels, as to any exhaustive treatment of the subject.

It did not, however, seem to me that there was anything inconsistent with what I had said in committing to paper certain notes and reminiscences on that subject which might amuse some readers, be profitable to others if things go well, and, whether they go well or ill, add a little to the literature of one of the three great joys of life. A man must have a mighty conceit of himself if he thinks that he can add much worth adding to what has been already written of Women and Song. But except in song itself (wherein, alas, I have but critical and not creative skill), and in ways rather general than particular, I must say I think Wine has been stinted of its due literary sizings. There are noble exceptions, Thackeray perhaps the greatest of them. But the serious books on wine have, as a rule, been rather dull, and the non-serious books and even passages not very "ingoing." I have known a most virtuous person, a true wine-lover and a man of great talent, speak in prose of "Carte Blanche" (or no matter what colour) as if it were a kind of champagne like *brut* or *œil de perdrix;* and even the minor singers—I do not speak of Panard or Tom Brown, who are not here "minor," of Peacock or Thackeray himself—are apt to be vague in their commendation of "rosy" and "sparkling," and in that fashion generalised drinks. They seldom give us the "streaks of the tulip" as they should. So that a little preciseness may help, if only on a small scale and in a discursive fashion, to make the subject ripe and real to some extent, if not to the extent it deserves.

This notion of mine first took positive shape owing to the requests received from the editor of an enterprising, but alas, too short-lived periodical, the *Piccadilly Review*. He actually published two of the chapters which should follow (the first and second). But the paper expired, with the third printed and the three next written in its dying grasp.*

I had from the first signified my intention of re-publishing, and Sir Frederick Macmillan had most kindly extended or modified (whichever be the proper word) his request for a big book to a provisional acceptance of this little one. So, recognising the clear risks, I set about it, with what result time may show. It is possible that someone, not a hopeless *bo*bolitionist, may say, "Mr. Saintsbury appears to have spent a great deal of money on mere luxuries." If I meet this "by anticipation" (as some people say when they want to save themselves the trouble of a letter of thanks, having previously tormented others with one of request) it is not out of pusillanimity or a guilty conscience. But I would request readers to observe in the first place that the outlay here implied or acknowledged was spread over rather more than half a century; and secondly, that, as I have more fully explained in the little book itself, I very rarely bought more at a time than a single dozen of each wine named, nay, half a dozen or even odd bottles by way of experiment. In wine, as in books and other things, I have tried to be a (very minor) Ulysses, steering ever from the known to the unknown. Thirdly, for nearly twenty years of the time I was a journalist and in other ways a working man

---

* I have to thank the courtesy of its executors for restoring to me these fragments.

of letters—a state of life to which Thackeray's ejaculation, "Grudge myself good wine? as soon grudge my horse corn," doth more particularly and specially apply; while for full another twenty I occupied a position in which, as one received much hospitality, it was not merely a pleasure but a duty to show some. But I offer these as explanations, not excuses. There is no money, among that which I have spent since I began to earn my living, of the expenditure of which I am less ashamed, or which gave me better value in return, than the price of the liquids chronicled in this booklet. When they were good they pleased my senses, cheered my spirits, improved my moral and intellectual powers, besides enabling me to confer the same benefits on other people. And whether they were bad or good, the grapes that had yielded them were fruits of that Tree of Knowledge which, as theologians too commonly forget to expound, it became not merely lawful but incumbent on us to use, with discernment, when our First Mother had paid the price for it, and handed it on to us to pay for likewise.

As I have thus become almost wholly serious, there may be no great harm in continuing to be so for the rest of this preliminary canter. There was a time, not so very long ago, when one could afford to treat the adversaries of honest drinking with a good-natured and rather lazy contempt. They punished themselves, and they could not hurt us. But that time has passed. The constituencies have been flooded till they have become incalculable; the general commonsense of the country has been weakened by a washy overflow of so-called education; statesmen, never the most trustworthy of persons, have become utterly untrustworthy; and the great institutions which once were towers of refuge and strength against popular delusions have opened their gates to any rising of the waters. One was once pretty sure that whether a

Bishop or a Judge was or was not personally a mirror of sanctity or a pattern of wisdom, mere silly and eccentric fads would find no favour with the one, and mere popular clamour receive no attention from the other. Everybody must decide for himself whether it is so now. But without venturing on any particular *scandalum magnatum*, it may be suspected that some people will entertain doubts on the point. Therefore it is well to keep the weather-eye open on this subject as on others, particularly because of one consideration.

This is the extraordinary, though no doubt in many cases unconscious, *dishonesty* of the so-called Temperance party. All fanatics and all faddists are dishonest. A.M.D.G. is only the exaltation to a blasphemous superlative of their invariable and indeed constitutive habit of mind. But it is a question whether the most Jesuitical Jesuit of the most heated Protestant imagination has ever outdone a thorough-going temperance advocate in the endless dodgings and windings, suppressions and suggestions of his method. These phenomena are, of course, best studied, not in the extreme Prohibitionists, who have the honesty of Habakkuk Mucklewrath, but in the members of societies, which, professing to desire only restricted hours, limitation in strength of drink, heavy taxation, etc., are really working for prohibition itself by steps and degrees. Except "Conscientious Objection" there was nothing more disgusting in the last five years than the duplicity of the cries, "Oh! surely you won't drink *during* the war," and "Oh! you can't think of drinking *after* the war." To guard against them it may be well for good drinkers to fortify themselves with the following facts, every one of which may be vouched for.

(1) There is absolutely no scientific proof, of a trustworthy kind, that moderate consumption of sound alcoholic liquor does

a healthy body any harm at all; while on the other hand there is the unbroken testimony of all history that alcoholic liquors have been used by the strongest, wisest, handsomest, and in every way best races of all times, and the personal experience of innumerable individuals in favour of the use. One of the most amazing audacities of these fanatics is the assertion that "even moderate drinking shortens life." A moment's thought will shew any clear-headed person that this cannot be proved without an exhaustive biological and clinical record of every moderate drinker since the beginning of time, unless there is a sophistic "sometimes" slipped in, which renders the proposition practically valueless.* Stopping a horse in order to save someone else's life sometimes shortens the stopper's; and going to church on an inclement morning may do so. Moreover, that moderate drinking *always* shortens life, while it is insusceptible of proof, is, and must ever be, susceptible of *dis*proof. Everyone knows, or may know if he chooses, instances of moderate drinkers who have reached ages far beyond the average age of man, in a condition of bodily health which compares with that of most, and of intellectual fitness which should shame that of nearly all, teetotallers. One supposes that this monstrous inexactitude is founded on some kind of physiological experiment: and indeed, if you give, say, a mouse, even a small quantity of absinthe, or raw potato spirit, you probably may say that, "moderate" drinking has shortened life. But otherwise the statement is one which no honest man should make, except as one of opinion, and no rational man credit, either as opinion or fact.

---

* "Quantification of the predicate" has been scoffed at. But in political logic it would often be valuable, and in the above instance it is a touchstone. [**"Quantification of the predicate"**: A term of logic introduced by Sir William Hamilton (*OED*, s.v. "quantification").—*Editor*]

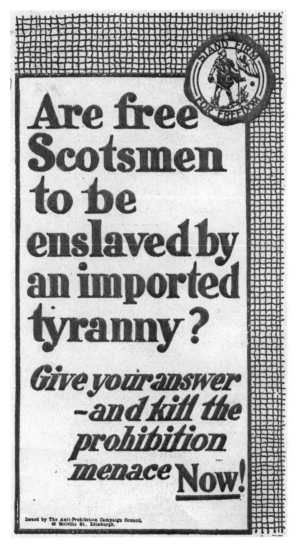

FIGURE 2. Scottish antiprohibition advertisement (*St. Andrews Citizen*, 13 October 1923).

(2) The alleged costliness of these drinks is entirely due to legislation, and most of the money apparently given for them is really spent to carry on the system of the State, thereby relieving unpatriotic (and extremely ungrateful) teetotallers of their just quota. A bottle of whisky used to cost, at normal prices without duty, some few pence to produce; and a gallon of good small beer could at the same time be brewed *with tax* for fourpence.

(3) The argument about diversion of foodstuffs is equally, though in a different way, fallacious. Grapes certainly are food of a kind, but they are not a staple; the sugar used for brewing is not eatable sugar; wheat is practically never used for brewing or distilling; and, as has been shewn during a long period of sanity, of good work, and of good but not preposterous wages, there is no difficulty whatever in providing the whole world with plenty to eat and plenty to drink at the same time and at easy rates.

(4) As to abuse, *abusus non tollit usum* is the simple and sufficient reply to the fallacies drawn from that.* But one may go further than this and boldly say, with a certainty of saying the truth, that for every evil deed that fact or fancy or the unscrupulous exaggeration of partisans can charge on alcohol, it has prompted a hundred good and kind ones; that for every life it has destroyed or spoiled it has made thousands happy; that much of the best imaginative work of the world has been due to its influence; and that it has, as has been amply shewn of late, given "more power to the elbow" of stout workers and fighters in the best of causes.

But we will not protest too much, and just finish this proem with something that does not in the least savour of apology. It is sometimes forgotten that only one of the two peaks of Parnassus was sacred to Apollo, the other belonging to Dionysus. The

---

* The supposed connexion with crime is reserved for the "Conclusion."

present writer has spent much of his life in doing his best, as he could not produce things worthy of Phœbus, to celebrate and expound them. It cannot be altogether unfitting that he should, before dropping the pen altogether, pay such literary respects as he may to the other sovereign of the "duplicate horn."

•

NOTE TO THIRD EDITION

This little book was reprinted with such unexpected rapidity that it was impossible for the author, without undue delay, to make a few corrections and add a little comment on its original reception. This reception was astonishingly and almost alarmingly favourable. I remembered, like my half-namesake Borrow, a certain uncomfortable text of "Woe"; and indeed the Fates did take some toll, unnecessary to specify, without long waiting. But the greediest author should have been satisfied and, if that were impossible, have had the edge of his appetite taken off by most of the reviews, not to speak of private acknowledgments. One disappointment, at least for a considerable time, I underwent. I had hoped for a little "merry war," as Mr. Kipling has it, with some champion of Pussyfoot. But such few blows as for a long time touched my pretty publicly exposed shield were curiously feeble, and even if meant to be dealt with the sharp end of the spear, obviously the work of clumsy instruments and prentice hands. The book, whatever its faults, certainly did not express or imply a desire (which one of the Pussyfoot *shirri* imputed to me) to "see guests under the table" at the close of the dinners it described:

and the fact, suggested by the same or another as my test of an Earthly Paradise, that "you could get blind drunk in Guernsey for sixpence" was only mentioned to emphasise the want of connection between serious crime (of which there was none there) and alcoholic cheapness. When, however, advocates are driven to this kind of advocacy, they are best left alone.

The encouragements I received were not limited to approval in reviews and letters—some of these latter from old friends of whom I had lost sight, and with whom wine, in its usual benevolent and beneficent fashion, thus reunited me. They sometimes took a very agreeably practical form. A gentleman of Liverpool, Mr. Holden, who represented the Spanish Produce Company of Cable Street, in that good city, wrote to me to ask if he might correct my ignorance (*v.* p. 154) of Spanish *cider* by sending me some. As in the other cases to be mentioned, I did not hesitate about accepting so good-natured an offer, and some very handsome bottles of "Sidra Champagne" with a picture of a piper ("Gaitero") on the label duly arrived. They were not exactly "Guipuzcoan," like Burton's, but came from Villaviciosa in the Asturias (the "Capital of the Filberts" of George Borrow himself), and so also represented Northern Spain.* The liquor did not disappoint the expectation raised by its receptacles. It was rather of the Herefordshire than of the Devonshire type, but exceedingly well flavoured, of good body, without being heady, and keeping the balance between too sweet and too dry with great success.

This, however, was not the end of my Nemesis-provoking windfalls. Messrs. Hedges & Butler, the well-known merchants

* If any one would like to know the makers' names, they were Valle, Ballina y Fernandez.

FIGURE 3. William "Pussyfoot" Johnson, a leading figure in the American Anti-Saloon League who agitated
for prohibition in England after the passage of constitutional prohibition in the United States (Ernest Hurst
Cherrington, ed., *Standard Encyclopedia of the Alcohol
Problem*, vol. 3 [Westerville, OH: American Issue Publishing, 1926]).

of Regent Street, in the same kindly and complimentary fashion, informed me that they *did* possess some of the old original
Constantia (*v.* p. 111) bottled in 1862, and requested my acceptance of a flask or two. My own acquaintance with the wine was
actually of older date than that just mentioned, for it must have
been some years before my father's death in 1860: and anyone

who understands the spirit of this booklet will understand also the interested impatience with which I waited till the gift could be fairly tried. I wanted, naturally, to see what it was like: but I wanted still more to see if I remembered rightly what it *had* been like. No disappointment came. I think—and its great age in bottle would in any case make this likely—that my recovered Constantia was a little paler in colour and more delicate in body than her ancestress of the fifties. But the flavour was "true," and I had neither mistaken it earlier nor forgotten it later. Charles Kingsley in *Hypatia* makes the naughty Prefect Orestes speak of Syrian wine as "honey and fire." The curious combination of honey- and grape-flavour in Constantia had remained in my memory, and if the fire did not now blaze or scorch, it glowed and warmed right well. Even with this, the genial pour of the gracious rain did not cease; for a representative of the great house of Sandeman* asked me to accept a brace of the most beautiful birds that ever fell to the longbow of a man of letters—two tappit-hens of that 1904 port of which I had only been able to praise the early development (pp. 71, 73). Ah! how I wished for the vessel described at p. 167, so that at last it might have accommodated its just quantum of nectar. But in the whole body of actual circumstances I could not have done either bird of Bacchus due honour at once; whereas when subjected to the process of decanting into

---

* As I have mentioned in the book, I have enjoyed more of Messrs. Sandemans' wine than of any other shipper's. As I have not mentioned, the three "supernacular" ports of '70, '72, '73 (p. 70) were, I believe, all of their shipping, and the only relic of my ancient cellar (stored in safe custody, I hope, but when to be drunk I know not) is a jeroboam of their '81, twice (see p. 65) rescued from dispersion.

flasks of less magnificent dimensions the wine came to my aid
again and again.

> So gentle and gracious are the compliments that pass
> between the folk of the meyny of the God!

If this document ever comes into use certain corrections of text
will have been or have to be made. My chief blunder of fact was
the remark (p. 70) that there was no evidence whether Barham was
speaking of port or claret in his 3 + 10 years' prescription. It was
a just penalty on me for not having taken sufficient care that my
copy of *Ingoldsby*—a possession from boyhood and with early impressions of the illustrations—was excepted from the sale of my
library and included in the salvage therefrom. He *does*, of course,
mention port just before. I have accordingly made correction.

No other important mistake of fact occurs to me, though I
have set right some minor slips of pen and press: but perhaps I
should plead more or less guilty to some *paraphthegmata*, as the
great rhetorician Aristides might have called them—"things I
ought not to have said." I have, I believe, wounded some worthy
feelings in what I have written about White Port, and I *was* excessive: for it is not nasty, and is undoubtedly a good invalid's
wine. But I never could see it without almost involuntarily and
uncritically (and perhaps expletively) saying "*Why* [the some-
thing] aren't you *red?*" Several good persons, again, who have
travelled have remonstrated with me on injustice to wines of
Touraine and its neighbourhood. I ought to have said that I have
never drunk them *in France*, thus giving them the direct (I intended an indirect) benefit of my remarks elsewhere on wines
that perhaps do not travel well.

As to the more serious part of the booklet, the refusal or delay of any but negligible Pussyfoot reply prevents rejoinder. I will

only mention one curious anecdote* buttressing my remarks on the impudence of the "moderate drinking shortens life" argument. A correspondent told me that some years ago there was a meeting of the governing body of Leicester Infirmary which was attended, among others, by no less than four governors over ninety, who outlived that age by years varying from 2 to 8, and not one of whom was an abstainer.

Perhaps one little concession to vanity may close this. A most well-wishing commentator seemed to be somewhat disturbed at the order of the wines in some of my *menus*, and to think that I had left it to the *chef* I mentioned. This was never the case; I should have brooked no such dictation either in regard to his own dishes or to my wines. The procession of the *dinner* wines is always deliberate. The *after*-dinner, as being set on the table together, may sometimes be more apparently—but not really—out of order.

---

* Perhaps adding one new example of the amazing audacity of the scarcely camouflaged Pussyfoot. A few days before revising this "Note" I saw, in a place already known to me as a good covert for this kind of fox, the statement that alcoholic drinks were "fatal to a life of study." It would be indecent to insist on any private reasons which I may have for amusement at this. I will merely remark that whosoever wrote it must, if honest, be utterly ignorant of the history of "study" and students, in any and every branch of learning, science, scholarship or whatsoever name may be given to the exercise of the intellect. Unless, indeed, he was using the word "fatal" in the rare sense of Dryden's charming "Address to the Duchess of Ormond":

"For beauty still is *fatal* to the line."

i.e. "fated." But this would have been, in the more ordinary sense, fatal to his argument, not to mention that Pussyfoots and poetry are rarely acquaintances. [*"fatal* to the line": "To Her Grace the Duchess of Ormond," *Fables Ancient and Modern*, line 31.—*Editor*]

But I will obey the rather peremptory question of King David and "speak no more of my matters" or of other matters in this place. If I allowed myself to be tempted, as another kind critic suggested, to discuss such things as "beeswing," there were no end. But I may inform him that I once sought in vain for silk or samite of its colour to form part of a vesture for the lady of my house. I never could find an exactly satisfactory representative to qualify bodice, underskirt and "trimmings" for an overdress of silver-grey in a confection which I had imagined.

G. S.

BATH, *October* 23, 1920.

I. ORIGINS

The late Mr. J. R. Planché, dramatist, antiquary, Somerset Herald, and I believe excellent person generally, was not such a good poet as Dante or as Tennyson; and when he wrote, very late in life, in an address to Youth,

> "I can do almost all that you can do,
> And I have what you have not, the Past,"

he might be thought to be blaspheming the doctrine of "Nessun maggior dolore" and

> "That a sorrow's crown of sorrow is remembering happier
> things."

But after all he had Horace with "Non tamen irritum," and Dryden with his magnificent adaptation,

> "For what has been, has been, and I have had my hour,"

on his side. At any rate, the other doctrine of "make the best of it," if base when applied to sublimer things, is grateful and com-

forting in the case of the lesser outrages of Fortune; and, if you
have lost your cellar, there is still some satisfaction to be got out
of your cellar-book.

The external aspect of this particular record, as it lies before its
owner, is, like that of many other things of some internal pre-
ciousness, not imposing. It is merely an ordinary "exercise book"
cloth-backed, with mottled-paper sideboards outside, and unruled
leaves within, undecked with the pompous printed page-headings
for different bins and vintages, and the dispositions for entering
consumption and keeping an eye on the butler, which the regular
cellar-book boasts. It had been one, I think, of a batch, most of
which were devoted to base purposes of lecture-notes, translations
of ancient and modern authors, etc., etc. But it happened to be at
hand and still blank when that owner first came into possession of
a cellar, better deserving the name than the cupboards which do
duty in most middle-class London houses; and so it was promoted.
The actual entries in it cover, with some intervals due to domestic accidents, a period of exactly thirty-one years (the duration of
some agricultural leases, I think), from 1884 to 1915. But the cellar, in the sense of the collection of wine which it represents, was
some years older in formation than the record, and was founded
in a great year for many things, wine itself included, the year 1878.

The foundation, I think I may say without vanity, or (since it
has ceased to be) without undue provocation to Nemesis, took
place under fair auspices, though it was then but a little one, ex-
tending only to a few dozen of various kinds besides ordinary
claret. I started it with purchases from a certain excellent firm, then
established on the north side of Pall Mall, who supplied my club,
and with whom I had had a very few dealings before I came back
to London. The managing partner was an old Scotsman, whose
ideas were very sound and whose manners could be very agreeable. We discussed the firm's wine-list for some considerable time;

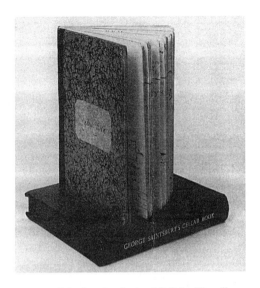

FIGURE 4. Saintsbury's cellar book (Michael Broadbent, *Saintsbury the Progenitor* [London: privately printed, 1993]).

and when I had made my scanty but careful selection, he accompanied me not merely to the door of his room but to that of the outer office. As we shook hands on the threshold he said to me, with the little bow which has almost disappeared:—"Mr. Saintsbury, Sir, if ye ask anyone to dinner and tell them where ye get your wine, we shall not be ashamed." No doubt these things are, in two senses, vanity; but I confess that the wings of peace fluttered and flattered my soul as I walked past Marlborough House. Only, such speeches impose. I felt that I had a new duty on me; never to insult the pure society of these liquids by introducing unworthy companions to it. To say this is, of course, like publishing banns; it invites any unkind person to get up and say, "You gave *me* bad wine." But I trust I should find compurgators.

The cellar-book, as I have said, did not start for a few years after this, and when it did, most of the good wines which had earned me that compliment had done their good office. Only two, I think, survived. One was a Burgundy—Richebourg '69—of which my friend in Pall Mall had remarked: "It ought to be good. The man we get it from sits up at night with a thermometer before it is bottled." And, so far as I remember, that thermometer was justified of its information.

This wine was not more than nine years' old when I bought it; but Burgundy is quick in maturing. The other was of a far older vintage, and one of the three or four most remarkable juices of the grape, not merely that I ever possessed but that I ever tasted.

As to this point my merchant and mentor, despite his general approval of my judgment, and despite also the fact that the wine was the most expensive I bought from him, did not quite agree. "Yes, it's great in its way; but it's a *coorse* wine," he said. But I understood this as merely a piece of chivalrous partisanship, for he was (and no shame to him) a devotee of Bordeaux, and when he wanted anything heavier, of Port: and this was a red Hermitage of 1846. The Hermitage of the year before must have been made just before I was born; and I thought it very nice of the vines, whose ancestors are said to have been of Shiraz stock imported by the Crusaders, to have kept this produce till I was alive and ready for my first birthday present. For it was really a wonderful wine. When the last bottle of it was put on the table before I again broke up my household in London for a time, it was just forty years old. Now most red wines, if not all with the exception of Port, are either past their best, or have no best to come to, at that age. And with all respect to the late Mr. George Meredith and some other persons of less distinction, I think that even those who have forty years' old Port in their cellars had much better drink it. But my Hermitage showed not the slightest mark or presage of enfeeblement. It was, no doubt (to translate, without "betray-ing," my friend's harsh epithet mildly), not a delicate wine; if you want delicacy you don't go to the Rhone or anywhere in France below Gascony. But it was the *manliest* French wine I ever drank; and age had softened and polished all that might have been rough in the manliness of its youth.

You had to be careful of it in some ways; one of the best-known of all my friends had very remarkable experiences as a conse-quence of neglecting my warnings, and consuming whisky instead of brandy with his soda after it. But there is no good in any man, woman or wine that will allow liberties to be taken with them. To champagne before it, it had no objection; nor, as hinted just now, to brandy afterwards. But it was uncompromisingly Gallic in its patriotism. They had only about a dozen and a half of it left in the wine merchant's cellars, and I bought the whole of it. But with a small supply like this and the certainty of nothing more like it (for it must be remembered that this was pre-oïdium and pre-phyl-loxera wine, and that the vineyards, by the time we drank it, had been ruined and replanted), it was rather a "fearful joy" to take a bottle of it from the dwindling company. However, I was not in a position to give dinner parties every week, nor, to speak frankly, did my company always deserve to have it set before them; so it lasted some years. It had, like all its congeners, a heavy sediment, and required very careful decanting; but when properly brought to table it was glorious. The shade of its colour was browner (people used, *vide* Thackeray, to call the red hocks "brown") than most of the Hermitages I have seen; but the brown was flooded with such a sanguine as altogether transfigured it. The bouquet was rather like that of the less sweet wall-flower. And as to the fla-vour one might easily go into dithyrambs. Wine-slang talks of the "finish" in such cases, but this was so full and so complicated that it never seemed to come to a finish. You could meditate on it; and it kept up with your meditations. The "gunflint" which, though not so strong in the red as in the white wines of the district, is supposed to be always there, was not wanting; but it was not importunate and did not intrude too much on the special Hermitage touch, or on that general "red wine" flavour which in some strange way is common to every vintage from Portugal to Hungary, vary as they may in character and merit otherwise. I do not say it was the best wine I ever had; that position I may be able to allot later.

Perhaps I may add something, though it may seem trivial or fantastic. I tried it with various glasses, for it is quite wonderful what whimsies wine has as to the receptacles in which it likes to be drunk. The large, slightly pinched-in "dockglass," half filled, suited it as indeed it does almost any wine. But whether it was mere whimsy on my own part or not, I always thought it went best in some that I got in the early seventies from Salviati's, before they became given to gaudiness and rococo. They were glasses of about the ordinary claret size, but flat-bottomed, and with nearly straight sides, curly-stemmed, with a white but rather cloudy body, an avanturine edge (very light) and deep blue knobs, small and sparsely set, in one row below it. They were good for all the great French red wines, but better for Burgundy than for Claret, and better for Hermitage or Côte Rotie than for Burgundy.

Alas!

The wine is gone, and with the wine went they, though many years after it. But of some other wines that they held and saw at the same time or later, we may talk further in other chapters.

Perhaps, however, a word or two on some matters connected with the above may not be offensive or superfluous. As may be supposed, I was not exactly a novice when I went to Pall Mall in 1878.

I think I must have acquired some knowledge of good wine and an unlimited horror of bad from my father; for though he died when I was very young, and in his later years drank very little (chiefly, as I may again mention later, the modest Marsala, which used to suffice professional and city men of the mid-nineteenth century, and but a glass or two of that), I possess, among my few memories of him, a cellar-book of earlier date with quite respectable entries. When I went to Oxford I joined no regular Wine Club for some private reasons, but used to give modest port and sherry "wines" in my own rooms, *not* imitating one of my most distinguished and amiable instructors, who was said as a freshman to have produced two bottles, taken them up to the table, shaken them both, and then said, "This is port and this is sherry; which will ye have?" One had one's share too of those feasts at certain more or less famous hostelries, where the bills used to run with a combination of detail and laconism: "To share of dinner, sherry, hock, champagne, claret, port, brandy *and breakages—£- -s. -d.*" I do not think I ever bought much wine in Oxford, remembering Dr. Portman's caution about "the other shop," and having dealings with an old friend of my father's in town. But I remember a good brown sherry of Guy & Gammon's.

From Oxford, after a brief interval at Manchester, with neither time nor means to invest in the gifts of Bacchus, I moved to Guernsey, where, as I have endeavoured to acknowledge elsewhere, things were as agreeable in this respect as in all others. Not only was liquor cheap, but it was *not* nasty.* I have mentioned some

---

* Except some smuggled German potato spirit which an intelligent Customs officer, as he told us afterwards at whist, took from a newly planted cabbage bed. It was said to be all but absolute alcohol, and in taste "more frightful than words can say," as poets observe in their unimaginative moments.

FIGURE 5. Elizabeth College, Guernsey, where Saintsbury was classics master from 1868 to 1874 (editor's collection).

specialties in later chapters, and I will only add here that while my six years of sojourn there convinced me that plenty and cheapness of alcoholic liquor did not tempt to abuse of it, they also showed me that this same cheapness was a remarkable preservative of quality. The genuine article was so moderate in cost, and the possible profit on selling it was so limited, that adulteration was hardly at all tempting. Let me add that as the islanders included an unusually large proportion of persons of fair income, ancestral houses, and gentle blood, hospitality was abundant and the means of exercising it excellent. There can be no insult in recalling the fact that during the quarter-century of the great French wars the Channel Islands were the chief entrepôt of foreign-made drink—never mind whether in connection with what is called smuggling or not. Barely half a century more had passed when I went to Guernsey, and I do not think the last bottle of the old stocks had been drunk out.

But if Guernsey treated me well, Elgin, to which I went for some two years in 1874–6, treated me in this respect almost better; though of course one had to pay more for one's actual purchases. In that blameless Hyperborean district, what my predecessor at Edinburgh, Professor Masson, was soon after to call "the savage observance of whisky toddy" (though this was only humorous irony like Lamb's on tobacco) lacked not observers. And the worship of the wine of the country did not exclude that of other cheerers. I never drank better claret or champagne than I had given to me "up there"; and it was there that I began, on a very small scale and interrupted by the shortness of my stay, to form a sort of cellaret though not a cellar, and to study the subject as well as others in a manner worthy of it and of them. Alas! my first library and my first cellar had to be relinquished, as my last cellar and my last library were, in the same country of Scotland, forty years later. But it was in Elgin that I made my first separate study of a great English writer—Dryden; in Elgin that I began to read Elizabethan literature more than sporadically, and in Elgin that I laid the foundation of a real cellar, by selecting, not merely buying as offered, a "classed" claret in the shape of '64 Ducru-Beaucaillou and a special champagne in that of '65 Krug.

My larger adventure there, like so many others, did not flourish (for reasons quite unconnected with the cellar), and vicissitudes followed, till, setting Chaucer at nought, I "fled *to* the Press," not from her, was most agreeably welcomed, and became in case to start a new collection of books and wines in the good year '78— the year of the second *Poems and Ballads*, and of the best Léoville

Barton *I* ever drank (though Anthony Trollope thought '64 the
ne plus ultra thereof); the year, finally, of which the Judicious Poet
wrote to somebody or something unnamed:

> A year there was of glory,
> Of promise false and fair
> When Downing Street was Tory,
> And England foiled the Bear;
> When all the wine succeeded
> From Douro to Moselle,
> And all the papers needed
> The wares I had to sell;
> When, friends with love and leisure,
> Youth not yet left behind,
> I worked or played at pleasure,
> Found god—and goddess—kind;
> Played my last rubber cosy,
> Took my last miss at loo,
> When all my world was rosy,
> But when I knew not—You!

And certainly, though one did know the *Poems and Ballads* in the
year itself, one did *not* yet know the Léoville. So perhaps the poem
was written to *it*, and not to a lady-love, as might seem more likely
to hasty observers.

II. SHERRY AND MADEIRA

The first batch of these notes was, as it were, prefatory and promiscuous; it is time to be more methodical. And that being so, no reasonable person should quarrel if we begin with Sherry, even as the truly good and wise usually do at dinner.

It will be remembered that the Chevalier Strong—speaking, it is true, to some extent interestedly, but from wide experience and a good taste and heart—warned Laura Pendennis on the eve of her marriage, that there was nothing more important to her husband's welfare than *pure* "sherry." And no doubt there was at that time, and has been since, a great deal of sherry that no honest and competent person could call "pure." Although I am myself no lover of modernity, I do not think there is, or was at any rate a short time ago, quite so much bad sherry about as there used to be. I remember in the middle of the sixties, when Sunday lunching places in London were rare and I had as yet no club, being driven to feed with an Oxford friend at a small tavern or chophouse in Piccadilly. The scorch and the twang of what they miscalled "Vino de Pasto" abide in my palate's memory to this day. And it was and is all the more wicked because Sherry is plenteous in quantity and singularly various in kind.

I have always thought that Manzanilla* and the other lightest growths and shipments of Xérès and San Lucar and their neighbourhood receive far too little practical attention in England. The Spaniards, I am told, drink them in large, tall beakers like our own old-fashioned beer-glasses (curiously enough it is on record that Fletcher the dramatist's "maid had her sack in a beer-glass," but this was pretty certainly not Manzanilla); and I can strongly recommend the practice. Drunk thus, the wine provides a real beverage; it goes with anything from oysters (with which Chablis, though orthodox, does not please me, while champagne, though it has Thackeray's sanction, seems to me a sin without a solace) to anything short of "sweets." Many of the other light Spanish wines of this class (of the Riojas, etc., we may speak separately) are excellent; for instance, the lighter Paxarettes—that wine which most literary people to-day associate only with Sir Telegraph in "Melincourt," and of which it seems "dry" America sent us the other day a batch of butts. But some of the finer kinds are really supernacular—the best "Tio Pepe," for instance. Only, he who indulges in them must remember that they are an exception to the general rule that "Sherry improves in the decanter." When they are opened, the finer ones especially, they must be drunk. I have known a bottle of Tio Pepe become appreciably "withered" between lunch and dinner.

* The Spanish traveller, Packe, quoted in Whymper's *Scrambles*, attributes the peculiar flavour of Manzanilla to an admixture of *Artemisia nevadensis*. This seems odd in the case of *wine*; but I may have something to say on Artemisias in the chapter devoted to liqueurs. [**Whymper's Scrambles:** Edward Whymper (*Scrambles amongst the Alps in the Years 1860–69* [London, 1871]) prints a list of plants found in the Sierra Nevada of Spain by Charles Packe, including "*Artemisia nevadensis* (used for giving the flavour to the Manzanilla sherry)." I know of no evidence for the use of the plant in Manzanilla sherry.—*Editor*]

Next to "Uncle Joseph" in my book—indeed, as having occupied the same bin—I find entered a wine than which, except that both were sherry and both pale in colour, it would have been impossible to discover or even invent a greater contrast. The entry is, "Pale Rich; Bot. 1865; Gee's sale, Torquay." My friends the Messrs. Collier, of Plymouth, had bought it, and knowing that I liked good "oddments," handed it over to me. I think, but am not sure, that it was Wisdom's shipping. It *was* rich, very rich, almost a liqueur; but not in the least fulsome, and of a flavour which I never tasted in any other sherry. There is a well-known wine of the class called "Nectar de Xérès," some of which lay in the next bin in my cellar to this, but I always thought that the unnamed liquid deserved the title better; and an elect lady of my acquaintance (when ladies *do* know anything about wine, there is no mistake about their taste)* used to prefer it to any other that I could give her.

One might jangle a long time on Montillas and Olorosos, Amorosos and that so vilely traduced Vino de Pasto itself; one

---

* In another case a hostess of mine, (alas! now dead) tasting some Burgundy which her husband had put before us, looked at me and said, "Isn't this corked?" Being less honest than Mr. Philip Firmin, I did *not* say anything rude, and equivocated. But she would have no "transaction," and as she went out of the room (she was small, and like all small ladies, especially when they are pretty, very firm in manner) she laid her hand upon her husband's shoulder and said, "———! you *must* send that bottle away and have another." I can see at this moment, after many years, a great single diamond, which she used to wear slung on a loose gold chain, swinging forward and flashing as she bent to say it. [**Mr. Philip Firmin:** Philip Firmin, the hero of Thackeray's *The Adventures of Philip* (1861– 82). Being entertained by Lord Ringwood, Philip is offered claret, but, "on tasting his glass, called out, 'Faugh! It's corked!' 'So it is, and very badly corked,' growls my Lord, with one of his usual oaths. 'Why didn't

FIGURE 6. Gonzalez, Byass Nectar label (Amerine Collection, Special Collections, Shields Library, University of California, Davis).

might, perhaps, give a friendly hint to an ingenuous writer, such
as those who think "Carte d'Or" a special brand of champagne,
that "Solera" is not a particular *kind* of sherry. The Spanish wine
merchants, or their English clients, have, moreover, a pretty taste
for giving feminine names to this wine. My cellars (and even cup-

some of you fellows speak? Do you like corked wine?' There were gallant fellows seated round that table who would have drunk black dose, had his Lordship professed to like senna" (ch. 18, end). Since Philip is later left a large legacy by Lord Ringwood because he is the only one of Ringwood's relatives who has never toadied to him, this piece of impoliteness is well rewarded.—*Editor*]

boards) have seldom for forty years been without a certain "Margarita," from some vaults in "Bristol cit*ee*," which were originally recommended to me by an actual Margaret, its namesake and fellow-citizen; and an "Emilia," an "Isabel," and a "Maria"(more than one, indeed, for there is a *Tia* Maria, to match the Tio Pepe) have kept her company at various times without quarrel or jealousy. Even a "Titania" appears in my book. But these are fantastries. Amontillado must not, perhaps, pass with such light notice. The name has, of course, been far more widely taken in vain than that of Vino de Pasto, which is, after all, itself more general; and for the true, at least the perfect Amontillado flavour, you may have to wait not a little time, while you certainly could not get it, even before the present "dear years," for a little money. Perhaps some people have forgotten, or never knew, how comparatively recent the taste for dry sherries is. It preceded, indeed, for a fairly long time that for dry champagne, but in both cases the "dry"— alas! that the word should have acquired a new and blasphemous signification in the context!—is evidence of a general revolution in taste. It is, of course, true that people say "sack" is "secco," and point to the old addition of sugar. But our ancestors of the sixteenth and seventeenth centuries had uncommonly "sweet teeth." We of the nineteenth century shed them, but the surprising fuss about sugar and jam recently looks as if they were coming back again.

The medium sherries—neither quite austere nor quite luscious—are, perhaps, more the wine of all occasions than anything else; and may be taken to utmost satisfaction with food or without it, at any time in the day, except the first thing in the morning and the last at night. But I own to an affection, mingled with regret, for the "old golds" and the "old browns" of yesterday, not to mention again such extraordinary things as the "pale rich" already spoken of; and I own also that I think, though by no means accustomed to bewail things past more than reason,

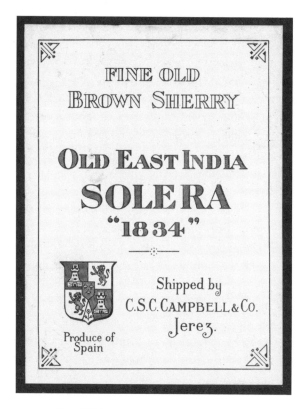

FINE OLD
BROWN SHERRY

OLD EAST INDIA
SOLERA
"1834"

Shipped by
C.S.C. CAMPBELL & CO.
Jerez.

Produce of
Spain

FIGURE 7. Fine Old Brown Sherry (Brady Collection, Special Collections, Shields Library, University of California, Davis).

that they really have "gone off." Whether, in consequence of their diminishing popularity, less care is used in their preparation; whether there is some change in the natural wines themselves as there certainly has been in some others, I cannot say. But I can indicate with some precision the difference I perceive between the old "East Indias" of fifty years ago and their representatives to-day. In those old wines the special flavour and the general "richness" seemed to be thoroughly and inseparably blended; you knew that the wine was not "natural," but somehow or other it might have been. Nowadays, wines of ostensibly or nominally the same class, however old they may claim to be, and however much money you may pay for them, suggest a "graft"—a stock of sherry with some particular character, and an inset of sweetening and flavouring super-induced. Which is a pity.

To finish with sherry, or at least the sherries on my list, let me note a wonderful Pedro Ximénès, stamped "Sherry," and furnished to me with the ticket "very old in 1860," by my constant friend in these ways, the late Mr. John Harvey, of Bristol, respecting whose cellars and those of his successors it may certainly be said:—"There's *nothing* rotten in the *street* of Denmark." It was not a wine for babes; but was curiously interesting to grown-ups in wine-lore.

It may seem irreverent to give so famous, and at its best so exquisite, a liquor as Madeira merely a postscript to the notice of its supplanter, which, by the way, it had itself supplanted. The proceeding is due neither to ignorance nor to contempt. For, in the first place, my father had many West Indian friends, and in early days I can remember actual apologies for giving one admirable Madeira—instead of contemptible "Gladstone" claret. And, in the second, I know no wine of its class that can beat Madeira when at its best; the very finest Sherries of the luscious kind—even "Bristol Milk" and "Bristol Cream" themselves—cannot touch it. But here, though by no means in other matters, I can echo Swift's, "Sir, I drink no memories"; and I fear that the very best Madeira is, and always has been since the pre-oïdium wines were exhausted, mainly a memory. I had some of these (both "London Particular" in origin, and from their special landing place in the West) when my cellar-book started, but I seldom cared to replace them with their degenerate successors, and that for two reasons—First, the degeneracy itself; and, secondly, the increased acidity. I suppose Madeira always *was* acid: these southern white wines generally are. Marsala certainly is, and though the best sherry escapes, the old practice of "liming" sack (the object of which I have known some people fail to understand) speaks volumes. Now, I am sorry to say that I have myself put into a glass of modern Madeira, from most unimpeachable providers, a little spoonful of carbonate of soda, with a result of frothing that could hardly be surpassed by sour beer. But let us not end on this uncheerful note. Certainly a real old Bual or Sercial of the times before 1850—I have drunk 1780 Madeira when it was nearly ninety years old and in perfection—was a thing to say grace for and remember. In fact, I think Madeira and Burgundy carry combined intensity and complexity of vinous delights further than any other wines. There is possibly something of the unlawful about their rapture, something of the "too much"—and accordingly they are the goutiest of all juices of the grape, whether pure or sophisticated.

The extraordinary *adaptableness* of sherry, glanced at above, may deserve a few more words. It does, perhaps, lend itself too freely to "mixtures." "Sherry cobbler" is indeed a most excellent drink. I was taught to make it when I was an undergraduate by no less a person than the late "Father" Stanton, who was as good a fellow as he was a godly man; and the preliminary process of "cataracting" the wine and the ice and the lemon from two properly handled and not pusillanimously approximated soda-water tumblers is a beautiful and noble occupation. But though my adolescence almost coincided with the greatest popularity of "sherry and bitters," I never cared very much for that, and "sherry and seltzer" has always seemed to me a mistake. The lighter sherries do not

FIGURE 8. London
Particular Madeira
(Amerine Collection,
Special Collections,
Shields Library, Univer-
sity of California,
Davis).

FIGURE 9. Messrs. Cossart, Gordon's *estufas*, Madeira; the wine is heated in the
process of its preparation (Henry Vizetelly, *Facts about Port and Madeira* [1880]).

need dilution, and the heavier appear to me to suffer a sort of "break-up" of their ethers in submitting to it. Since the scarcity and monstrous price of whisky I have not infrequently given sherry "pegs" a fresh trial, but with little satisfaction. In fact the unusual range of alcoholic strength, and the great diversity of flavour and body in the different sherries make dilution almost unnecessary, except for persons who must have "long drinks." As remarked above, Manzanilla will carry you nearly through dinner, and others of the lighter class will go all through, though they may not be drinkable in quite such volume. I once even attempted a fully graded *menu* and wine-list with sherry only to fill the latter—a "sherry dinner" to match the claret feasts often given by lovers of Gascon wine. It was before I began to keep such documents, and so I am not quite certain of the details. But if I were reconstructing such an entertainment now, and had the wherewithal as I once had, I should arrange it somewhat thus: Manzanilla with oysters; Montilla with soup and fish; an Amontillado with entrées and roast; an Amoroso or some such wine with sweets; and for after dinner, the oldest and brownest of "old browns," say Brown Bristol Milk, which in its turn doubly suggests a finish to this notice. The very darkest sherry I ever possessed, indeed that I ever tasted or saw, was an 1870 wine specially yclept "Caveza," which I bought when it was more than twenty years old, and of which I still had some when it was over forty. It was not an absolutely first-class wine, but good enough, and remarkable for its extraordinary, and not easily describable colour—almost black except against the light. This brought about an incident slightly comic. I was giving a dinner-party in the early nineties, and a decanter of this wine was put on the table. Whereupon one of my guests (a medical man not quite so amply possessed of convivial amiability as some others of the faculty) proceeded positively to lose his temper over it. "It was not sherry; it couldn't be sherry; there never was sherry of that colour; it must be queer-coloured port mislabelled." Neither his host's assurances, nor those of his fellow guests, nor appeal to his own taste and smell would satisfy him; and things were getting almost unpleasant when I managed to turn the conversation.

III. PORT

That Port should follow Sherry is, or ought to be, to any decent Englishman, a thing requiring no argument. My cellar, if not exactly my cellar-book (which, as has been said, did not begin till some years later), was founded in this eminent respect on a small

· supply of 1851 (I think, but am not sure, Cockburn's), whereof my friend in Pall Mall, but from Scotland, who supplied it, ingenuously said that for his part he liked rich port, but that for a medium dry wine he did not think it could be surpassed. Nor have I, to my remembrance, ever drunk much better than this, or than some magnums of the same shippers and vintage which succeeded it, and

· were bought at the sale of that air-travelling victim, Mr. Powell, of Wiltshire. Indeed, I think '51 was the finest port, of what may be called the older vintages accessible to my generation, that I ever tasted; it was certainly the finest that I ever possessed. The much

· talked of 1820 I do not think that I ever drank *securus*, that is to say, under circumstances which assured its being genuine. Some

· '34, with such a guarantee, I have drunk, and more '47, the latter from when it was about in perfection (say, in 1870) to a date the other day when it was some sixty years old and little but a memory, or at least a suggestion. But '51 in all its phases, dry, rich and medium, was, I think, such a wine as deserved the famous and pious encomium (slightly altered) that the Almighty might no doubt have caused a better wine to exist, but that he never did.

For some years, however, after the book was started I did not drink much port, being in the heat of my devotion to Claret or Burgundy after dinner. I cannot find that I ever possessed any '54, which, though not a large or very famous vintage, some not bad judges ranked with '51 itself, but I have records of '58, '61, of course '63, '68, '70, '72, '75 and '78 in the first division of my book, and before the interval in which I did not keep it regularly. During that interval I was accused and convicted of acute rheumatism, and sentenced, as usual, to give up port altogether—which was all the harder as I had just returned to my natural allegiance thereto. The result was that several dozens of what was going to be one of the best wines of the century, Dow's '78, comforted the sick and afflicted of a Cambridgeshire village and that the only "piece" of port that I ever laid down—a quarter-cask of Sandeman's '81—was taken back on very generous terms by the merchants who had supplied it. They gave me an additional five per cent. per annum on what I had given for it.

However, other people had to be provided for, and I did not myself practise total abstinence. I seem, from menus preserved, though the book was in suspense, to have trusted chiefly to three kinds, no one of which perhaps would have been highly esteemed by a person who went by common opinion, but which had merits. One was a wine of uncertain vintage, believed to be '53, and probably Sandeman's, but certainly very good. Another was a Rebello Valente of '65. Now '65, like '53, has no *general* repute as a vintage, and some people think Rebello Valente "coarse." I can

FIGURE 10. Walter Powell, the ill-fated balloonist, from the sale of whose cellar Saintsbury bought Cockburn's 1851 port: ". . . the finest port . . . that I ever tasted" (*Illustrated London News*, 24 December 1881).

only say that this, for a "black-strap" wine, was excellent, and I
confess that I do not despise "black-strap." But the gem of the
three was a '73, which had been allowed to remain in wood till
it was eight or nine years old, and in bottle for about as much
longer before I bought it. It had lost very little colour and not
much body of the best kind; but if there ever was any devil in its
soul that soul had thoroughly exorcised the intruder and replaced
him with an angel. I had my headquarters at Reading at the time,
and a member of my family was being attended by the late Mr.
Oliver Maurice, one of the best-known practitioners between
London and Bristol. He once appeared rather doubtful when I
told him that I had given his patient port; so I made him taste
this. He drank it as port should be drunk—a trial of the bouquet;
a slow sip; a rather larger and slightly less slow one, and so on;
but never a gulp; and during the drinking his face exchanged its
usual bluff and almost brusque aspect for the peculiar blandness—
a blandness as of Beulah if not of Heaven itself—which good
wine gives to worthy countenances. And when he set the glass
down he said, softly but cordially, "*That* won't do her any harm."
But I am not entirely certain that in his heart of hearts he did not
think it rather wasted on a lady, in which, as I have said, *I* think
he was wrong.

I found out, at any rate, or chose to find out, that it did *me* none,
or *si peu que rien*, and regretted my precipitancy in getting rid of
the '78 and '81. But in ten years I had three house-moves and no
good cellar; so that I simply used up what wines I had got and supplied deficiencies for immediate use only. When, in 1895, I settled in Edinburgh, it became possible, and to me desirable, to make
larger provision; and I set about it, though in a way perhaps not
the most "provident" in another sense. If you lay down a considerable quantity of an approved vintage port, just ready to bottle,
you get it, or did get it, very cheaply. For nearly a hundred years

before the war the price averaged some thirty to six-and-thirty shillings a dozen; it seldom or never plays the tricks that claret, in growing up, will sometimes do; it will treble its value in twenty or five-and-twenty years, and when it is matured, if you want to get rid of it, it will fetch full price. On the other hand, if you buy small lots of matured wines for your own amusement, you will pay a good deal for them, and broken dozens, or even larger lots sold at auctions will go for a song, while small lots of immature wines will go for whatever is worse than a "song." However, you have your amusement meanwhile, and must be prepared, as usual, to pay for it.

Between 1895 and 1915 I collected in this way small lots of most of the best back-vintages from '70 onward, with a few older still: and laid down a dozen or two of several sorts of the best that followed from '96 to '08 (I had bought but not cellared '11 before I gave up housekeeping). At one time I had, I think, about fifty or sixty different kinds of port, though seldom more than a dozen of each, sometimes only two or three bottles. The financial result when the cellar came to be sold was disastrous; but the amusement during the twenty years was great. You could continually try different vintages of one shipper, or different shippers of the same vintage, against each other; and as each year made a difference in the good wines, and these differences were never exactly proportionate, the permutations and combinations of experiment were practically infinite, and always interesting in the trial, even if disappointing in the result. To find '70 and '73 always maintaining and improving their place to the very last bottle, when tears would have mingled with the wine but for spoiling it; to see the '90's catching up and beating the (as it seemed to me) always over-rated '87's: or to pit against each other two such vintages as '96 and '97 from the same shipper—these were intellectual as well as merely sensuous exercises, and pleasing as both.

One of the results of this extensive and continuous "sampling" was the conclusion that the exclusive devotion of some wine-merchants to particular shippers is rather a mistake, and that the superior position accorded in the market to some of these shippers— Cockburn and Sandeman especially—is not universally justified. It is true that from the two shippers just named, and, perhaps, from one or two others, you will hardly ever get bad wine; but you do not get from them quite the same variety of good that you do from an enlarged range. I have done justice to Cockburn advisedly, and in the large number of Sandemans that I have had I have rarely been disappointed. But I don't think I ever drank—I certainly never had—a better '87 than some Smith Woodhouse; and I have seldom gone wrong with Graham, which I have heard experts (or supposed experts) patronise as "very fair *second*-class." There is no shipper's wine that I have found better than the best of Dow, '78 and '90 especially; Warre is almost always trustworthy; and Croft generally. Martinez and Offley, both famous names, have justified themselves with me, and so has Taylor, especially for somewhat rich wines. But the best rich that I ever had was, I think, a Cockburn of '81. Good wines I have had, in particular "Zimbro," of Feuerheerd's, but never, I think, the very best; and Kopke's famous "Roriz" did not seemingly appeal to me, for I find none in the book.

On another point of great interest, the possession of so large a number of different vintages and shipments enables one to give a pretty well-based opinion; and that is the extreme uncertainty of the keeping qualities even of a fortified wine like port. I have already hinted, and may now state more precisely, my belief that no red wine will keep much more than fifty years without "going

FIGURE 11. The new port lodge of Silva and Cosens, Oporto, Portugal (Henry Vizetelly, *Facts about Port and Madeira* [1880]).

off." It is true that Barham was (as I had forgotten in the first edition of this book) speaking of port only when he wrote—

> "And I question if keeping it does it much good,
> After ten years in bottle, and three in the wood."

But to claret this applies more strongly, though I think it applies to port, if not commonly, oftener than the general public supposes. The best and most robustly and skilfully prepared wines, such as '51, '63, '70, '73, '78, '81, '87, '90, and most '96's with some '97's, probably arrive at their best between twenty and thirty. But it is sometimes difficult to foresee how long they will keep at it. The most curious experience I had of this may finish the paper. Early in the year 1900 I bought from my Bristol friends some small parcels of the very best ports then available, including '70 (a really magnificent wine), and both '72 and '73. Comparatively few people may know of '72, but its price was then the same as that of the more famous '73, and for some time I thought it the better of the two, and got more of it; and this held for a year or two. But when the '72 had turned its thirty, the superior vitality of the younger wine began to tell, and in a few years more it was better than ever, while the more delicate "Ventozello" of '72 had certainly ceased improving and was even slightly senescent.

So no more, save a postscript, of "the Englishman's wine"; though I should like to talk of a curious Dow, as deep in colour as a wine bottled at thirty months, but otherwise completely "tawny" in character; of the '04's and their wonderfully rapid development (some which a friend gave me at Belfast, when it was not near Barham's limit, might have made a Sinn Feiner into a good citizen); of many other things. They are, to blend two lines of Mr. Swinburne's, "past as the shadows on glasses"—the glasses in which they themselves were drunk; but the memory and the delectation of them remains.*

I subjoin a list of the ports in my cellar at different or the same times.

* One of the most agreeable incidents of my life in connection with Port is quite recent. Soon after I had published something about wine in the *Athenæum*, and since America "went dry," two students of that misguided country wrote to me saying that they had found it impossible to refrain, after reading the article, from sallying forth, purchasing some so-called port wine (I hope it was not very bad), and drinking my health in it. It would be difficult for a teacher to have a more gratifying testimonial to the efficacy of his teaching; especially when he remembers the boasts of Prohibitionists as to bringing on prohibition by sowing pseudo-scientific tarradiddles in U.S. school-books. [**published something about wine:** "The Bounties of Bacchus," *Athenæum* (21 November 1919): see the appendix.—*Editor*]

Shippers and Years

Cockburn	Dow	Croft	Sandeman
1851	1870	1875	1863
–81	–78	–85	–67
–84	–87	–87	–70
–90	–90	–94	–72
–96	–96	1900	–73
1900	–99	–04	–78
	1904		–81
			–87
Martinez	Warre	Graham	–90
1880	1878	1881	–91
–87	–84	–84	–92
1900	–87	–96	–97
	–90	–97	1900
	1900		–08

Silva & Cosens	Taylor	Smith Woodhouse	Feuerheerd
1887	1884	1887	1873
–90	–87	–96	–96
–96	–90	–97	–?
1901	1900		(bot. 1902)
–02			

Offley	Rebello Valente	Tuke Holdsworth
1887	1865	1890
–92	–90	

Gould Campbell	Burmester*	Uncertain	•
1892	1900	1853	
1900		−58	
		−61	
		−68	
		−70−74	
		−73	

(NOTES ON PORT LIST.)

It should be observed that the relative frequency with which the names of shippers occur does not invariably involve a higher estimate on my own part, owing to the fact noticed in the chapter on the subject, of the partiality of some wine merchants for some shippers. This is especially the case with Sandeman and with Silva & Cosens, though I need hardly say that I find no fault with my advisers' taste in either case, especially in the first. And I have been informed, rightly or wrongly, that for some years past Dow's marks, which I think on the whole I have personally preferred to any others, have been in Messrs Silva's hands.

The wines of uncertain origin, it need also hardly be said, were bought merely on their merits. The '70, bot. '74, was a very curious wine, somewhat "blackstrappy" and even "public-housy" in character, but by no means to be contemned. Some of the later vintages, which I had in full bottle size, I never tasted, including one or two of the '96's and '97's, and I think all the 1900's and their successors. But the pints were "morigerant" even up to the already-mentioned 1904, though mine was not quite so good as my friend's.

---

* This wine, the only one of the shipper's that I ever bought, was sold before I tasted it.

Taking shippers and vintages all round, I should say '51, '58, '63, some '67, '70, '72, '73, '78, '81, '87, '90, were the best of those I drank in thorough condition. To make a still "shorter leet," as they say in Scotland, I think '51, '70 and '90 supplied the three best ports I have ever had. But though I don't exactly *envy* the people who bought my wine at prices which would scarcely buy Tarragona now—for Envy is not one of the heaviest of my quite heavy enough list of Deadly Sins, and I humbly hope for no long detention with wired-up eyes if I have the luck to reach the scene of that purgation—I think they made uncommonly good bargains.

For Port—*red* Port, as one of its earliest celebrants after the Methuen treaty no less justly than emphatically calls it, White Port being a mere albino—is incomparable when good. It is not a wine-of-all-work like Sherry—Mr. Pendennis was right when he declined to drink it *with* his dinner. It has not the almost feminine grace and charm of Claret; the transcendental qualities of Burgundy and Madeira; the immediate inspiration of Champagne; the rather unequal and sometimes palling attractions of Sauterne and Moselle and Hock. But it strengthens while it gladdens as no other wine can do; and there is something about it which must have been created in pre-established harmony with the best English character.*

---

* One thing it should not be asked to do, and that is to act purely as a thirst-quencher. I remember two stories illustrating this in a tragi-comic manner, though the tragedy predominated in the first, the comedy (with some romance) in the second. Mozley in his *Reminiscences*, I think, tells how a predecessor of his at Cholderton contracted a sad habit of excessive drinking. It appears that, in old days at Oriel, they used, as poor Hartley Coleridge found to his cost, to devise traps and torments for their probationer fellows (more recently I have heard of nothing worse at other colleges than expectation of salad-making). This man's

trial was cataloguing the library. It was in a state of dust not very creditable to the "Noetics," who had, however, hardly then arisen, and this
dust had to be "laid." The youngster, perhaps too proud of his new status to drink beer, fled to port—then still the milk of donhood, as Greek
was its unthreatened mother-tongue—and allowed the *Apeiron* to violate the law of the *Peras*. The other story is unpublished, and not so sad.
A Canadian lady once told me that, when she was a girl, she was playing
lawn-tennis with other maidens in the gardens of the late Professor Goldwin Smith "over there." It was a very hot day, and he came out and good-
naturedly asked them if they would not like something to drink. (Goldwin Smith had a reputation for acerbity; but I can say that, on the only
occasion when I met him—as being an old *Saturday Reviewer* he revisited his former haunts at the Albany, and my editor admitted me to the
interview—he was as agreeable as any man could be.) Well, after a few
minutes, during which the damsels naturally became thirstier than ever,
their host reappeared, bearing on a mighty silver salver glasses of—port
wine! They were not—or at least she was not—so ungracious as to refuse it; but it did not exactly meet their views. [**Mozley:** *Reminiscences
Chiefly of Oriel College, and the Oxford Movement*, 2 vols. (London, 1882).
Thomas Mozley (1806–93) was an undergraduate at Oriel College, Oxford, where he was the pupil and friend of John Henry Newman, whose
sister Mozley married. The story, in chapter 9 of the *Reminiscences*, is
about Joseph Pickford, who held the living of Cholderton before Mozley. Pickford, as a probationary fellow of Oriel, had been set to work on
the task, not of cataloging, but of shelving some thirty thousand volumes
in the Oriel library, which, by long neglect, had been subjected to "fermentation, germination, secretion, humectation, and exsiccation, and all
kinds of natural processes." Mozley does not present Pickford as a heavy
drinker but as a miserly, disagreeable fellow. **Hartley Coleridge:** the
poet's son. He lost his Oriel fellowship on grounds of intemperance, lack
of discipline, and association with doubtful characters. Hartley himself
thought that he had been persecuted. See Earl Leslie Griggs, *Hartley Coleridge: His Life and Work* (London: University of London Press, 1929),
pp. 82, 88. **"Noetics":** A group of young theological turks at Oriel College in Mozley's day: from the Greek *noesis*, "knowledge." ***Apeiron . . .***

Peras: Greek antonyms: *peras* means "end, limit, boundary"; *apeiron*, a term from pre-Socratic philosophy, means "unbounded, limitless." **Goldwin Smith:** Smith (1823–1910) had been an original member of the staff of the *Saturday Review*, founded in 1855. He wrote for it until 1858, when he became Regius Professor of History at Oxford. In 1868 he went to Cornell University as one of the founding faculty of that institution. In 1871 he migrated to Toronto, married a rich widow, and remained there for the rest of his life. Smith was throughout his life engaged in controversy in the cause of liberal reform; in Canada he was a champion of Canadian independence. **the Albany:** The *Saturday Review* under its editor Walter Pollock had its offices in Albany, in Piccadilly.—*Editor*]

IV. CLARET AND BURGUNDY

To write on these two glorious wines, giving them only some thousand words apiece, may seem audacious and profane, even with the limitation of the texts to the contents of a small cellar during a few years. But it has to be done; and the pleasure at least of doing it is not lessened by the fact, unpleasant in itself, that for a good many years past the writer has been unable to drink either. For his conscience is clear and his gratitude unmixed, inasmuch as, for full forty years earlier, he never missed an opportunity of drinking his fair share of the best of both that came in his way.

I did not begin my cellar at a very good time (the latest seventies and early eighties) for Claret of the best class. The great '58's—respecting which Thackeray had enquired "Boirai-je de ton vin, O comète?" and Fate had answered "No"—were very dear, not very plentiful, and getting a trifle old. '64 was in perfection, but very dear likewise: and one was in danger of laying down those costly and most disappointing '70's, which, though they lasted in a rather unusual fashion and were drinkable at forty years old, were always more or less what wine-slang calls "dumb." Until the '74's and '75's were ready one had to pick up odd lots of crack vintages,

and what one could of others which had turned up unexpected
trumps. One of these latter, a '71 Lafite which hailed from Pall
Mall, was a great stand-by; some '62 from the Powell sale, already
mentioned, of the same premier wine, as it is vulgarly esteemed,
a little less so. (For my own part I think the best Latour rather
better, and a thoroughly "succeeded" Margaux quite as good, while
the outsider rival, Haut Brion—"Ho Bryen" as Pepys called it a
quarter of a millennium ago—can be wonderful. I remember
some Haut Brion of a friend's (it was '84), which for a short time—
it did not, I think, "hold" well—was at least the equal of any claret
I ever drank.)

Of the "regulars" of this period I see I had a beautiful Margaux of '58, and an almost equally beautiful Pichon-Longueville
of '64, a Montrose (one of the least common of the second-
growths in England, but charming at its best) of the same year,
and another Margaux of '68. Of those unsatisfactory '70's I had
at various times Lafite, Latour, Margaux, Haut Brion, Pichon-
Longueville, Lagrange, and Croizet-Bages. The seven wines,
taking only a dozen of each, cost, at the high prices then ruling
for claret, about thirty pounds. I might have had three times the
quantity of a sound *bourgeois* wine, much above *ordinaire*, for the
money, and no disappointment.

These things, however, will happen: and, especially on the
"small quantity, many kinds" principle, you get good compensa-
tion. I once bought some magnums of '75 Mouton Rothschild,
rather before it had established its reputation, at an extremely
moderate price, and I need hardly tell anyone who knows claret-
history what it turned out to be. I don't think I ever had a better:
and it gave me one agreeable triumph. The late M. Beljame, one
of the best of men, of scholars, and of foreign speakers of English, was dining with me. During dinner I had, perhaps rashly,
said that I thought we got some of the best French wine in En-

gland, and he replied politely but doubtfully, "Yes, you get some of the best, and," with a little hesitation, "some of the worst." So I laughed and waited. When he had the Mouton in his glass I said, "Now is *that* 'from behind the fagots' or not?" And he bowed, as only a Frenchman can bow, and turned the phrase back into its native French with an emphatic "Oui" before it.

As long as the '74's and '75's lasted nothing quite touched them; but I have always thought that the knowing ones seldom did justice to the '78's. It was customary to see and hear them described as "coarse"; but they were certainly (to play a little on words) the last "fine" wines for many years, if indeed there has been anything since equally deserving the epithet. With '78 *Château* Lafite I was indeed unlucky, for I bought, without sampling, several dozens of it when it was eighteen or twenty years old, and found that it had evidently been kept in too hot a cellar. But I had some magnums of Léoville, already spoken of, and some others of Beychevelle of this year, than which I never drank any better representatives of those two admirable wines; and I also lit upon one of the "bastard" Lafites, to borrow, without impoliteness, the term applied technically to lower class Montrachet—Lafite-Carruades—which had been originally bottled in or for Ireland, and which certainly justified the reputation of Irish claret. One very much preferred it to what used to be called "Scotch claret"—a generous and potent but decidedly "doctored" liquor, sold without name of vineyard, and suggesting a considerable admixture of the black wines of Cahors or thereabouts. This, however, had, I think, been practically obsolete for many years, even before the Caledonian deserted the purer kinds. After '78 there were catastrophes on catastrophes of mildew and the like, till you came to the strong, yet like the '70's rather hard and dumb, wines of '87, and the delightfully fresh and flavoury but rapidly withering '88's and '89's. But the last wines (for the '99's and '00's never seemed to me good for very much, and I have not tried later vintages owing to the causes mentioned) that I possessed and really rejoiced in were the '93's. The Latour of this year and the Rauzan Ségla, when eleven years old, were super-excellent; Montrose, Larose, Mouton Rothschild and Palmer were at the worst satisfactory; and I found something more than mere satisfaction in two outsiders—Gentiles, as it were, or at least trans-Jordanians to the pure Israel of Medoc— to wit, Pape Clément and Haut Brion Larrivet.

One thing may be noticed before turning away from a wine on which I could write a dozen or a score of these chapters, and that is the extraordinary drop in prices which this book of mine shows, and the cause of which people may assign at their choice to the falling off in the goodness of the liquor, or the falling off of the taste for it in Great Britain. As for the latter fact, I need only say that before I left Edinburgh,* the headquarters at one time of claret-drinkers, it was practically useless to open a magnum of claret for a dinner party of twelve or fourteen people, unless you selected your guests on purpose. And as for the price, taking the same growths at the same age of (1) the good vintages

---

* The first Lord Kinross, when he was Lord President, once told me that in his early days at the Scottish Bar it was customary for knots of four frequenters of the Parliament House, when a vintage promised well, to lay down as many hogsheads of the best reputed first or second growths, dividing the produce in bottles among themselves (a hogshead of claret makes about 23 dozen, so the subscribers would have that quantity apiece of the vintage, divided into lots of between 5 and 6 dozen of each growth). He added that he did not believe any of his brethren did any such thing at the time we were talking. [**Lord Kinross:** John Blair Balfour (1837–1905), the first Baron Kinross, the leading advocate in Scotland, and a Liberal politician, was Lord President of the Court of Session in Scotland from 1899 to 1905. His early days at the bar would have been in the 1860s.—*Editor*]

in the seventies, (2) the '93's, (3) the '99's and '00's, I should say that there was a drop of at least twenty-five per cent. between the first two, and a further drop of more than the same extent between (2) and (3). Even now, when all wine is at abnormal and preposterous prices, I see hardly anything, in the better classes of claret, quoted at figures parallel even to those which obtained thirty years ago.

If Claret is the queen of natural wines, Burgundy is the king: their places being taken in the other realm of the artificial by Madeira and Port. I was, during the keeping of this book, permitted by the kindness of my already mentioned friend, the late Mr. John Harvey, to be possessor of a small quantity of Romanée Conti '58. It was five-and-twenty years old when I bought it, and in absolute perfection: indeed, more than one good judge agreed with me that it was almost impossible to conceive anything more perfect in its kind. It is the fashion of course to put Clos-Vougeot at the head of all Burgundies, and very delicious Clos-Vougeot can be: but I never drank any specimen thereof equal to this for the combination of intensity and delicacy in bouquet and flavour, for body, colour and every good quality of wine. Indeed, Clos-Vougeot, excellent as it is, seems to me often, if not always, to have the excellences of claret rather than those of Burgundy; it does not "hold to the blood of its clan" quite firmly enough. The '69 Richebourg which I mentioned in the first of these articles was also a fine wine, though it could not approach the Conti. The two were succeeded after some time (for one does not every day, unless one is both a millionaire and a Hercules, drink Burgundy of this class, though I cannot imagine a better *viaticum* in fetching Alcestis from the shade or any other difficult adventure) by others. The book was not kept in those times. But I find in *menus* of the date of the interval a Musigny of '77 and a La Tâche of

'86, both of which I remember as delightful; as well as a Romanée of '87 which was good but which was a little injured, for me if not for others, by the memory of its great forerunner. Warnings of gout on my own part, and the annoyance of finding more and more people leave such treasures in the decanter, prevented my buying much Burgundy latterly. My last batch was a comparatively humble Corton of 1881, bought when it was nineteen years old for sixty-eight shillings a dozen, and quite cheap at its price. It lasted for at least a dozen years longer, and never went off at all.

But in the earlier days the Richebourg was accompanied by a bevy of less distinguished representatives of the Slope of Gold and its neighbourhood—Corton again, Pommard, Santenay, Chenas and others—beverage wines which you paid some forty shillings a dozen or less for, and you could drink without reproach of conscience, even by yourself. The bin was the occasion of a pleasant occurrence, which I may tell to the glory of my family, and perhaps for the amusement of the reader. One of my father's sisters was a very old lady, who lived by herself in a remote part of the country on no large income, and (as the phrase goes) in a very quiet way. Having some trouble with her eyes, she came up to town to consult an oculist, and naturally stayed with me. The oculist, finding nothing organically wrong, but only a certain weakness of age and constitution, recommended her to drink Burgundy. I gave her on successive days some of the Richebourg, telling her frankly that it was a very expensive wine, and some of a sound Pommard, which could be had for between half and a third of the price, that she might choose and order some from the merchant, who, as it happened, supplied both. I had imagined that the first figure would either frighten or shock her; but she said with perfect simplicity, "I think, my dear boy, the best always *is* the best," and ordered a small supply of the Richebourg forthwith.

One more Burgundy story, perhaps, to finish with. A vast number of years ago a friend of mine, who had some official business with one of the great rose-growers in the neighbourhood of London, asked me if I should like to go with him. We went down by train, and after the business was done and the gardens thoroughly surveyed, were entertained with a most copious and capital lunch, or rather early dinner. To vary a poem which Mr. Gladstone once adapted to rally his great rival and "the farmers of Aylesbury," "with the salmon there was sherry, with the mutton there was beer"— some of the best draught Bass that I remember. But when we had done justice to it all, our host produced a bottle of very special Burgundy—Chambertin,* I think—which had been given to him by a correspondent at Dijon itself. It would never have done to re-fuse it; nor perhaps (for we were both young men) had we much inclination to do so. So we submitted to "the sweet compulsion" and took our leave. But then came the question, "What to do next?" It was a warm summer afternoon; and, though England produces nothing better than beer and France nothing better than Burgundy, it is difficult to imagine two beverages which agree worse together. Had we taken the train again we should probably have fallen asleep, and been waked ignominiously and in a flustered condition by the ticket-collector. So we made up our minds to walk the ten or twelve miles, and did it. I remember that for the first part of the way I felt as if there was a thin India-rubber or air-cushion beneath the soles

---

* It may have been noticed that I do not mention any of this famous wine as in my own possession. The fact is that it has never been a favourite of mine. It may be blasphemous to call it "coarse," but it seems to me that it "doth something grow to" coarseness, as compared with those pre-ferred above. It was Napoleon's favourite; and the fact rather "speaks" its qualities, good and not so good. ["**doth something grow to**": Shake-speare, *Merchant of Venice*, II, ii, 18.—*Editor*]

of my boots. But there is hardly anything that you can't "walk off," and we walked off this pleasing but perilous predicament.

(List of "Classed" and other clarets in cellar at various times. The "outside" vineyards are italicized.)

1864— Ch. Margaux
1862— 	" Lafite
1864— 	" Pichon-Longueville
	" Montrose
1868— 	" Margaux
	" Dauzac
1869— 	" de Beychevelle
	" Kirwan
1870— 	" Lafite
	" Latour
	" *Haut Brion*
	" Margaux
	" Pichon-Longueville
	" Lagrange
	" Croizet-Bages
1871— 	" Lafite
1874— 	" Léoville-Barton
	" Rauzan
	" Palmer
	" Giscours
	" Branaire-Ducru
1875— 	" Mouton-Rothschild
	" Durfort
	" Duhart-Milon

1878—	Ch. Lafite	
	” Latour	
	” Léoville-Barton	*Magnums, and both*
	” de Beychevelle	*quite admirable.*
	” Langoa	
	” Dauzac	
	” *Lafite Carruades*	
1883—	” Margaux *(magnums)*	•
1884—	” Durfort	
1887—	” Lafite	
	” Cos d'Estournel	
	” de Beychevelle	
1888	” D'Issan, La Lagune, Beychevelle,	
1889	Clerc-Milon, *Smith Haut Lafite*	
1891—	” Mouton d'Armailhac	•
1892—	” Duhart-Milon	•
1893—	” Latour	
	” Rauzan-Ségla	
	” Montrose	
	” Gruaud-Larose	
	” Mouton Rothschild	
	” Palmer	
	” de Beychevelle	
	” *Pape-Clément*	
	” *Haut Brion Larrivet*	
1895—	” Palmer	•
1896—	” Léoville-Poyferré	•
1899—	” Margaux	

1899— Ch. Mouton Rothschild
    " Pichon-Longueville
    " Gruaud-Larose-Sarget
    " Léoville-Lascases
    " Cos d'Estournel
    " Langoa
    " Calon Ségur
1900— " Margaux
    " Léoville
    " Langoa
    " Pontet-Canet
    " Pape-Clément

(NOTES ON CLARET LIST.)

Some additional notes on a few of these may be interesting. The magnums of Margaux 1883 may surprise connoisseurs, for the year had a very bad reputation, mildew having attacked the vines. I saw them in an auction-list years later, and, having made a bid for a few, was offered the whole lot—several dozen—at an absurdly moderate price, 3s. 6d. to 4s. per magnum. They were actually *premier vin*, château-bottled and in quite good condition, though the wine was light in body and not very full in flavour. I drank them, while they lasted, in place of ordinary Medoc of about the same price, and a very good bargain they were. About the same time or a little later, when I was not keeping my cellar-book regularly, a bottle or two of, I think, Langoa, dating from the mildew years, developed an extraordinary malady, arising from the presence of what I believe the chemists call caproic acid. The stuff tasted and smelt abominably *hircine*.

The wines italicised above are, of course, inhabitants of the Court of the Gentiles—outsiders as regards the official list—though Lafite *Carruades* is, I believe, actually a neighbour of the greater vineyard. Haut Brion *tout court* every one who knows anything about claret is acquainted with, and it is spoken of above. Haut Brion *Larrivet* is not much below the chief of the clan. Another Gentile, Smith Haut Lafite, was unnoticed among the examples of those two curious years, '88 and '89. They "came up as a flower" and faded like one—but for freshness and passing pleasure of flavour and bouquet—for drinking at a draught—they were charming. Browning's "A Pretty Woman" is the poem that reminds me most of them.

Some readers may be surprised at seeing Pontet Canet figure only once in the list, and that only among the 1900's. It became, in the odd way in which things do so become, a "literary" wine a good many years ago; but I never cared for it. Almost all the wines of its own (Fifth) class that I know seem to me as good or better—Batailley, Dauzac and Mouton d'Armailhac decidedly better. Of other classed wines which do not figure at all in the above list, but which I have possessed or at least drunk at different times in my life, Brane-Cantenac and Ducru-Beaucaillou have left best memories among the second growths; Malescot Saint-Exupéry among the third; Branaire-Ducru and Le Prieuré among the fourth. Of all the elect—between 50 and 60—only some half score are quite unknown to me, and these include, I think, no seconds; only Ferrière and Marquis d'Alesme among the thirds; but Saint-Pierre, Talbot, Pouget, Marquis de Terme and Rochet among the fourths; and Grand-Puy, Pedesclaux, Belgrave and Camensac among the fifths. And I should not have left them untried if I had ever seen them in any wine-merchant's list during the time when I could drink claret.

I have said nothing about the wines of Saint-Emilion—even

the noted "Cheval Blanc"—because I have never cared much for them. But I certainly do not wish to say anything against them. And to mention all the good non-classed wines, Medoc or not, that I have drunk and enjoyed would be endless. In the days above mentioned—the Time of Roses—I have had divers half-hogsheads of such wines bottled in half-litres or Imperial pints for ordinary drinking, and thanked the Lord therefor. Some such wines—for instance, a good *premier bourgeois* Margaux—will turn out just as well as any but the best classed growths, and might be drunk "before the dear years" with no sense of extravagance. Perhaps no wine's name has been more taken in vain in England than Saint Julien's. He must be a fortunate claret-lover who has not sometimes made grimaces over a bottle so labelled* at the average British hostelry. Exactly why this poor district has been so abused I do not know. It is true that some of the very best vineyards (Léoville, Larose, Ducru-Beaucaillou, Lagrange, Langoa, Beychevelle) are situated there. But Margaux (one of the silliest examples of "facetious and rejoicing ignorance" about wine that I remember was a jibe at the difference of Margaux and Château Margaux) and Pauillac (which actually has two of the three first growths, Lafite and Latour, with the scarcely inferior Mouton Rothschild and Pichon-Longueville to back them up, and not a few excellent fourths and fifths) have very much fewer tricks played on them, and others, except Saint-Estèphe, hardly any at all. Perhaps relative abundance of produce gives the reason.

I have endeavoured to keep clear of the most commonplace topics in these notes. Perhaps, however, something should be said on two such. I have lived through two or three different phases of at-

---

* There is one label in particular which is very common, and which I learned long ago to shun. But the peculiarities of the law of libel prevent my specifying it.

titude to the temperature at which claret should be drunk. There was the Ice Age—certainly a barbarous time. It is well that Browning's "Bishop Blougram" was not an Anglican prelate, for his directions to my sometime colleague in journalism, Mr. Gigadibs,

Try the cooler jug,
Put back the other, but don't jog the ice,

are very harrowing. Icing good claret at all is, as has been said, barbarous; but the idea of subjecting it to processes of alternate freezing, thawing and freezing again is simply Bolshevist. Some readers may remember "marsupial" claret jugs with a pouch for ice. Then came the warming period, determined by not always well understood imitation of French ways. (It is in one of Sandeau's books, I think, that an uninvited guest complains of the claret being unwarmed and the champagne un-iced.) Unfortunately, people used to put it close to the fire and parboil it. Now, and for some time, the books have recommended nothing more than bringing it up in time to let it get the temperature of the dining-room, which is sound enough. As for Burgundy baskets, they are pretty instruments, and may be useful—when the cork is not first drawn with the bottle perpendicular. But to make them of any real good, the *whole* of the contents should be poured into successive glasses, at only the necessary inclination, till the sediment is reached, and no tilting back permitted.

V. CHAMPAGNE AND
OTHER FRENCH WHITE WINES

Who was the author of the celebrated, or once celebrated description, "A man who likes (or 'who would say he likes') dry champagne"? It indicates a period so far back that only the oldest of us remember it. It is true that you may find the offer of "champagne, sweet or dry" in books of still earlier date, but the "dry" there was, I believe, *still* dry Sillery. However, the change came: and it was not finally accomplished when my cellar-book was started. The head of the great house of Roederer was, even later, said to have declared that as long as *he* lived there should be no bowing to the dry Baal in his cellars; and, at any rate in the country, Clicquot was more often still sweet—not to the "Russe" extent, which was only good for savages or children, but yet not dry. Indeed I remember how, when I confessed to my Pall Mall mentor in the opening interview, that I did not share the prevailing mania for Pommery, he looked at me approvingly and said, "*I'*d nearly as soon have a bra-a-andy and sod-d-a!" Nevertheless if you only keep sufficient wine-flavour in dry wines (they are apt to lose it) nobody of catholic taste would desire their abolition, though one may regret the moderately rich and full-flavoured variety as an alternative.* And as a matter of fact, the earliest pages of my book show Pommery itself and Heidsieck Monopole, Perrier Jouet's "Club Dry" and even Dagonet's "Brut Exceptionnel." This last used to be (I think it has gone off lately) a considerable favourite with me, though I have heard some people say they would rather drink camomile or calumba. And, taking well-known brands all round, I do not know that I was more faithful to any than to Krug. I began my fancy for it with a '65, which memory represents as being, though dry, that "*winy* wine," as Thackeray describes it, which Champagne ought to be, but too seldom is. And when, just fifty years after that vintage, I drank farewell to my cellar before giving up housekeeping, it was in a bottle of Krug's Private Cuvée, 1906.

Still, I had no monomania on the subject. I think there were few of the greater brands that were not represented by a modest dozen or two at one time or other in my cellar; and the very best I ever had was a Perrier-Jouet, obtained through the same kindness which supplied me with the Romanée Conti already mentioned. It was a wine of the great vintage of 1857, and was sup-

* The optimists who hold that there is in all evil good may point to the effect of U.S. "dryness" in acquainting *us* with "Goût Américain" champagne. It seems to me (I am sorry to shock Mr. Walter Leaf, both as a scholar and as a colleague in scholarship of two intimate, though alas! now dead, friends of mine; but at least I did *not* give "30s. a dozen" for my specimen bottle) a not unhappy compromise between asperity and mawkishness. ["**Goût Américain**": Depending on whether North or South America is meant, Champagne of this description may be slightly or very sweet. **Mr. Walter Leaf:** (1852–1937), chairman of the Westminster Bank by profession and a noted Homeric scholar by avocation; he translated *The Iliad* (1892) with Saintsbury's friend Andrew Lang. I do not know what other of Saintsbury's friends worked with Leaf, nor what the allusion to "shocking" Leaf might mean.—*Editor*]

THE NEW SCHOOL.

Uncle (who is rather proud of his Cellar). "NOW GEORGE, MY BOY, THERE'S A GLASS OF CHAMPAGNE FOR YOU—DON'T GET SUCH STUFF AT SCHOOL, EH! EH! EH!"
George. "H'M—AWFULLY SWEET! VERY GOOD SORT FOR LADIES—BUT I'VE ARRIVED AT A TIME OF LIFE, WHEN I CONFESS I LIKE MY WINE DRY!" *(Sensation).*

FIGURE 12. *Punch* on the new taste for dry Champagne, "a change not finally accomplished" when Saintsbury began his cellar book (*Punch*, 12 April 1862).

posed to have formed part of a parcel originally shipped for Queen Victoria, and designated "t.c." that is to say *très coloré*. When I bought it, May 1884, it was twenty-seven years old, of a deep amber colour, and nearly but not quite still, though not at all ullaged (alas! there are some people who do not know that ullaging sometimes improves champagne. But they, as the Colonel said to the Cornet who did not know that age improved it, "have a great deal to learn"). It was so majestical that one was inclined to leave it quite alone, and drink it like a slightly sparkling liqueur. But I was tempted—not I think exactly or wholly by the devil—to try if the immense dormant qualities of it could be waked up. At that mo-

ment I also had some '74 of the same shippers, than which there
can have been few better—just in perfection, ten years old, all raw-
ness gone, but sparkle in fullest force. So I married them, and the
voice that breathed o'er Eden did not refuse to repeat itself, *mutatis decenter mutandis.*

"The bigger the better" is, though a common, not a universal
rule; it does not, for instance, apply to fish, nor to mutton, nor
to some other things edible and not edible. But it generally applies to receptacles of wine, and to those of champagne very specially. Jeroboams, or to be accurate, double magnums, to which
the term Jeroboam, properly applying to a *six* bottle vessel, is often
by courtesy vouchsafed, are costly and risky, for a corked one is
no joke of a loss. They require a properly adjusted company to
drink them, and an intelligent Ganymede or Hebe (I have known
Hebe do it beautifully) to pour them out. But you never get such
good wine as in or from them. As for vintages, I thought the '70's
(with which, in the way of laying down, I started) very good indeed, but Champagne vintages are perhaps better known than
any others, so that there may be no need to waste time on them.
Sometimes there were interesting conflicts of adjoining years,
especially in '92 and '93, and later in '98, '99 and 1900. The knowing ones usually went for '92, which was, if I remember rightly,
the smaller and selecter vintage. I had some good wines of it—
Pommery and Krug and Roederer among them. But the vintage
that I laid down most of, and liked, I think, almost best of all,
was '93. It took, in some cases, a long time to develop; the Clicquot, at eight and even nine years old, had a peculiar bitterness.
But this worked itself out; it became a very perfect wine; and
though its seventeenth winter was certainly not "sweet," as seventeen is supposed to be, it then had all other excellences that
such a wine ought to have, and retained them till over twenty.

Nor were the others, as each came to perfection, much behind it. I find special notes of admiration on Moët, Ayala, and St. Marceaux—the last a shipper rather undervalued, I think, south of Tweed, though respected duly north of it. As for the three competitors of the end of the century, I should select Clicquot '99 as the best of a dozen good ones.

But champagne is—or was*—everybody's wine, and needs little talking. Nothing, perhaps, does you so much good if you do not drink it too often; but, for my own part, *"toujours champagne"* would nauseate me in a week or less. One thing, as a pendant to what was said on the price of claret, may be added: and that is, that as Bordeaux put its prices down Reims sent them up. In the late seventies one was seldom asked more than ninety shillings for the very best vintages, ready to drink, at eight or nine years old. Five-and-twenty years later ninety-five and a hundred were demanded for wine just sent over, and wanting years to fit it for drinking.

Perhaps, too, I should here say something, as in the Claret chapter, on the question of temperature. Ladling bits of raw ice into a glass of champagne at dinner is no doubt again barbarous; though hosts who have given their guests doubtful wine may be glad to see it done. Nor do I myself approve of the ice-pail; for extreme cold certainly hurts flavour. But there is no doubt that most people *do* like their champagne cold; indeed, even on some bottles of white Bordeaux, you may find directions to "ice." It is also certain that cold assists the "pick-me-up" character of sparkling wine. Matthew Arnold, in one of his letters, notes how "the cool champagne at dinner" relieved a previous touch of the heart-weakness, which was in the end to prove fatal to him. For my own

---

* I don't think I have drunk it a dozen times in the last three years, or thrice in the last twelve months.

part, I have always found that, except in extremely hot and close weather, wrapping the bottles in a cloth wetted with water fresh from the tap (or better still, a well), and placing them in a draught for a short time, gives all the coolness necessary, and does not "numb the ethers."

It is, perhaps, too bold to attempt to deal with the three great groups of white Bordeaux, Burgundy and Hermitage, those of the Loire district, and the innumerable *petits vins blancs* of the rest of France, in the tail of a chapter. But the restriction of these papers to a single small collection makes it less impudent. The last-named group are almost unobtainable in England, and, indeed, might not travel. I never cared much for the wines of Anjou, Touraine and their vicinage, either sparkling or still. Medical favour has for the last two or three decades greatly popularised Graves and Barsac, but it has always seemed to me that no wines lose more by crossing the channel. On the other hand, the fuller Sauternes travel very well, and in their way are noble.

I say "in their way," because there is a curious difference between white and red wines, as it seems to me. The last glass of your bottle of good Claret or Burgundy (I mean of the bottle when you drink the whole) is as good as the first. I am not sure that it is not better. But the first glass of the corresponding white wines—be they Château Yquem or Montrachet themselves—is a great deal better than the last; indeed, this last has a tendency to "sicken," as is also the case with white Hermitage, and with the heavier hocks. At least, that is my experience; and I have found many, though not all, good drinkers disposed to agree with me.

Still, all these wines, when good, are very good gifts indeed, and if you find that too many glasses spoil their effect, the obvious remedy is to drink fewer. I should, indeed, never drink them—with the possible exception of white Hermitage—*after* dinner; and

the fact that Thackeray did so once—at somebody else's suggestion, it is true—seems to me almost the only blot on his wine-
record. But the lighter—not *too* light—kinds, such as good Carbonnieux or Olivier of the western branch, or a good Pouilly of
the eastern, are admirable dinner wines. And, *in themselves,* such
wines of the greater clans, as Châteaux Yquem, Coutet or Latour
Blanche, as Montrachet, and even a very good Meursault ('70 of
this was first-rate),* all of which made their home with me at different times, are always memorable. With an unnamed Haut
Sauterne of '74, bottled by one of the oldest Edinburgh merchants, but bought at somebody's sale, I have specially fond associations. It was a very rich wine, being about thirty years old when
I first had it; in fact, it was too rich for some tastes. But once there
came to "the grey metropolis" a Finnish lady—a most perfect
representative of non-Aryan beauty and anythingarian charm—
to whom not only all men, but what is more wonderful, most
women, fell captive the moment they saw her. She was dining with
us once, and confided to me, with rather a piteous *moue,* that, in
this country, champagne was "so dreadfully dry." Fortunately I
had remembered beforehand that the warlocks and witches of the
North like sweet things; and had provided a bottle of this very
Sauterne, of which I had a few left. She purred over it like one
of Freya's own cats (let it be observed that I do *not* think Freya
was a Finnish goddess), and I promised her that I would keep the
rest for her. But alas! she left Edinburgh in a short time, and after no long one I heard that she was dead. The wine lost half its
flavour.

* The same lady who praised my "Pale Rich" Sherry (*v.* Chap. II.)
was good enough to remember most *donnescamente* (as Dante says) this
Meursault, many years afterwards. [*donnescamente: Purgatorio,* XXXIII,
135: "with womanly dignity," "graciously."—*Editor*]

Sparkling white Burgundy can be very good,* the best of all the imitations of Champagne. I have spoken of the lighter still wines. As for Montrachet,† it is very great, though, as someone says, I think in Freytag's best novel, it "makes one's veins swell like whip-cord." With white Hermitage I have twice been lucky—once with a lighter wine, Château Grillet or Grillé, which used to be a favourite here in the days of the Regency, and once with a heavier, La Frette. This last was one of the ornaments of my cellar. It

* Some which we used to get in Guernsey *before* the war of 1870 (the supply stopped then) was the cheapest *good* sparkling wine I ever had. It cost, unless my memory plays tricks, but thirty shillings a dozen, certainly not more than thirty-six shillings; and the shop where I bought it—a queer emporium of furniture, curiosities, second-hand books and Heaven knows what else—was the only place where I ever heard Victor Hugo speak. For sparkling *red* Burgundy I have never cared; nor indeed for any red "fizz." "Old Rose" champagne was sometimes delicious, but it was not *red*; and its modern deeply "pinkified" representatives please me not much. The true *œil-de-perdrix* tint is not, I think, "synthetically" attainable. But a perfect "partridge-eye" champagne might almost deserve, on the pattern of "pheasant-eye" narcissus, the epithet "poetic." [**Victor Hugo:** Hugo lived in self-imposed exile on Guernsey from 1855 to 1870. Saintsbury was on Guernsey from 1868 to 1874. *œil-de-perdrix* **tint:** "partridge eye"; brownish-red or pale pink, or, as Frank Schoonmaker says, "a sort of combination of very pale pink and bronze" (*Encyclopedia of Wine*, 6th ed. [New York: Hastings House, 1975]); characteristic of certain sparkling wines, of Meursault, of the wines of Neuchâtel in Switzerland, and others. **the epithet "poetic":** The learned name of the common, or pheasant's eye, narcissus is *Narcissus poeticus.—Editor*]

† This magnificent and formidable wine has three degrees or qualities, *Aîné, Chevalier* and *Bâtard.* The last is not the least noteworthy of the denizens of Sinister Street; the Chevalier I do not think I ever drank; but the "eldest" certainly deserves his pride of place. [*Aîné, Chevalier* and *Bâtard:* That is, the "elder," the "knight," and the "bastard." André

was a '65, and was nearly thirty years old when I bought it at a sale in Edinburgh, but before I went to live there, a friend taking some of the batch off my hands. It was not "done for" twenty years later still, when it had reached its full half-century; but it wanted re-corking, and the "gun-flint" taste had grown too strong for most people. At its very best, it was unique—a worthy sister to its twenty years elder, and at this time departed, *red* brother, celebrated in Chapter I.

Jullien explains that the three grades, though coming from the same place and from the same variety of grape, differ on account of the exposure of the vineyards (*Topographie de tous les vignobles connus,* 5th ed. [Paris, 1866], p. 137). *Aîné* is no longer in use, but the classifications *Bâtard-Montrachet* and *Chevalier-Montrachet* are.—*Editor*]

VI. HOCK, MOSELLE AND THE REST

German wine has of late naturally shared the unpopularity of German everything—naturally, but not wisely. The true attitude in such matters was long ago put in the "War Song of Dinas Vawr":

> His wine and beasts [*provide*] our feasts,
> And his overthrow our chorus.   •

Not that Hock, as indeed was hinted in a former chapter, has ever ranked with me among the "First Three," or even the first five or six greatest wines. The "palling" character of its attractions, when at its supposed finest, precludes that. I was once favoured with half a dozen single bottles of the very finest Hocks in ordinary commerce—wines, the cheapest of which would have "stood you in," as the old phrase went, some ten shillings a bottle at the old prices, and the dearest nearer a sovereign. Except for curiosity's sake, I would much rather have had a similar collection of good second-class claret; and after the first two glasses of each Rhine wine, it would have been no sacrifice in me to leave all the rest to any compotator.

In fact, despite the wonderful first taste of the great "Auslese"   •

wines, I think both Hock and Moselle best as beverage drinks; for in these lower qualities, the overpowering and almost barbaric volume of flavour does not occur, and they are very fresh and pleasant quenchers, going well with most sorts of food. In days when it was still lawful to drink bottles of wine in the plural, I should have said that a bottle of hock at dinner, and a bottle of claret after it, was a decent and moderate allowance, and likely, as one of Scott's people allows of something else, "to bring a blessing with it." But for finer purposes I should, once more, regard them as chiefly curiosities; and accordingly, they never figured largely in my wine-lists.*

What has been said of Hock applies with little change to Moselle. The wines of Ausonius's favourite river have long had a deserved reputation for flowery flavour; unfortunately they have—of late years and even decades—acquired another, also well deserved but much less enviable, as being the most abominably "faked" of all real or pretended juices of the grape. Whether it was partly due to green unknowing youth or not, I cannot say, but I certainly seem to remember a time when Sparkling Moselle, though apt to be a little over-sweet, was a pleasant and seemed a wholesome liquor. I once, in company with a friend, made a light but agreeable meal at Oxford in the time of fritillaries, on a bottle of it; one of those nice china vases full of ice, which looked like giant conjurors' eggcups; and some wafers. It also went excellently with a most opposite accompaniment, certain sardine sandwiches, which they then made very well at the "Mitre." But after 1870 the

---

* *Sparkling* Hock I liked little, and never bought. The "Cabinet *Sekt*," which the interesting tenant of Amerongen patronised so strongly, was "a very *German*" champagne. [**tenant of Amerongen:** Kaiser Wilhelm II of Germany, whose first refuge in Holland after his abdication and flight in 1918 was the town of Amerongen.—*Editor*]

general curse of insincerity, overreachingness and fraud, which even such a prophet of prophets of their own as Nietzsche recognised as hanging on Germany, attacked with particular ferocity the banks of the river whose various charms and benefits—its beauty and its variety, its wine and its trout and its grayling—the poet sang fifteen hundred years ago. Sparkling Moselle became a thing to be very carefully chosen or avoided altogether; the "floweriness" of both sparkling and still had a horrible suspicion of the laboratory; and I once attributed (the faculty not disagreeing) a persistent attack of an unpleasant kind to an unduly prolonged sampling of the lighter sorts. Nor did I ever much affect the loudly-trumpeted Berncastler Doktor. Still, I own that a really good Scharzhofberg is a very fine wine; and that some of the beverage kinds from Piesporter to Graacher are mighty refreshing. But it may be well to warn those who cellar it that light Moselle, when young, is very apt to *cloud*, though it should, if good, clear later.

By the way, is there any *red* Moselle?

For the *red* hocks, however, I must put in a word, both in justice to them and in charity to my fellow-creatures. They—not merely Assmanshäuser, which certainly is the best, but Walporzheimer, Ober-Ingelheimer and others—are specifics for insomnia after a fashion which seems to be very little known, even among the faculty. Many years ago, when I was doing night-work for the press, and even after I had given that up, when I was rather unusually hard run at day-work, I found sleep on the off-nights as well as the others in the former case, and often in the latter, not easy to obtain. I was not such a fool as to take drugs, and I found hot grog or (what is not in itself inefficacious) strong beer, conducive to an uncomfortable mouth, etc., in the morning when taken only a few hours before. But a large claret glass or small tumbler of red hock did the trick admirably, and without deferred discomfort.

Somewhat akin, I suppose, to these red Hocks are the still red champagnes, which are very rare in England, but are very nice wines, and quite unsurpassed for what doctors might call neurotic dyspepsia. I think they first came to my knowledge as prescribed for Prosper Mérimée in the illness which preceded his death: and after long looking for them in vain, I was lucky enough, some five-and-thirty years ago, to pick up, at the Army and Navy Stores, some still Red Verzenay of 1868. I have never seen any since in lists.

In the same bin with it once lay some Côte Rôtie—more easily procurable with us, but not very commonly seen on English dinner-tables. Something of what was said in the first of these papers as to Hermitage extends to this, and to Châteauneuf du Pape, and to many other less famous red wines of the south of France. They were, I believe, special favourites with Victor Hugo; and there is a certain Hugonic character about them all, though it never, except in Hermitage itself, rises to anything that suggests the full inspiration of the *Châtiments* or the *Contemplations*. It is more congenial to the novels in prose.

Other oddments of France put themselves forward—Saint-Péray, very pleasing now and then for a change; red sparkling Burgundy, which as noted above, I never found to be a success; while white sparkling Bordeaux is an anti-natural perversity, the invention of which deserved Dante's circle of the fiery rain. Then there is Picardan, the northernmost wine of France and the worst. This I never admitted to my cellar, but I have drunk it. And there are some French wines, well spoken of by French writers, which I have never come across, such as *vin d'Arbois*, a growth, I think, of Franche-Comté, as to which I have in vain sought particulars.

The outsiders of the Peninsula I never cellared much, but have

Picardan
Vieux

———

Ce vin délicieux produit
du vieux sol français, est
comparable aux meilleurs
vins d'origine étrangère

IMP. J. LE HÉNAFF & Cⁱᵉ. Sᵗ ETIENNE

FIGURE 13. Picardan, the "worst" wine of France, Saintsbury thought; but what wine did he mean? (author's collection).

tried sometimes. White Port I must say I think nearly deserving of the curse above pronounced on sparkling claret; but the faculty occasionally prescribe it. Calcavell*os* (or -*a*), which our ancestors used to drink more than we do, can be grateful and comforting. I never found the light Bucellas, which was rather popular some years ago, very satisfactory; indeed, except Manzanilla and its kin, already spoken of, at one end of Spain, and white Rioja (a capital beverage liquor) at the other, the very light wines of the Iberian soil are to me rather suspect. I remember the dysentery after Najara, a story oddly confirmed by a mining engineer whom I met once in a hotel smoking-room, and who told me that his English miners, in much the same district of Spain, always suffered from that unpleasant complaint if they drank the common country wines. But I once drank a kind of Portuguese claret or Burgundy (was it called "Priorato"?) which was far from contemptible. Tent and Alicant seem never now to be used with us for profane purposes; and I will not discuss Tarragona except to observe that in our present wine-famine it appears to have been promoted from that name to "Spanish Port," and from some half-crown an imperial quart to five shillings a bottle. But how many of my readers know Ampurdam? I never met it except long ago in the Channel Islands, where it was common. It looked and tasted rather like the curious compound called "matrimony," which the thrifty throats of the earlier nineteenth century used to consume. Few decent middle-class households then were without their standing decanters of port and sherry, which, when the port was getting rather stale, were mixed together as remnants, and so nothing was lost. When Ampurdam (which is an actual place name) was new, it was very fiery and rather disagreeable, standing to Port itself much as Picardan does to Sherry. But at fifty or sixty years old it became by no means despicable.

The word "Iberian" was used just now from a memory of a phrase of Thackeray's, "Iberian or Trinacrian wine," and "Trinacrian" of course leads us straight to Marsala. I cannot say that I have much personal affection for this wine, despite all the literary and historical associations of Sicily from Theocritus to Nelson. But it has with me merits of early use (see chap. i.); it was probably the first wine that I tasted. At one time, too, I was allowed to save occasional glasses of it for the purpose (illegal, I suppose) of attempting to distil brandy in one of my retorts—for, like many other boys, I used to play at chemistry. The illicit result, I remember, was far from intoxicating and very nasty. The best wine of the Marsala class that I ever drank was some brown Syracuse that we used to get in Guernsey; it might have passed for a very rich, but by no means very coarse, brown sherry. The dry Marsalas are often fearfully acid. But on the whole the pleasantest association I have with this wine dates quite recently, from the actual disappearance of my cellar itself. I had, for some special purpose, procured a gallon jar of Marsala from one of the big Stores, but had used very little of it. When the sale was over, and bins of odd bottles of the best ports for the last forty years had fetched something like a couple of pounds a dozen, this despised vessel, not above three-quarters full, went for more shillings than it had cost when it was untapped. It was (worse luck for me) before the war—though its first year was over—had brought about the present preposterous prices of wine; and these anomalies are characteristic of auctions. But when I see Marsala quoted at sixty, seventy, and eighty shillings a dozen, I say, "Well, at any rate, this one wine did make *me* a profiteer!"

Of colonial wines I need not speak, for they hardly figure in my book at all; while I never drank any American. The great irruption of Greek and Hungarian kinds occurred before my time of collection, though at Oxford and afterwards I tried a certain number. The Greek were, as a rule, insufferably beastly. When, many years after, I happened to read Folengo's admirable description of the wine which "ventris penetralia *raspat*," I recognised their quality at once. You could not say this of Hungarian, even putting aside Tokay, which itself will probably never recover the disappearance of those Hapsburgs, with whom it was so inseparably connected. Republican Tokay would be a contradiction in terms. But to tell the truth, it never was a wine: only a prince of liqueurs. The commoner vintages were not intolerable; you *could* drink Carlowitz if you tried, and the Austrian Vöslauer was not to be despised. But I never quite got over a scientific lecturer, who contended that the chemical analysis of Château Lafite and that of some Hungarian *ordinaire* being quite the same (at least he said so), it was absurd to give five pounds a dozen for the one when you could get the other for twenty shillings. He was probably the spiritual father of the gentleman who told us the other day, after much orthodox experiment, that drinking without eating really made you more drunk than drinking with or after eating.

As to Italian, I suppose it does not travel well, though Chianti, like Carlowitz, can be drunk. I remember some very "wersh" sparkling Asti; but I think I preferred it to some sparkling Lacrima Cristi, which suggested ginger beer alternately stirred up with a stick of chocolate and a large sulphur match. However, none of the things mentioned since Marsala ever figured in the cellar whose memoirs I have been summarising; indeed, I should have held most of them unworthy of it. So let us wish it—at least as regards its most dignified contents—good-bye. I really think it was lovely and pleasant in its life, and the memory of it borrows its own bouquet and flavour. Many bottles went into it full, and came out empty or to be emptied. I only wish I could have used the empties, especially the jeroboams, in the pelting of any Pussyfoot who would make our dinner-tables dry places, and deprive our hearts of that which God sends to make them glad. Of some other good creatures which kept the wine company and of things connected with the cellar itself and the whole subject we may yet speak.

But, before passing to these, it may be right, since they have

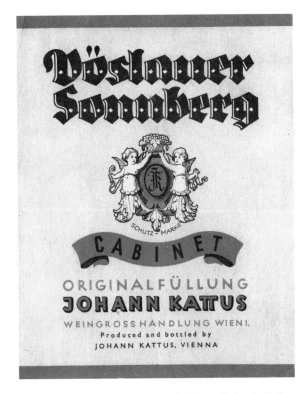

FIGURE 14. Vöslauer, a wine "not to be despised" (Brady Collection, Special Collections, Shields Library, University of California, Davis).

sometimes, though not often or largely, found a home with their betters, to mention those generally poor things, "British Wines." I say "generally," because I have known ginger wine which was not a despicable liquor. A good Oxford man and good country clergyman, who was a very old friend of my family, and in whose house I more than once found hospitality, instruction and on one

FIGURE 15. Labels for Lord Bute's British wines; they would be drunk, Saintsbury wrote, only as a "penance" (Hugh Barty-King, *A Tradition of English Wine* [Oxford: Oxford Illustrated Press, 1977]).

occasion my first acquaintance with the *Oxford and Cambridge Magazine*, used to have some made at home, which he called his "sermon-writing essence," and which was capital. And another person whom I could trust, my friend Mr. E. B. Michell, mildest-mannered of men, great with fist and scull, and one of the last of falconers before the Lord, told me that a tenant of his father's used

to make rhubarb wine which was really worth drinking. "Raisin wine" can be doctored into something not unlike a coarse Tent; and "orange" into something by no means distantly suggestive of sherry and bitters. But all these are amiable "fakings," brandy being the chief accessory to the fact. "Currant" *is* a poor creature— a dreadfully poor creature, though consecrated by the baby lover at the Holly Tree Inn—and as for "cowslip," I should wish it kept for the less Arcadian Arcadia. Of elder wine, though it need not be actually and immediately nasty, I am bound to say that, when I think of it, I always think likewise of the West Indian prelate who related his experience with some too hospitable members of his flock. "They gave me," he said, "some wine—very nice wine; and then some cigars—very nice cigars. I think that, later, we had some rum—very nice rum. But, do you know," and one can imagine the innocence of the pontifical smile, "that afterwards I was positively *ill*."*

Of English or Welsh grown wine that would really *be* wine—grape-juice glorified—if it could, I have spoken in a note to my *History of the French Novel*.† Whether anybody else has emulated the late Lord Bute in the trouble he took to introduce or revive this, I do not know. But judging from an experience of the actual Vinum Buteanum, I should say that a decent Marsala (and as will have been seen, I do not rank Marsala very high) was far preferable.

MISCELLANEOUS NOTES ON THE LAST SIX CHAPTERS

Before quitting the subject of wine proper, there are a few omitted points on which I may be permitted to say a word or two "promiscuous," as the vulgar have it.

It may seem odd that I have said nothing, in the chapter on Champagne, as to Saumur, Vouvray, and the Swiss imitations. These last I have never drunk. As to the first, I should feel inclined to borrow the saying of the innocent accomplice to whom a villain had imparted a share of stolen Champagne. Interrogated as to the various liquors which had been given to him, he said that there was one which was "like ginger-beer, but not so nice."

---

* I believe elder wine can be made less deleterious by putting an equal quantity of brandy in it. But why not drink the brandy by itself?

† In connection *(v. sup.)* with Picardan.

If he had said this of Saumur I should not have found much fault with him. Vouvray has not the same coarseness, but seems to me feeble.

I wonder if there exists anywhere a bottle of the old original Constantia? I am happy to say that in my youth I once drank it. (I am sorry for anyone who has not, once at least, drunk both real Constantia and real Tokay.) It has not, I believe, been made for many decades, the modern products of the vineyards so called being quite different. But it was of the sort to last. The late Bishop Creighton, who when vicar of Embleton in Northumberland was permitted to sample the famous Trevelyan cellar before it was committed to the sacrilegious hands of Dr. Richardson, fully confirmed my ideas as to white wines lasting much longer than red. And it is at least said that the stronger Rhenish and Bavarian wines will keep for centuries.

Old West Indians used to hold that Madeira ought to be drunk not merely *warmed* but *warm* in this climate; I suppose as a sort of restoration of the conditions to which it was accustomed.

At the time of the Champagne riots not long before the war, I asked a wine merchant of large experience whether it would not be possible to import the products of the outlying districts of the province—seeing that their discontent at the absorption of these products by the shippers of Reims, Epernay, etc., and the re-sale at much higher prices, led to the trouble—and to sell them as such. He answered that no merchant would dare to do it, the public being so much under the thrall of names that the stock would be left on the hands of anyone who did. If, as one suspects, the curious secondary firm-names under which some of these great shippers used to send out wines, cheaper than their official *cuvées*, covered outliers of this kind, they were sometimes excellent. But, in fact, no liquors required greater care than Champagnes at 60s. or 70s. per dozen before the war. They could in some cases be fit to put before anybody: in others it would be unpleasant to give a definition of fitness in the person who deserved to be set down to *them*.

I was doubtful, in writing the Claret chapter, as to saying something about the rather frequently discussed question of the official classification of Bordeaux wines, and its relation to their merits "as it strikes a contemporary" foreigner. Perhaps a few words may be added. No one, I suppose, would turn out any of the three (or, if you admit Haut Brion, *four*) "firsts." The most popular promotion from the second class would no doubt be Mouton Rothschild, and from what I have said above, it will be pretty clear that I should not, in that position of examiner which I have so often held in other matters, be eager to blackball. But the very same difficulty which so often occurs in the other cases referred to presents itself here. If Mouton Rothschild is to have its first, why not Rauzan? If Rauzan, why not Léoville, which, as noted above, Anthony Trollope thought pure nectar? If these two, why not Pichon-Longueville, which in at least one instance I have known superlative? Once, too, I should have put before even these four that Larose which some have called "the lady of clarets," which Thackeray in his early days made "Sawedwardgeorgeearllyttonbulwig" couple with Lafite as a guess for his host's weally nectaweous wine; and which he later selected as Mr. Pendennis's best, wickedly wasted by clumsy Philip. But for many years I sought in vain for a Larose that was quite up to its old mark. So much for "seconds," though more might be said of them. But, sifting the thirds, why, one may say, should Lagrange, Langoa and Palmer be definitely postponed to Cos d'Estournel and Ducru-Beaucaillou? Descend further, and I at least should say that Beychevelle, by no means once in a way only, has been the equal of any third and some seconds, though it is only classed as a fourth; while of its actual class-fellows I hardly know one that is better to my knowledge than Mouton d'Armailhac, a fifth. Lastly, to go beyond the class-list in one instance only, why is that charming wine Château Citran "gulfed"? But of wrangling about this (as about all class-lists without exception) there were no end.*

* Something may be expected on the question—What, if anything, should be taken and eaten with after-dinner wine? I am afraid that the "whets" of our ancestors were rather stimulants to drinking (which no-body but an abstainer or a drunkard should require) than meliorants of appreciation. Their chief modern representatives—olives and devilled biscuits—are not bad, but I have never, despite a due devotion to Pallas, been such an enthusiast for the olive as some of my friends. And the *devilled* biscuit, a capital thing in itself, is rather violent for a fine wine. Plain Passover bread, or those "Thin Captains," which somewhat resemble it, seem to me best of all. Nuts pass, of course, but most "soft" fruit is questionable. Grapes go not ill, but I have sometimes felt a moral qualm, in marrying a grape too nearly to what is in a way its grandmother. Some accept peaches and nectarines; I rather doubt, though I am very fond of the latter. Strawberries have many votes, and some good stories, in their favour. But the one fruit which seems to me to go best with *all* wine, from hock to sherry and from claret to port, is the medlar—an admirable and distinguished thing in and by itself, and a worthy mate for the best of liquors. [**"whets"**: something eaten or drunk before dinner as a stimulant to the appetite, especially a small drink of liquor. **olives . . . Pallas**: By tradition, Pallas Athena gave the olive tree to Athens.—*Editor*]

VII. SPIRITS—HOLLANDS AND WHISKY

There is perhaps no division of any cellar, past or present, actual or possible, which to-day excites in the mind of a pious pilgrim to Lantern-Land such mixed feelings as that devoted to the produce of fermentation *plus* distillation. And when fond memory brings the other light of other days before him, the pilgrim must be a man of most angelic mildness if the predominating element of the mixture is not something like indignation. The present writer was informed, not long before the war broke out, by *two* trustworthy experts, that eighteen pence a gallon or threepence a bottle was an outside and indeed extravagant cost to fix for everything concerned in the production of most excellent spirit at proof. Now you get (when you *can* get it) stuff watered to 30' *under* proof at half a guinea. But let us, if possible, forget this tragedy, and return, if not to the blissful times and places elsewhere recorded, when and where you could buy a tumbler of Hollands for threepence, to more recent conditions, when in England and Scotland, excellent brandy cost five shillings a bottle; none but fancy or extra-old whiskies more than four; and gin, whether "squareface" or London or Plymouth, not much more than half a crown.

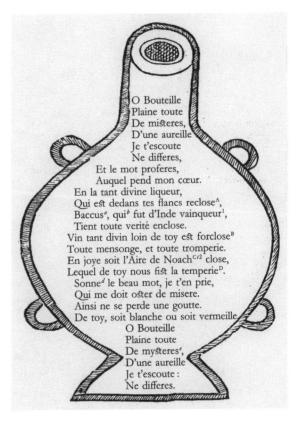

FIGURE 16. "The Holy Bottle" sought by Panurge and Pantagruel in Lantern-Land (François Rabelais, *Gargantua and Pantagruel*, bk. 5).

When my cellar, if not exactly my cellar-book, was started, I had recently returned from a two years' sojourn in the north of Scotland, where, it is needless to say, I had become something of a judge of whisky; and the loss of the unblended product, direct from the Morayshire distilleries, was a real privation. I had never cared, and do not to this day care, much for the advertised blends, which, for this or that reason the public likes, or thinks it likes. And it was then difficult to get any other in London; a personal friend, himself a distiller, who allowed me to have some of his ware "neat," begged me not to mention the fact, as he was under a sort of contract only to supply the big middlemen. So for some time, though, of course, I always kept some whisky going, I did not drink much. Fortunately I had acquired in Guernsey, and not lost in Scotland, a taste for Hollands, which was easily procurable, and of which thenceforward my cellar was never destitute, till, at the final sale, I was fool enough to part with half a small cask-full for about seventeen shillings a gallon, not much over the price that it was to fetch per bottle two or three years later.

The British cellar-owner of the upper and middle classes at the present day does not as a rule know much about Hollands; but it is a very excellent, most wholesome, and, at its best, most palatable drink. It is true that it varies very considerably; and its flavour is so pronounced that some people can never reconcile themselves to it, while others, who have liked it, lose the taste. The most frequently met with and best known—De Kuyper's, familiarly denominated "J.D.K.Z." or "square-face" simply—requires great age to mature it, and, as generally sold, is rather harsh and fiery. Wynand Fockink is more expensive, but always to be trusted; its stone *litre*-jars reposed and were replaced for many a year in my cellar. Bols, like Wynand Fockink best known to us for liqueurs, is also a sure card, and also rather dear. Two excellent shipping firms, from whom I often filled bins and casks, were Collings and Maingay (both pure Guernsey names, but established in Holland), whose gin I obtained from two different merchants in Plymouth and in Edinburgh, but never saw elsewhere, and Jansen's, on which latterly in Edinburgh I chiefly depended. But the very best Hollands I ever had in my life had gone through unusual experiences. It will be remembered that, a good many years ago, a man-of-war (the name of which has slipped my memory) was wrecked between Malta and Gozo. After a considerable time her contents were salved, and certain cases of Hollands, which had been supplied by Messrs. Collier, of Plymouth, were taken back by them. Naturally, some bottles were spoiled; and the curious corn-husks (rye or buckwheat?) in which they are usually packed had suffered. But where the corks had held, the waters of "the tideless, dolorous, midland sea" had proved themselves kind foster-mothers, and the gin was the softest and mellowest I ever tasted. Messrs. Collier were good-natured enough to let me have a case, in which I think not more than one or two bottles had suffered the worser "sea-change," and been ousted, while all the rest had undergone the better and remained. I wish I had had twenty cases instead of one.

But though I never deserted Schiedam, and, when I was ordered off claret about 1905, established a little stock-cask thereof, it was inevitable that, having returned to Scotland ten years earlier, I should revert to the "wine of the country," and should increase my relative consumption at the same catastrophe. The people who buy a bottle of "Green Rhinoceros" or "Purple and Yellow" as they want it, and are satisfied with that, though no doubt they might drink much worse liquor, know little about whisky. Nor do those who think that very old whisky is necessarily very good whisky know much more. One of those grocer-merchants, who dispense good liquor in the Northern Kingdom, and who sometimes have as much as a hundred thousand gallons stacked in their own bonded warehouses, once told me in confidence that he didn't himself care for *any* whisky that had been kept by itself in cask for more than fifteen years. "It gets *slimy*," he said; and I am bound to say I agree with him. In bottle, of course, it escapes that fate; but then there it hardly improves at all. The more excellent way—formerly practised by all persons of some sense and some means north of the Tweed—is to establish a cask of whatever size your purse and your cellar will admit, from a butt to an "octave" (14 gallons), or an "anker" (ten), or even less; fill it up with good and drinkable whisky from six to eight years old, stand it up on end, tap it half-way down or even a little higher, and, when you get to or near the tap, fill it up again with whisky fit to drink, but not *too* old. You thus establish what is called in the case of sherry a "*solera*," in which the constantly aging character of the old constituents doctors the new accessions, and in which these in turn freshen and strengthen the old. "It should be pretty good," said a host of mine once in a country house beyond the Forth, "it comes from a hundred-gallon cask, which has never been empty for a hundred years." This is the state of the blessed, to which all cannot attain. But with care and judgment it can be approached on quite a modest scale. I have done it in octaves for both Scotch and Irish whisky, and in ankers for Hollands and brandy, during such time as was allowed me. I think of their fair round proportions now with unsoured fondness.

The prettiest cask, however beautifully varnished (a process which I venture to think an error, for it must check the natural perspiration of the wood) and adorned with the most exquisitely silvered tap, will not turn bad whisky into good; and it is time to discuss the varieties of this admirable liquor in both its forms, wherein "Scotus," to alter Claudian's juxtaposition "*æmulat* Iernen." There once for a time was "Welsh" whisky, manufactured, I suppose, under a mistaken belief that Celtic surroundings would suffice, but we will not reason of it, only mention it and pass. Transatlantic varieties, now threatened with extinction, may have a note later. For my own part, I am as impartial as an Englishman should be, and can afford to be in this instance, between *the* Two. Indeed, I used, while it was still possible for persons not millionaires or miners to do so, to drink one at lunch and the other at dinner, completing the "Quis separabit?" with English gin at night. But I think it must be allowed that the "Scotch drink" has more numerous and more delicate *varieties* of character than the Irish.

When I lived in Scotland the total number of distilleries was said, I think, to exceed two—certainly one—hundred; though not a few of the smaller were not working, as a consequence of the great whisky "crash" of some years earlier. Morayshire alone, the non-metropolitan county which I once knew best, had some scores. But a good many, especially in the south, dealt with grain spirit, and I am speaking only of malt.* Taking all those that I have

---

* With *one* more recent exception, the Whisky Commission of some years since was perhaps the most futile Commission on record, though it was not so mischievous as its successor. "Grain" *is* only good for blending, or for mere "drinkers for *drunkee.*" [The first inquiry into the matter of Scotch whisky was not by royal commission but by a select committee of the House of Commons in 1890. For some time the traditional malt whiskies of Scotland had been blended with so-called grain whiskies made from maize, rye, or oats, and these blends had, for the first time, given "Scotch" whisky a market beyond Scotland. The question was whether unmalted grain whisky distilled by patent (continuous) stills could be called "Scotch whisky" in competition with the traditional whisky distilled from malted barley in pot stills. The committee decided in favor of the grain distillers by concluding that whisky was whisky, and that neither the materials that went into it nor the methods by which it was made needed to be specified (*Report of the Select Committee on British and Foreign Spirits*, Parliamentary Sessional Papers, 1891, XI). In 1908 the question was renewed and was then referred to a royal commission, which reported in 1909; in effect it reaffirmed the findings of the 1890 committee. If a whisky was distilled in Scotland, it was Scotch; anything beyond that was a matter of taste. Saintsbury's description of the commission as "futile"

tried, I should say that some certainly stand above the rest. I used to endeavour to supply my cask with, and to keep independent jars of, the following:—Clyne Lish, Smith's Glenlivet (half the distilleries along and about the Spey from Grantown to the sea tack on the famous Glen to their own names, but "Smith's" is the accepted premier), Glen Grant, Talisker, and one of the Islay brands— Lagavulin, Ardbeg, Caol Isla, etc. The picturesquely named "Long John," otherwise Ben Nevis, is less definite in flavour than any of these, but blends very well. Glendronach, an Aberdeenshire whisky, of which I did not think much forty years ago, improved greatly later; and I used to try both of these in my cask. But I always kept separate supplies of all, and amused myself with these, alone or variously blended, at intervals. A friend of mine from Oxford days, now dead, held some mixed Clyne Lish and Glenlivet of mine to be the best whisky he had ever drunk.

In conclusion, I think I have noticed, in the forty-five years since I began to study whisky, that the general style of most if not all kinds has changed, owing to the comparative disuse of "toddy," and the substitution of whisky-and-soda, or potash. The older whiskies were darker in colour, from being kept in golden sherry or madeira casks, rather sweeter in taste, and rather heavier in texture; the newer are "lighter" in both the first and the last respect, and much drier in taste. But the abominable tyranny of enforced

---

is given some color by the fact that it interviewed 116 witnesses over thirty-seven days of hearings and published 724 pages of testimony in order to conclude to do nothing: see the *Final Report of the Royal Commission on Whiskey and Other Potable Spirits*, and its *Minutes of Evidence*, Parliamentary Sessional Papers, 1909, XLIX. Incidentally, the commission's report always spells the word *whiskey*, never as *whisky*, which makes one wonder how venerable is the rule that Scotch whisky never has an *e* in it? But perhaps the spelling is evidence of the commission's incompetence?—*Editor*]

FIGURE 17. The Glenlivet: the "accepted premier" of Speyside whiskies (Brady Collection, Special Collections, Shields Library, University of California, Davis).

"breaking down" to thirty below proof has spoilt the ethers of the older whiskies terribly.

There is, as indeed I have hinted, no "wrong to Ireland" intended in not noticing its produce first. I have postponed it, not that I love it less, but because I do not know quite so much about it. I have never *lived* in Ireland, only spending there a few "B.B.B." days, as they say on the placards of dissenting chapels (I extend these in the case mentioned to "Brief, Bright and *Beatific*"), and though I have tried a fair number of Irish whiskies,

FIGURE 18. The Lagavulin Distillery, Isle of Islay (Alfred Barnard, *The Whiskey Distilleries of the United Kingdom* [London, 1887]).

and have never been without some, they are much fewer than the Caledonian brands. My book contains entries of both the Jamesons, John and William; of Roe, Power, and E. and J. Burke from Dublin; of Persse and another unnamed from Galway; of Coleraine, Comber, and one or two not named from Belfast and the north; and of some (good but not further identified) from Cork. (I may mention by the way that the very best Irish whisky I ever remember, which was given me by my old friend Colonel Welman, Brigade-Major in Guernsey many years ago, also came from Cork.) There may have been one or two others, but these were what I chiefly "kept going." Of their respective characters I have not much to say. Irish whisky wants, I think, more keeping than Scotch, and the famous "J. J." especially is seldom thoroughly good before it is ten years old. Some of the best I ever had was some *William* Jameson of nearly twenty. But when it is good, it has the national characteristic of being (with the same limitation) singularly ingratiating. No spirit makes you appreciate so fully that beautiful line,

> And the soft wings of Peace cover him round

which Marryat (or Howard) unwittingly illustrated by the incident of Rattlin the Reefer being sheltered from the stramash on the harbour of Cork itself in the embraces of the Misses O'Toole. Scandal has said that it sometimes crosses the larger bay outside and returns as Cognac. Whether there ever was any truth in this, I cannot say. A charming poem on this new "Return of the Wild Geese" might be written. But it is literally true that on two different occasions I myself, whose palate is not, as perhaps these pages may show, quite unexercised in such things, have taken what was supposed to be brandy for Irish whisky.

Of Canadian and American whiskies I have promised a notice, but shall not say much, though my cellar has seen several. Walker's well-known Canadian Club is the least unpalatable that I have tried; though for some samples of American I have given more money than I ever paid in the good days for the best of the home brands. It was said, I think, in the whisky enquiries of some years ago, that the high colour and strong flavour of these spirits is due to the practice of singeing the insides of the casks. It may be so or may not. But the real fact is that the American, if not the Canadian kinds, are obviously prepared for drinking as liqueurs or cocktails, not for mixing. As such they are not repulsive; they are less good, but not loathsome, as rather sweet toddy; very nasty with cold water; and worse with soda or potash. That they are or were generally drunk "neat" is, I believe, the fact; and if any rational comparison of the state of America and England in regard to alcoholic liquor were made, this fact would have to be taken into "high consideration."

Note on Toddy.—This, even in Scotland, now almost prehistoric compound, ought to be made, according to Morayshire rules, in a fashion opposite to that usually imagined to be correct. You put in the hot water, sweetened to taste, first, and let the sugar melt thoroughly; *then* you add the whisky. And, of course, you do not "swig" it brutally from the rummer or tumbler, but ladle it genteelly, as required, with a special instrument made and provided for the purpose, into a wineglass which has been brought, again specially inverted beforehand in the rummer or tumbler itself.

VIII. SPIRITS—BRANDY, RUM
AND GIN, WITH SOME EXOTIC THINGS

Brandy is, no doubt, in a certain sense—even in more than one—the most excellent of spirits—"Aqua *Vitae*" by excellence. It comes, to speak scholastically, from the noblest source—the grape. It passes through the most dignified stages, for it is wine before it is brandy, and therefore presumably drinkable, while I do not envy anyone who drinks the initial forms of whisky, "feints" and "forshotts," though the latter (as to the spelling of which I confess doubts) is remarkably good as an embrocation for rheumatism. It is the object of the most reverential treatment; for residents in the district say that the small farmers who distil it do not part with their older treasures without personal reluctance. And whether it is the most pleasantly drinkable or not (I own that I myself get much sooner tired of brandy and soda than of whisky and potash) it can acquire as a liqueur the finest flavour, and is unapproached as a medicine. All alcoholic drinks, rightly used,* are good for body

* Even absinthe, the most open to abuse, is sovereign sometimes, as for instance, after sea-sickness. [**absinthe:** A greenish spirit flavored with absinthe (*Artemisia absinthium*, or wormwood), anise, and other herbs.

and soul alike; but as a restorative of both there is nothing like brandy.

Like other excellent things, however, it does not admit of much talking. There is good brandy, and there is, though it is almost a contradiction in terms, bad brandy; but there is no great variety in the good, except that produced by purity and age. Outward differences, of course, there are; and a few of origin and kind. As far as the latter are concerned, the decree has long gone forth that all brandy—at least all French brandy—is to be *called* Cognac; though how much of it actually comes from the Charente is quite another question. "Armagnac" brandy, a genuine place-name with an interesting historical association (you may drink Armagnac after Burgundy now and they won't quarrel) used to be honestly sold in the Channel Islands as such. I never saw it quoted or offered in England. "Eau de Vie de Marc," a sort distilled from grape husks as well as juice, is sometimes procurable, and not to be despised

---

On the grounds of its danger to health, its sale was progressively banned in European countries, beginning with Belgium in 1906, Holland, 1909, Switzerland, 1910, and France, 1915. "The wormwood," so the fourteenth edition of the *Encyclopedia Britannica* states, "acts powerfully upon the nerve-centers, and causes delirium and hallucinations, followed in some cases by idiocy." Absinthe was the favorite drink of the *poètes maudits* of the *décadence*, and to flirt with its destructive powers a mark of imaginative grace. How potent the wormwood in absinthe may actually have been is disputed: the high alcohol content (typically around 70 percent) must have had a good deal to do with the supposed power of the drink, and unrestrained habits of indulgence a good deal more. Apart from its toxic effect, the contribution of *Artemisia* to absinthe was its bitterness; the dominant flavor of the drink was that of anise, and anise-flavored aperitifs have long been substituted for absinthe in those places where absinthe used to be drunk.—*Editor*]

as a liqueur, though it does not "mix" well. I have had it in my cellar. Not there, nor in England at all, have I seen rose-coloured brandy as I have in French country districts. But like all other spirits it is of course originally white, and I have myself possessed some of that.* With us, as those who know a little about the history of the subject are aware, "Pale" brandy, which is now the rule, was something of an exception till about the middle of the nineteenth century. "Brown" is perhaps now taking its place as such. I always kept some brown brandy in my cellar, for it is better as a liqueur than pale, and very much better for the composition of that grand old stuff beloved of Mr. Pickwick, and doubtless part-cause of his virtues—hot brandy and water. But with soda water it is a mistake, and I trust that another great man in fiction (which is only another kind of fact), Dr. Opimian, of whom it is recorded that he took his brandy at night with hot water in winter and soda water in summer, provided for the difference. He was certainly right in preferring brandy at this time. Indeed, the three spirits

---

* It is curious that gin is the only spirit that has as a rule been allowed to remain white, except in such cases as "raspberry gin," which was popular in the eighteenth century, and "clove gin," which I never saw, but which I suppose must have taken some colour as well as taste from the spice. I have noted above white rum and white brandy, but not, I think, white whisky, which however is quite to be mentioned "for the sake of honour." I have drunk it in Scotland, and have had it of excellent quality from Bristol. But I think the best that I ever drank was at the Ulster Club in Belfast, a hospitable institution fit to be adorned with various laurels. It stands to reason that whisky left in such a condition will be drier than that which has been casked in succession to anything but the driest sherry. And I own I think dryness a great merit in Scotch if not in Irish usquebaugh or "scuback," as the French were wont to *estropier* the word brought by Jacobite exiles from the two whisky countries. Hollands, especially when very old, is often straw-coloured.

noticed in this chapter have an advantage over those of the last chapter as "nightcaps." Whisky, at least in the case of some people, has a tendency to keep the drinker of it, except in rather immoderate quantities, awake.*

It was most pleasant, during the late war, to read the unvarying testimony of all qualified and unprejudiced authorities to the invaluable services of the rum ration, which, in defiance of fanaticism and in compliance with common sense and experience, was issued to our men. The merits, virtues and interests of rum are very great and unusually various. That it is "good for de tomac," as it (under a false name, to be sure) was of yore asserted to be on

---

* In the text I thought it well not to couple non-French brandy with French. But for completeness others, some of them not despicable, should perhaps be mentioned here. Of "British" brandy I have known little (at least of what called itself so), and have not desired much further acquaintance. But I should like just to have tasted the formidable specimen possessed by the great Mr. Moulder in *Orley Farm.* Australian I used to drink occasionally for some years as an economy, and it is not bad; but after a time I got tired of it. Spanish can be very good. I do not desire anything much better than Domecq's "Fundador" of 1874; though perhaps by this time it may suggest the caution of a candid wine-merchant as to "Waterloo" Sherry. "We call it so; but I cannot undertake to state mathematically the proportion of 1815 in it." Even the lesser degrees of this brandy—bearing "vines" instead of "stars" as badges—can be well spoken of. [*Orley Farm:* Trollope's Mr. Moulder is a traveler for the firm of Hubbles and Grease, of Houndsditch, doing business in "tea, coffee, and British brandy." Moulder is proud of his private stock: "He had got some brandy—he didn't care what anybody might say about Cognac and eau de vie; but the brandy which he had got from Betts' private establishment seventeen years ago, for richness of flavour and fulness of strength, would beat any French article that anybody in the city could show" (*Orley Farm*, chs. 6, 24). **Domecq's "Fundador":** Brandy produced by the sherry firm of Domecq since 1874.—*Editor*]

a famous occasion, may be unhesitatingly asserted and counter-signed. It is certainly the most carminative and comforting of all spirits. Everybody knows that hot rum and water is sovereign for a cold, but perhaps everybody does not know exactly how the remedy should be applied. This is the *probatum*. You must take it in bed; premature consumption merely wastes the good creature. It should be made, in a large rummer-glass, as hot as you can drink it (hence the advice of the rummer—for a mere tumbler may burn your hands), not too sweet, but so strong that you sink back at once on the pillow, resigning the glass to the ready hands of a sympathising bedside attendant, preferably feminine. If you do not wake the next morning, possibly with a slight headache but otherwise restored, there must be something really the matter with you.*

And it must never be forgotten that without rum that glorious liquor called punch—that liquor "nowhere spoken against in the Scriptures"—that wine of midnight—cannot really exist. Brandy punch (though in perfect punch there *should* be brandy), whisky punch, gin punch are all misnomers. "No bishop, no king" is a wise maxim; but (for there have been kingdoms which were not Christian) it is not such an eternal verity as, "No rum, no punch."

The most remarkable rum I ever possessed was some white or

---

* The feeble-minded or hypocritical may substitute "sal volatile punch," *i.e.* hartshorn, hot water, lemon and sugar. It is not bad, but far inferior to rum.

The recipe above intended for real punch is as follows:—three parts of rum, two of brandy ("Ensign O'Doherty" substitutes arrack), one of lemon juice, and six of hot water, the quantity of sugar being a matter quite of taste. I never knew this mixture found fault with by respectable persons of any age, sex or condition, from undergraduates to old ladies, at any hour between sunset and sunrise. [**"Ensign O'Doherty"**: One of the pseudonyms used by the Irish journalist William Maginn (1793–1842).—*Editor*]

rather pale straw-coloured spirit, which I bought at a sale in Edinburgh; which had belonged to Wallace of Kelly, a somewhat "legended" laird of the earlier nineteenth century; and which was said to have been cellared in or before 1845, my own birth-year (I had a little brandy of the same date once, but sacrificed all save a thimbleful of it to pious purposes under stress of Dora the Detestable). It was still excellent with hot water, but was perhaps best as a liqueur, though it may have been rather too tarry for some tastes. Precious, too, was some Wedderburn of 1870 which I used to get from my friends Messrs. Harvey, and which was not the less agreeable because 1870 itself was the first year in which I ever abode, for more than a few hours, by the gorge of the Avon. But I cannot help regretting the darker rums of older days: nearly all rum is pale now. The dark rum certainly *looked* better when diluted: and the eyes have a right to be pleased as well as the palate. I think its flavour was fuller too, and allied itself better with that of its constant friend the lemon. It is asserted, with what truth I know not, that the methods of distillation have altered. But it is still famously good; we could repair much of our long injustice to the West Indies by drinking more of it; it is quite free from the hypocritical but colourable objection that the making of it wastes food stuffs—indeed the more rum the more sugar—and if we ever get fair taxation and uncontrolled trade again it might be quite cheap. I have often wished to drink Java and Queensland rum, but have never been able to get hold of either, though I have seen some good-looking dark Australian stuff in the Tantalus-case of an Exhibition.

Nor have I ever disdained the humble and much reviled liquid which is the most specially English of all spirits; which, as observed before, you used to be able to procure at its best for not much more than half-a-crown a bottle; and which now, owing to the witchcrafts and (for I must be permitted biblical freedom)

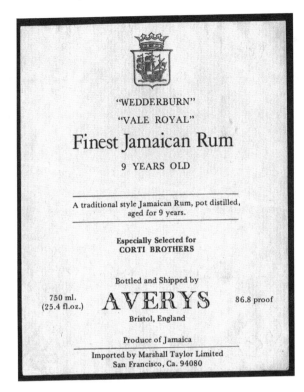

FIGURE 19. Wedderburn from Jamaica; Saintsbury regarded it as "precious" (Brady Collection, Special Collections, Shields Library, University of California, Davis).

whoredoms of "Dora" with persons unnecessary to mention,* has recently cost half-a-guinea. I have always been sorry for gin. By popular abbreviation from "Geneva" (itself a corruption of the

---

* The young man in Tennyson's poem was rather a feeble person; but he showed a prophetic strain of wisdom in saying "I *will* not marry Dora." [Tennyson, "Dora," line 22.—*Editor*]

still prettier *genièvre*) it acquired a name which is unfairly suggestive of traps and snares. First the neglect, and then as usual the hasty action, of the legislature brought it into extreme discredit nearly two hundred years ago; and Hogarth, one of the best of artists and fellows, but not precisely of thinkers, made that bad name worse. Further neglect and further stupidity saddled it with the odious association of "gin *palace*"; and the irrational opprobrium actually reached such a height a hundred years ago that even men who represented themselves in the *Noctes Ambrosianae*, as drinking oceans of whisky, upbraided Hazlitt for drinking gin; while, not far from the end of the nineteenth century, Anthony Trollope by no means caricatured fact when he made, in *Ayala's Angel*, a vapourish girl be shocked because her uncle, host and practically saviour from destitution, drank gin and water in place of the port which he had to give up to meet the expenses of her stay.

Now there is no more real reason for all this obloquy than there is for abusing water because the Inquisitors employed the water-torture, or because pirates and Bolshevists have made people "walk the plank." No doubt there is bad gin. I daresay the gin that was drunk in Gin Lane at a penny a glass was rather terrible. Its very powerful flavour masks adulteration rather easily; and I daresay again that which was sold "for drunkee" was vilely doctored. But to continue the argument used just now, people have committed hideous crimes with razors and pocket-knives, and both these implements, as well as many others, have been forged and sold by honest persons though they were made of worthless steel. "In its natural and healthy condition," as Lamb said of the above-mentioned Hazlitt (and as, for he was fond of it, he might have said of actual gin itself) gin is a capital spirit. When well made both its taste and its odour are very agreeable; it is admittedly one of the most wholesome of all the clan, and a real specific for some

FIGURE 20. Old Tom, the "sweeter and heavier" style of gin (Bella Landauer, *Some Alcoholic Americana* [New York: Harbor Press, privately printed, 1932]).

kinds of disease. There is perhaps no liquor more suitable for hot weather than gin and soda with a slice of lemon—"the British soldier's delight," as they used to call it in the barracks where I stayed in the sixties; and though I was obliged to call gin-punch a misnomer as an appellation, I should not much mind how cold I was if I could have a good tumbler of it to dispel my shivers.

There is not very much to say about different kinds of gin, though almost every distiller or refiner of it has fancy flavourings of his own. As it *is* "refined," and not simply distilled, it gains little if anything from age; and if the Northern Cobbler had broken down and tasted his big bottle, I do not know that he would have found it as "meller" as he expected. But when good it is a good creature always. I used generally to keep three kinds of it— "Old Tom," the sweeter and heavier variety; "unsweetened London," which seems to me the best gin-of-all-work; and "Plymouth," the most delicate in flavour and perhaps the wholesomest. Some gins, though I do not want to scandal their makers, strike me as over-flowery in taste.

A few words may be added on some less common spirits, which I have had from time to time in bin or on shelf. Arrack, which at one time seems to have been as common in English cellars as brandy or rum, and much commoner than whisky, is seldom seen now; and I once came just too late for a Scotch one, which had been ancestrally famous for it. What I have had in my own possession was a not disagreeable cross between rum and Irish whisky—good enough neat, but better in the "rack punch," for which it used to be chiefly employed, and which, at Vauxhall, seems to have started enquiries whether its name was derived from its alleged constituent, or from its consequences next morning. The Norwegian "Aquavit," which used to flow so freely (*vide* that delightful book, *Forest Life: a Fisherman's Sketches in Norway and Sweden*), but to which styptics have been applied by modern churlishness, seemed to me, in the specimens I have had, a weak and not very delicious whisky, as indeed its older name of "cornbrandy" implies. I think much better of its connection, Vodka— the most tragically associated of all liquids, for the absurd withholding of it probably had much to do with the Russian Revolution,

while the inevitable reaction made that Revolution, when it came,
more terrible. "Raki," which I suppose is like arrack, I never tried;
nor "plum spirit"—indigenous to the brave little country, which
used to "spell itself with a *we*," and has not bettered the spelling
more recently.*

* One note more, to the last chapter rather than to this. The atroc-
ities of "Dora" have naturally revived illicit distilling. It is said that some
of the results are quite good. But although I consider the offence a natural consequence of the present persecution, I must confess that the only
whisky of this kind that I ever drank was incredibly nasty.

IX. LIQUEURS

It may perhaps have been noticed by anyone who does me the honour to read this little book that I am rather partial to alcoholic
liquors. No doubt they are bad things if you make yourself a slave
to them; but then most things to which you make yourself a slave
are bad—with some rare exceptions in the case of women, and
then only because a few of them accept the slavery as reciprocal.
I could, if I chose, bid adieu to all these liquors to-morrow without difficulty, though with very great regret.* I have recently, and
at various other times of my life, reduced my consumption to any
desirable point. I think those who can drink them and do not, fools;
but I think those who can't drink them and do, worse fools, and

---

* As the late Mr. Leland put it—in language perhaps shocking to
those who read without understanding, but not to those who can see the
allegory—

We'll get drunk among the roses, / And lie sober on the straw.

Nor do those who have most enjoyed the roses and the wine take the straw
and the sobriety least philosophically. Or, if anyone's nerves need more
sentimental treatment, here is a variant on the famous ballad-lament, for

unjust men too, because they bring scandal on an excellent creature, and consume that share of it which should go to others.

All which is not padding, but a relevant introduction to what I am going to say of Liqueurs—that of all the various species of their genus they can be least unconditionally recommended. They are, save occasionally for medicinal purposes, the most positive of superfluities and extravagances.* They are also, being as a rule both too strong and too sweet, the most questionably wholesome; and excess in them results in sufferings the most unpleas-

---

something had and lost, which will apply in this meaner matter and in others:

> O! had I wist, before I kissed,
> That love would be sae sair to *gain*—
> *I had played the game, just all the same,*
> *To win the pleasure WITH the pain.*

It has indeed been objected that this gives a discord on the minor key of the opening: but even the objector admitted that it was a right English mood and mode. [**Mr. Leland:** Charles Godfrey Leland (1824–1903), an American journalist and writer who spent many years in Europe. He was a member of the Savile Club and founder of the Rabelais Club, to both of which Saintsbury belonged. Leland is now best remembered for his *Breitmann Ballads* (1871). **WITH** *the pain:* The *Oxford Dictionary of Quotations* gives this stanza of the ballad thus:

> But had I wist, before I kist,
> That love had been sae ill to win,
> I had locked my heart in a case o' gowd,
> And pinned it wi a siller pin.—*Editor*]

---

* Especially when people ask, as (it may be interesting to posterity to know) they sometimes are asking now, thirty shillings for a *half*-litre bottle of *yellow* Chartreuse.

ant of all such sufferings. Nor do they possess the natural grace and charm—the almost intellectual as well as sensual interest— of the best wine. On the other hand, they are for the most part very pleasant to the taste; they are frequently very pretty to look at; and if there be any truth in the old and perhaps somewhat rash statement as to the connection between the wills or wishes of womankind and of the Divinity, they cannot be hateful to God. For nearly all ladies, and especially all young ladies, like them very much indeed. Also they have a good many other sorts of interest, from their great variety of kind and association. I never was myself much addicted to them, but I have usually had a bottle or two of a few of the best in my cellar while I had it.

Liqueurs are, as has just been said, extremely numerous; indeed, when I knew France (which as far as actual presence goes is a long time since, much too long for me to have had any chance of being useful there recently) almost every chemist in every small town had one of his own, which was sovereign for digestion and other things. Some of the less known ones had considerable merits: I remember a big bottle of "Berrichonne" which was quite nice. But the best of these minorities was one called "Génépi des Alpes," which, having originally met it in those isles, favoured of Bacchus, which have been so often mentioned, I succeeded in procuring from these latter till the supply somehow stopped. Like that of the majority of these minorities, its flavour was of the Chartreuse class,* but less peculiar and powerful: and it was also much weaker as a spirit.

* Although I have not the slightest knowledge of botany, I am tempted (leaning mainly on the arm of my almost life-long friend, Sir W. T. Thiselton-Dyer, but absolving him from responsibility for any slips of my own natural and unscientific pravity) to venture a quasi-botanical note on the probable source of these flavours. It seems that the genus Artemisia (by the way, the French *armoise* throws a twilight

Of the recognised seductions that accompany coffee after dinner, I suppose Chartreuse itself and Curaçao have the best claims to be the kings of the Liqueurish Brentford. The rivals or imitations of the first-mentioned are, even excluding the humbler ones just referred to, very numerous. Benedictine; Trappistine; a cer-

---

on the Goddess) contains four groups of very numerous species; but that all, or nearly all, the known flavourers of liquors belong to the group Absinthia; *A. Absinthium* itself being responsible for Absinthe and (partially?) for Chartreuse. *A. nevadensis* (see on Manzanilla) seems to be a variety of *A. camphorata*, a suggestive name; while *A. Barretieri*, another Spaniard, but of the Seraphidia group, is admittedly used for liqueur as well as for medicinal purposes. *A. mutellina* and *A. glacialis* supply Génépi: and I personally suspect them in Chartreuse. Of the other groups it is doubtful whether any flavours liqueurs, though the Dracunculi enrich cookery with Tarragon. The Abrotana or Southernwoods suggest capabilities in our way: but do not seem to be known flavourers. On the other hand *A. maritima*, one of the fourth group, or Seraphidia, is said by one 18th century authority to be "an ingredient of distilled waters," and by another (c. 1726) to be used by Dublin alehouse keepers ("When the early purl is done") to make their purl with. One wonders whether there was *A. maritima* in the purl which refreshed Peter Simple after that agitating night with the press-gang and the Amazons?; whether George Borrow would have objected to sea-wormwood in purled beer as he did to wormwood proper in plain ale?; and whether John Buncle, Esq., in those very days when he and his Dublin friends sang "Let us go to Johnny Maclaine's, and see if his ale be good or no," gave orders (the alehouse itself was by the sea-side) to have it purled with *A. maritima*—and plenty of gin? This last named plant and *A. sacrorum* (one of the southernwoods) Sir W. M. Conway found in the Himalayas; could an "Eau *Sacrée* des Lamas" or "Lamaseraïne" be made of them? In M. Levier's botanical promenade in the Caucasus I find only *A. campestris* var. *sericea* (one of the Tarragon group) and *A. splendens* noted as representing this Garden of Diana (some would say of Proserpine) there. Perhaps Prometheus

• tain "Père Kermann," which from a joke of mine about its legend-
wrapper my children used to call "Forty Years in the Wilderness";
• a red Italian Chartreuse or Certosa (far from bad) and others will
occur. But none of them approaches, for instruction in complex-
• ity and delight in appeal of flavour, the famous but now exiled

---

foresaw the dangers of the Green Muse, and kept her from the scene of
his torture and his triumph. Anyhow, the connection between moun-
tains and liqueurs through the genus Artemisia is interesting, and an instance of the innumerable interests which alcohol lends to life. As such
I have dwelt on it. My unwritten *History of Wine* would have dealt with
the somewhat Chartreuse-suggesting Ἀψινθίτης οἶνος of the Greeks;
and the question whether when Artemisia drank the ashes of Mausolus
they tasted like wormwood; etc., etc. (Later kindness from Kew adds many
Caucasian Artemisias *including* Absinthium.) [**Sir W. T. Thiselton-
Dyer:** William Turner Thiselton-Dyer (1843–1928), botanist and classical scholar; director of Kew Gardens, 1885–1905. Saintsbury's friendship with him went back to their days at King's College School. **a
twilight on the Goddess:** *Armoise* means "Artemisia." I cannot explain
the reference to "twilight." **Absinthia:** The four groups that Saintsbury
discusses are Absinthium, Dracunculi, Abrotana, and Seraphidia. **"When
the early purl is done":** A comic misreading of *Macbeth*, I, i, 3: "When
the hurly-burly's done" (R. H. Stoddard, ed., *Personal Reminiscences by
Barham, Harness, and Hodder* [New York, 1875], p. 130). Purl is beer in-
fused with wormwood. Dickens, "Six Jolly Fellowship Porters," describes
a tavern on whose doorposts is written "The Early Purl House"—from
which it appears that purl must be taken early. **Peter Simple . . . Amazons:** Captain Marryat (*Peter Simple*, ch. 10): the hero is part of a press-
gang and is roughly handled by women when the gang raids an alehouse;
on his escape he is taken to another house, where "the landlady made us
some purl . . . which I thought very good indeed." **wormwood proper
in plain ale:** George Borrow, *Wild Wales*, ch. 90: when he finds that the
ale he has bought from an old woman, who brewed it herself, is bitter
from wormwood, he asks, "Why do you put such stuff in your ale?" **John
Buncle, Esq.:** From a story by Thomas Amory, 1765–66. **Sir W. M.**

preparation itself. And it must be *green*; there is no such absolutely veracious application of a well-known maxim as that all yellow Chartreuse would be green if it could. As might be expected from its character and composition, it improves enormously with age; I kept some once for fifteen or sixteen years to its huge advantage. At the same time there is always something rather severe about it; it is not so engaging as not too sweet, but also not too dry or "thin" Curaçao. The very best of *this* amiable temptation that I ever possessed, or indeed that I ever drank, was some which used to be procurable at the well-known house of Justerini and Brooks in the vanished Opera Colonnade, between forty and fifty years ago. It also was green, but brown is perhaps the more germane colour, and white is not to be contemned merely for its whiteness. "Grand Marnier," the recent popular and expensive French variant on Curaçao, has never seemed to me quite its equal; but the Cape liqueur called Vanderhum is excellent.

To our grandfathers the chief companions or rivals of Curaçao were Maraschino and Noyau—both admirable things when they are not, as they both sometimes are, a trifle sickly. I think less ill of our Fourth king among my namesakes than some people do,

---

Conway: William Martin Conway (1856–1937), Baron Conway of Allington, art historian, collector, and mountaineer; his travels in the Himalayas in 1892 are described in *Climbing and Exploration in the Karakoram-Himalayas*, 3 vols. (London, 1894). **M. Levier's:** Emilio Levier, *À travers le Caucase: Notes et impressions d'un botaniste* (Paris, 1894). **Green Muse:** Absinthe. Ἀψινθίτης οἶνος: "Wormwood wine," mentioned by Greek medical writers such as Dioscorides. **Artemisia drank the ashes of Mausolus:** In the version of the story told by Aulus Gellius (*Attic Nights*, X, xviii, 3), Artemisia, after having built the Mausoleum for her dead husband, caused his bones to be burned and thereafter mixed some of his ashes in her daily drink.—*Editor*]

FIGURE 21. Père Kermann liqueur; the natives in the background
are presumably Brazilian (Amerine Collection, Special Collections, Shields Library, University of California, Davis).

• but I cannot approve of his fancy for maraschino punch. It is a blunder and a confusion; nearly as bad as drinking Château Yquem with
soda-water. But there is something very attractive in a maraschino
bottle with its straw envelope. And Martinique can hold its own with
• Zara; though Noyau condescends sometimes to rouge itself, while

FIGURE 22. Chartreuse from the years of the Carthusians' exile in Spain (Amerine Collection, Special Collections, Shields Library, University of California, Davis).

the wares of Luxardo and Drioli remain stainless. The "Water of Cherry" which in comparatively guiltless days the German made in his western districts, and the "Water of Gold" which he devised in his eastern, are or were by no means bad things. I hope that the rather unsettled fate of Dantzic will not dry up the fount of Goldwasser, which pleased sight and smell and taste alike.

Still further eastward and with still unhappier recent local memories, comes Kümmel—I suppose the most wholesome of all liqueurs, and not far from the nicest. "Ça pique dans le nez," says

one, I think, of M. Zola's young women; but certainly "ça chatouille le palais." "Parfait Amour" is an older-fashioned drink, but,
with the most careful protestation against any blasphemy of the
name which it takes in vain, I cannot say that I think much of the
thing. And as for Rosolio (I think it was Rosolio, but not the variety from which Samuel Titmarsh suffered), I have much too sharp
a memory of once incautiously opening a bottle of it over a fire-
place, so that the liquid dropped, and the flame catching it, ran up
and scorched my arm, to meddle with it any more. All these, and
not a few others—Cassis, Anisette, Crème de Menthe, "Cointreau,"
a pretty violet-coloured mixture from the Riviera which was popular some years ago, but of which I forget the name—have figured
for a time on a certain shelf which I used to reserve for such things.
But I have never possessed, drunk, seen, or in modern books heard
of, "Citron," which the lady used to "drink with His Grace and
Chartres." Does anybody know what it was? It sounds like a kind of
Curaçao made with lemon or actual citron-peel instead of orange.

However, I will not close this short chapter without saying
something of the supposed wickedest of all the tribe—the "Green
Muse"—the Water of the Star Wormwood, whereof many men
have died—the *absinthia tetra*, which are deemed to deserve the
adjective in a worse sense than that which the greatest of Roman
poets meant. I suppose (though I cannot say that it ever did me
any) that absinthe has done a good deal of harm. Its principle is
too potent, not to say too poisonous, to be let loose indiscrimi-
nately and intensively in the human frame. It was, I think, as a rule
made fearfully strong, and nobody but the kind of lunatic whom
it was supposed to produce, and who may be thought to have been
destined to lunacy, would drink it "neat." Of its being so drunk I
once had a harmless but very comic experience. The late Bishop
Creighton and I had contiguous lodgings, during the later part of
our undergraduate life at Oxford, in one of the old houses east of

FIGURE 23. Kümmel, "the most wholesome of all liqueurs" (Amerine Collection, Special Collections, Shields Library, University of California, Davis).

University and now destroyed. We used them practically in common, employing one sitting-room to eat and the other to work in. On one occasion we had had some men to dinner, and when the last went our good landlady, who had been hovering about on the landing in an agitated manner, rushed into the room crying,

"O! gentlemen, is that stuff poison?" We naturally requested further light. It turned out that a glass of absinthe, which had been poured out but not used, had been taken downstairs, and that our excellent landlord, sagely observing, as his wife rather reproachfully said, "It *must* be good if the gentlemen drink it," had quaffed it without water, but as she said "as he would gin," and had naturally found it rather too much for him. We calmed her fears and recommended a plentiful draught of water, adding in the most delicate way in the world, a caution that it was not invariably necessary to drink liquor that was left over; and dismissed her. Also we endeavoured—for Creighton was like Thackeray's Jones "a fellow of very kind feeling, who afterwards went into the Church," and I hope I was not less kind, though my destiny was more profane—not to laugh too much till she had closed the door.

A person who drinks absinthe neat deserves his fate whatever it may be. The flavour is concentrated to repulsiveness; the spirit burns "like a torch-light procession"; you must have a preternaturally strong or fatally accustomed head if that head does not ache after it. Moreover, you lose all the ceremonial and etiquette which make the proper fashion of drinking it delightful to a man of taste. When you have stood the glass of liqueur in a tumbler as flat-bottomed as you can get, you should pour, or have poured for you, water gently into the absinthe itself, so that the mixture overflows from one vessel into the other. The way in which the deep emerald of the pure spirit clouds first into what would be the colour of a star-smaragd, if the Almighty had been pleased to complete the quartette of star-gems,* and then into opal; the thinning out

---

* As yet only a triad—sapphire (which is pretty common), ruby (rarer), and topaz, which I have never seen, and which the late Signor Giuliano, who used to be good enough to give me much good talk in return for very modest purchases, told me he had seen only once or twice.

of the opal itself as the operation goes on; and when the liqueur glass contains nothing but pure water and the drink is ready, the extraordinary combination of refreshingness and comforting character in odour and flavour—all these complete a very agreeable experience. Like other agreeable experiences it may no doubt be repeated too often. I never myself drank more than one absinthe in a day, and I have not drunk so much as one for some thirty years. But the Green Muse is *bonne diablesse* enough if you don't abuse her; and when you land after rough handling by the ocean she picks you up as nothing else will.*

But an ordinary emerald in *cabochon* form, represents one of the stages of the diluted absinthe very fairly. [**Signor Giuliano:** Carlo and Arthur Giuliano, jewelers, of 115 Piccadilly (*Post Office London Directory*, 1911; the firm is not in the 1920 directory).—*Editor*]

* The once home-made "cordials"—Cherry Brandy, "Gean" Whisky, Sloe Gin, and one or two others—are rather flavoured spirits than liqueurs; and are much more wholesome than most of the foreign concoctions. There is a Copenhagen Cherry Brandy too, which deserves a good word. [**"Gean":** In Scottish dialect, the wild cherry. **rather flavoured spirits than liqueurs:** The terms *cordial* and *liqueur* appear to be interchangeable, *cordial* being more American than English. Attempts to distinguish consistently between the two terms break down, since both must mean a sweetened, flavored spirit: how sweetened, how flavored, and what kind of spirit may be answered in many ways. **Copenhagen Cherry Brandy:** The produce of the Peter Heering Company, sold as Cherry Heering. It is not, like Kirsch, distilled from cherries, but is a brandy flavored with cherries.—*Editor*]

X. BEER, CIDER, ETC.

There is no beverage which I have liked "to live with" more than
Beer; but I have never had a cellar large enough to accommodate
much of it, or an establishment numerous enough to justify the
accommodation. In the good days when servants expected beer,
but did not expect to be treated otherwise than as servants, a cask
or two was necessary; and persons who were "quite" generally took
care that the small beer they drank should be the same as that
which they gave to their domestics, though they might have other
sorts as well. For these better sorts at least the good old rule was,
when you began on one cask always to have in another. Even Cobbett, whose belief in beer was the noblest feature in his character, allowed that it required *some* keeping. The curious "white ale,"
or *lober agol*—which, within the memory of man, used to exist in
Devonshire and Cornwall, but which, even half a century ago, I
have vainly sought there—was, I believe, drunk quite new; but
then it was not pure malt and not hopped at all, but had eggs
("pullet-sperm in the brewage") and other foreign bodies in it.
   I did once drink, at St. David's, ale so new that it frothed from
the cask as creamily as if it had been bottled: and I wondered

whether the famous beer of Bala, which Borrow found so good at his first visit and so bad at his second, had been like it.* On the other hand, the very best Bass I ever drank had had an exactly contrary experience. In the year 1875, when I was resident at Elgin, I and a friend now dead, the Procurator-Fiscal of the district, devoted the May "Sacrament holidays," which were then still kept in those remote parts, to a walking tour up the Findhorn and across to Loch Ness and Glen Urquhart. At the Freeburn Inn on the first-named river we found some beer of singular excellence: and, asking the damsel who waited on us about it, were informed that a cask of Bass had been put in during the previous October, but, owing to a sudden break in the weather and the departure of all visitors, had never been tapped till our arrival.

Beer of ordinary strength left too long in the cask gets "hard" of course; but no one who deserves to drink it would drink it from anything but the cask if he could help it. Jars are makeshifts, though useful makeshifts: and small beer will not keep in them for much more than a week. Nor are the very small barrels, known by various affectionate diminutives ("pin," etc.) in the country districts, much to be recommended. "We'll drink it in the *firkin*, my boy!" is the lowest admission in point of volume that should be allowed. Of one such firkin I have a pleasant memory and memorial, though it never reposed in my *home* cellar. It was just be-

---

* This visit (in the early eighties) had another relish. The inn coffee-room had a copy of Mr. Freeman's book on the adjoining Cathedral, and this was copiously annotated in a beautiful and scholarly hand, but in a most virulent spirit. "Why can't you call things by their plain names?" (in reference to the historian's Macaulayesque periphrases) etc. I have often wondered who the annotator was. [**Cathedral:** William Basil Jones and Edward Augustus Freeman, *The History and Antiquities of Saint David's* (London, 1856).—*Editor*]

fore the present century opened, and some years before we Professors in Scotland had, of our own motion and against considerable opposition, given up half of the old six months' holiday without asking for or receiving a penny more salary. (I have since chuckled at the horror and wrath with which Mr. Smillie and Mr. Thomas would hear of such profligate conduct.) One could therefore move about with fairly long halts: and I had taken from a friend a house at Abingdon for some time. So, though I could not even then drink quite as much beer as I could thirty years earlier a little higher up the Thames, it became necessary to procure a cask. It came—one of Bass's minor mildnesses—affectionately labelled "Mr. George Saintsbury. Full to the bung." I detached the card, and I believe I have it to this day as my choicest (because quite unsolicited) testimonial.

Very strong beer permits itself, of course, to be bottled and kept in bottle: but I rather doubt whether it also is not best from the wood; though it is, equally of course, much easier to cellar it and keep it bottled. Its kinds are various and curious. "Scotch ale" is famous, and at its best (I never drank better than Younger's) excellent: but its tendency, I think, is to be too sweet. I once invested in some—not Younger's—which I kept for nearly sixteen years, and which was still treacle at the end. Bass's No. 1 requires no praises. Once when living in the Cambridgeshire village mentioned earlier I had some, bottled in Cambridge itself, of great age and excellence. Indeed, two guests, though both of them were Cambridge men, and should have had what Mr. Lang once called the "robust" habits of that University, fell into one ditch after partaking of it. (I own that the lanes thereabouts are very dark.) In former days, though probably not at present, you could often find rather choice specimens of strong beer produced at small breweries in the country. I remember such even in the Channel Islands. And I suspect the Universities themselves have been subject to "declensions and fallings off." I know that in my undergraduate days at Merton we always had proper beer-glasses, like the old "flute" champagnes, served regularly at cheese-time with a most noble beer called "Archdeacon," which was then actually brewed in the sacristy of the College chapel. I have since—a slight sorrow to season the joy of reinstatement there—been told that it is now obtained from outside.* And All Souls is the only other college in which, from actual experience, I can imagine the possibility of the exorcism,

Strongbeerum! discede a lay-fratre Petro,

if lay-brother Peter were so silly as to abuse, or play tricks with, the good gift.

* When I went up this March to help man the last ditch for Greek, I happened to mention "Archdeacon": and my interlocutor told me that he believed *no* college now brewed within its walls. After the defeat, I thought of the stages of the Decline and Fall of Things: and how a sad but noble ode might be written (by the right man) on the Fates of Greek and Beer at Oxford. He would probably refer in the first strophe to the close of the *Eumenides;* in its antistrophe to Mr. Swinburne's great adaptation thereof in regard to Carlyle and Newman; while the epode and any reduplication of the parts would be occupied by showing how the departing entities were of no equivocal magnificence like the Eumenides themselves; of no flawed perfection (at least as it seemed to their poet) like the two great English writers, but wholly admirable and beneficent— too good for the generation who would banish them, and whom they banished. [**last ditch for Greek:** By vote of Convocation on 2 March 1920, Greek ceased to be a compulsory subject at Oxford. Saintsbury of course voted with the minority. See his letter on the subject in the *Athenæum,* reprinted in *A Last Vintage* (London: Methuen, 1950), pp. 215–17. **Swinburne . . . Carlyle and Newman:** Swinburne's "Two Leaders," a double sonnet, in which Carlyle and Newman are addressed: "Last prophets of past kind . . . here your hour is done." So at the end of Aeschylus's *Eumenides,* the hour of the Spirits of Wrath is done.—*Editor*]

I have never had many experiences of real "home-brewed," but two which I had were pleasing. There was much home-brewing in East Anglia at the time I lived there, and I once got the village carpenter to give me some of his own manufacture. It was as good light ale as I ever wish to drink (many times better than the wretched stuff that Dora has foisted on us), and he told me that, counting in every expense for material, cost and wear of plant, etc., it came to about a penny* a quart. The other was very different. The late Lord de Tabley—better or at least longer known as Mr. Leicester Warren—once gave a dinner at the Athenaeum at which I was present, and had up from his Cheshire cellars some of the old ale for which that county used to be famous, to make flip after dinner. It was shunned by most of the pusillanimous guests, but not by me, and it was excellent. But I should like to have tried it unflipped.†

I never drank mum, which all know from *The Antiquary*, some from "The Ryme of Sir Lancelot Bogle," and some again from the notice which Mr. Gladstone's love of Scott (may it plead for him!) gave it once in some Budget debate, I think. It is said to be

---

* This was one of the best illustrations of the old phrase, "a good pennyworth," that I ever knew for certain. I add the two last words because of a mysterious incident of my youth. I and one of my sisters were sitting at a window in a certain seaside place when we heard, both of us distinctly and repeatedly, this mystic street cry: "A bible and a pillow-case for a penny!" I rushed downstairs to secure this bargain, but the crier was now far off, and it was too late.

† By the way, are they still as good for flip at New College, Oxford, as they were in the days when it numbered hardly any undergraduates except scholars, and one scholar of my acquaintance had to himself a set of three rooms and a garden? And is "The Island" at Kennington still famous for the same excellent compound?

brewed of wheat, which is not in its favour (wheat was meant to be eaten, not drunk), and very bitter, which is. Nearly all bitter drinks are good. The only time I ever drank "spruce" beer I did not like it. The comeliest of black malts is, of course, that noble liquor called of Guinness. Here at least I think England cannot match Ireland, for our stouts are, as a rule, too sweet and "clammy." But there used to be in the country districts a sort of light porter which was one of the most refreshing liquids conceivable for hot weather. I have drunk it in Yorkshire at the foot of Roseberry Topping, out of big stone bottles like champagne magnums. But that was nearly sixty years ago. Genuine lager beer is no more to be boycotted than genuine hock, though, by the way, the best that I ever drank (it was at the good town of King's Lynn) was Low not High Dutch in origin. It was so good that I wrote to the shippers at Rotterdam to see if I could get some sent to Leith, but the usual difficulties in establishing connection between wholesale dealers and individual buyers prevented this. It was, however, something of a consolation to read the delightful name, "our top-and-bottom-fermentation beer," in which the manufacturer's letter, in very sound English for the most part, spoke of it. *English* lager I must say I have never liked; perhaps I have been unlucky in my specimens. And good as Scotch strong beer is, I cannot say that the lighter and medium kinds are very good in Scotland. In fact, in Edinburgh I used to import beer of this kind from Lincolnshire,* where there is no mistake about it. My own private

---

* It came from Alford, the *chef-lieu*, if it cannot be called the capital, of the Tennyson country. I have pleasant associations with the place, quite independent of the beery ones. And it made me, partially at least, alter one of the ideas of my early criticism—that time spent on a poet's local habitations was rather wasted. I have always thought "The Dying Swan" one of its author's greatest things, and one of the champion examples of

opinion is that John Barleycorn, north of Tweed, says: "I am for whisky, and not for ale."

"Cider and perry," says Burton, "are windy drinks"; yet he observes that the inhabitants of certain shires in England (he does not, I am sorry to say, mention Devon), of Normandy in France, and of Guipuzcoa in Spain, "are no whit offended by them." I have never liked perry on the few occasions on which I have tasted it; perhaps because its taste has always reminded me of the smell of some stuff that my nurse used to put on my hair when I was small. But I certainly have been no whit offended by cider, either in divers English shires, including very specially those which Burton does not include, Devon, Dorset, and Somerset, or in Normandy. The Guipuzcoan variety I have, unfortunately, had no opportunity of tasting.

Besides, perry seems to me to be an abuse of that excellent creature the pear, whereas cider-apples furnish one of the most cogent arguments to prove that Providence had the production of alcoholic liquors directly in its eye. They are good for nothing else whatever, and they are excellent good for that. I think I like the weak ciders, such as those of the west and of Normandy, better than the

---

pure poetry in English literature. But I never fully *heard* the "eddying song" that "flooded"

> the creeping mosses and clambering weeds,
> And the willow branches hoar and dank,
> And the wavy swell of the soughing reeds,
> And the wave-worn horns of the echoing bank,
> And the silvery marish-flowers that throng
> The desolate creeks and pools among—

till I *saw* them.

stronger ones,* and draught cider much better than bottled. That of Norfolk, which has been much commended of late, I have never tasted; but I have had both Western and West-Midland cider in my cellar, often in bottle and once or twice in cask. It is a pity that the liquor—extremely agreeable to the taste, one of the most thirst-quenching to be anywhere found, of no over-powering alcoholic strength as a rule, and almost sovereign for gout—is not to be drunk without caution, and sometimes has to be given up altogether from other medical aspects. Qualified with brandy—a mixture which was first imparted to me at a roadside inn by a very amiable Dorset-shire farmer whom I met while walking from Sherborne to Bland-ford in my first Oxford "long"—it is capital: and cider-cup *(v. inf.)* who knoweth not? If there be any such, let him not wait longer than tomorrow before establishing knowledge, though we may say more of it here. As for the pure juice of the apple, four gallons a day per man used to be the harvest allowance in Somerset when I was a boy. It is refreshing only to think of it now.

Of mead or metheglin, the third indigenous liquor of South-ern Britain, I know little. Indeed, I should have known nothing at all of it had it not been that the parish-clerk and sexton of the Cambridgeshire village where I lived, and the caretaker of a vin-ery which I rented, was a bee-keeper and mead-maker. He gave me some once. I did not care much for it. It was like a sweet weak beer, with, of course, the special honey flavour. But I should imag-ine that it was susceptible of a great many different modes of preparation, and it is obvious, considering what it is made of, that it could be brewed of almost any strength. Old literary notices generally speak of it as strong.

---

* Herefordshire and Worcestershire cider can be very strong, and the perry, they say, still stronger.

XI. "MIXED LIQUORS"

What did Charles Lamb mean, in those "Confessions of a Drunkard," which oscillate in a rather ghastly manner between truth and fiction, irony and sincerity, art and nature, by "those juggling compositions which under the name of 'mixed liquors' conceal a good deal of brandy, etc.?" He cannot have meant punch, for he has already mentioned it separately. The phrase, with what follows, is hardly applicable to "bishop" and its class, or to "cups," but it must apparently mean something of one sort or another like these. At any rate, though things of the kind, except "Swedish punch" and one or two others, seldom occur in a cellar-book, they certainly cannot be made without things that do occur there; so it may not be improper to include here something about them, since they are "mixed liquors" in a special and, one would hope from Lamb's description of their namesakes, less deleterious sense.

Bishop itself would, from books, appear to have been in former days very specially an Oxford drink, but it certainly was not common there in my time. In fact, on the only occasion on which I did see and taste it, I made it myself in my own rooms, for joint consumption with a friend (not Creighton), who, as a matter of fact, actually did become a bishop later. It is, as I have found more people not know than know in this ghastly thin-faced time of ours, simply mulled port. You take a bottle of that noble liquor and put it in a saucepan, adding as much or as little water as you can reconcile to your taste and conscience, an orange cut in half (I believe some people squeeze it slightly), and plenty of cloves (you may stick them in the orange if you have a mind). Sugar or no sugar at discretion, and with regard to the character of the wine. Put it on the fire, and as soon as it is warm, and begins to steam, light it. The flames will be of an imposingly infernal colour, quite different from the light blue flicker of spirits or of claret mulled. Before it has burned too long pour it into a bowl, and drink it as hot as you like. It is an excellent liquor, and I have found it quite popular with ladies. I think it is said (but I have not the book at hand) to have played the mischief with Alaric Tudor, the sorriest, though not the most disagreeable, of *The Three Clerks;* but then it was made of public-house port, which was probably half elder wine and half potato spirit.

Of its titular superiors, "Cardinal" and "Pope," the former is only a rather silly name for mulled claret, while "Pope," *i.e.* mulled burgundy, is Anti-christian, from no mere Protestant point of view. *No* burgundy is really suitable for mulling, while to mull good burgundy is a capital crime. It is quite different with *vin brûlé,* a very popular beverage in Old France, and a regular Christmas and New Year tradition in the Channel Islands. When made of an unpretentious Bordeaux, it wants no dilution, of course, and if it is fairly stout wine, should want no fortifying. Some sugar it will certainly want, not to correct acidity, but to fill out body and flavour; a cloved and cloven lemon instead of the orange of bishop, a saucepan, a fire, and goblets. It will flame with less ghastly gorgeousness than the stronger liquor, but prettily enough, and it is exceedingly grateful and comforting. Indeed, virtues which it is not lawful to mention are attributed to it in Old French literature of the Pantagruelist variety.

· Was there any negus in the length and breadth of the land during the recent revival of Christmas festivities? A hundred years ago, as everybody who reads knows, it was omnipresent both at public entertainments (where it may be suspected that few landlords were as "liberal" as Mr. Jingle accused him of Rochester of being when

· he was presented with Dr. Slammer's card) and privately in houses before the bed-candles were taken. Even after dinner (*vide* Scott in *St. Ronan's Well* and the self-thoughtfulness of Mr. Winter-

· blossom) it seems to have held up its head with neat wine and punch. In my own time, and only in the earlier part of that, I re-

· member it at children's parties. Port negus is not bad, and is indeed a poor relation of bishop; but one would hardly take it except as a kind of emergency drink after being kept out late in snow or rain, after a long railway journey in an unwarmed carriage, or the like. Modern sherries of the drier and less full-bodied kind make negus impossible; with a full golden or brown you may make a fair alternative to the port mixture. Hot water ("screeching hot,

· ye divil") and sugar are the properties of the compound, lemon-slices, etc., its accidents. I have never been quite sure whether the "wine and water" so frequently mentioned of old, and in fact regarded as a sort of necessary ladies' nightcap, was negus, or merely cold "grog" of wine. Our ancestors, I regret to say, had rather a habit of putting water into wine—a proceeding partly connected with, and perhaps also partly explaining, their long sittings.

Flip and punch having been spoken of elsewhere, we may pass from winter to summer drinks, only premising that some of the bottled punches formerly obtainable were very deadly. I remember partaking of a bowl made from one such in Scilly, *anno* 1867, with a very agreeable, and soon to be hospitable officer of Her Majesty's 20th Regiment and an old Oxford parson, both of whom were the best of company. The basis of the compound seemed to be arrack, and it was by no means unpalatable. But hardly ever, I

FIGURE 24. Dr. Slammer defying Jingle before presenting his card:
had the negus been too strong? (Charles Dickens, *Pickwick Papers*
[1837]).

think, in all my life have I been so feelingly appreciative of the
Vauxhall "next morning" before spoken of, or of that experienced
by Mr. Tudor at the other end of Cornwall.

Cups, unless made of shocking stuff, or treacherously strong, involve no such punishment, and they are notoriously sometimes

constructed in such a fashion as to be little stronger than, if as strong as, "temperance drinks." On the other hand, they can be raised to much higher powers. I once invented one which was extremely popular, and had a curious history later. Instead of soda water I used sparkling Moselle, in the proportion of a pint of this to a bottle of claret, with thick slices of pine-apple instead of lemon, and one lump of ice as big as a baby's head.* It was astonishing how the people lapped it up, and nobody complained next day (I gave it at an evening party) of headache, though some ladies did say: "Wasn't that delicious cup of yours *rather* strong? I slept *so* soundly after it!" But that is not the history. Some years after I had invented it I gave the receipt in an article in the *Saturday Review*, which used at that time to confide to me most books on eating and drinking. Before long it began

---

* I think this mixture may be triumphantly vindicated against any charge of "confusion," such as may be brought against others, especially the once celebrated "Bismarck." Between the flavours of stout and of champagne there is no possible liaison. The former simply overwhelms the latter; and all the wine does is to make the beer more intoxicating and more costly. Thus the thing is at once vicious and vulgar. But the delicate flowery tastes and bouquets of the claret and the moselle make, in another sense, a real "bouquet," and the sparkle of the one wine gives just what the other has not. The advice about the "baby's head" may seem to run contrary not merely to that usually given in wine-catalogues and store-lists—"Do not put ice in cups," but also to my own remarks on icing claret and champagne. But I think there is a distinction. First, the "neat" flavour of the wine is, in cups, already submerged by the mixture of sugar, spirit, cucumber, borage and what not, and so is tolerably proof against mere contact with ice. Secondly, the progressive dilution by the melting ice does no harm, unless the more generous elements of the compound have been very stingily proportioned, which in this instance is certainly not the case. Thirdly, the floating iceberg rejoices the sight and, if it bobs

to appear in such books themselves, as indeed I had altruistically expected, for they are almost inevitably compilations. But the gradation of titles was very amusing. The first borrower honestly quoted it as "Saturday Review Cup"; the second simply headed it "Another Cup." But the third trumped both of them *and* me, for with a noble audacity he (or *she*, as I think it was) called it "My Own Cup."

Receipts for claret-cup are innumerable. Everybody has tasted it when it appeared to be composed of nothing but a little bad *ordinaire* and a great deal of soda water: and from this, in both Latin and English senses, "vile" mixture you may ascend to the most complicated prescriptions with sherry, brandy, liqueurs of various sorts, lemon, cucumber, borage (which always should be there, if possible), and half a dozen other things.

Champagne- and moselle-cups seem to me to come under the double sentence more than once applied in these pages. If they are made of good wine they are wicked; if of bad, unpardonable. Indeed, on the whole, it seems to me that no cup comes up to cider-cup, for the simple reason that there you are not contaminating but corroborating. A very little fizzing water, a good dose of stout well-flavoured sherry, just a *pousse* of brandy, with lemon and borage, will make *the* drink for hot weather, and the drinker will escape some inconveniences formerly hinted at as attending the drinking of "apple wine" neat.

Porter-cup and beer-cup I have only heard of, and do not much fancy, though of normally strong Bass and a little soda water I can

---

against them, the lips, especially if the container is one of those brown-and-yellow, straight-sided, three-handled "toby"-ware vessels which are cups' best (temporary) home. [**"Bismarck"**: Identical with "Black Velvet," i.e., a mixture of stout and Champagne.—*Editor*]

say: "*Bu* et approuvé," as in certain circumstances superior to bottled Bass itself.

In looking over this chapter I notice that I have said nothing here (nor anything earlier except in the case of true, that is to say beer-made, "flip") of mixtures with milk and eggs. For the milk-class I have no great affection. "Rum and milk" has been often celebrated in the words of Mercury, and sometimes in the songs of Apollo; but I do not think the rum is improved. Whisky and milk is rather better, especially if the whisky is very "smoky," for this corrects the mawkishness of the milk. I remember some, partaken of on a solitary walk in more than usually (for it was very early in the year) solitary Skye, from Uig by the Quiraing to Stenscholl. It seemed a thing in place, though the dispenser was a young person quite unbeautiful, extremely unkempt, and with no apparent knowledge of English beyond the name of the required mixture; and though the beach afterwards afforded neither golden cricket-ball nor coin-filled casket from the wreck of the *Carmilhan.* Brandy goes with milk even worse than rum; I never tried gin. As for "pullet-sperm in the brewage" once more, sherry-and-egg and brandy-and-egg ("cock-a-doodle broth") are well-known restoratives; and some have recommended a sort of prairie oyster, made by breaking a raw egg into a half-tumbler of rough red wine of claret type, and swallowing it without beating. But I cannot reconcile myself to the port and beaten-up egg which mountaineering books occasionally prescribe. The two flavours appear to me to "swear at" each other as trucelessly as do certain colours.*

With all these mixed drinks, however, and the more so with them the more mixed they are, there is perhaps, in the purged consider-

---

* For "purl" see note on "Artemisias" in the chapter on "Liqueurs." Theoretically, I believe it should be warmed with a red-hot poker: but the only experiment of the kind I ever made was far from successful.

ate mind of age, a doubt whether they are not vanities. Punch escapes by virtue of its numerous venerable and amiable associations, and, to speak frankly, of its undeniable charms; and at the other end cider cup, for the last reason, if not for the others. Bishop and *vin brûlé* diffuse an agreeable warmth, and so on and so on. (By the way "burnt sherry," though it has at least one great testimonial from Dickens, is not directly known to and is rather doubted by me, while *Hunted Down*, the same great writer's and good drinker's commemoration of burnt brandy, certainly does not favour it.) But they are all very liable to lead to the consumption of too much sugar, and sugar is as unwholesome to the possibly unscientific but practically experienced judgment as its derivative alcohol is healthful.* They all slightly suggest that mystical (but, the longer you live and the more you think, more profoundly justified) biblical curse on "confusion." Spirit asks for water (which thing is an allegory), but wine and beer ask for nothing but their own goodly selves, and somebody to drink, appreciate, and not abuse them. There was, as usual, an infinitely wider scope and range of action than that directly implied in the great sentence twice quoted in part already, "*Simple of itself;* I'll no pullet-sperm in my brewage." And yet I do not recant my exaltation of flip and some others, or my recipe for "Cup." One must be inconsistent sometimes.

---

* I had rather have the brewing and distilling done outside my body, instead of inside, as is the way of the abstainers.

XII. BOTTLES AND GLASSES

Something was said, in the opening chapter of this booklet, of certain special wine-glasses; and there has been mention of bottles—the containers, not merely the units contained—now and then. But there should, I think, be a little more on both points before we conclude. Bottles are extremely interesting things; and as for glasses and decanters, they can be delightful works of pure art. Without the former the bins of a cellar are as the walls of Balclutha, desolate; and there should in every cellar be a shelf of glasses, ready for the owner's private experiments or for his public liberality. One of my pleasantest cellar remembrances is that of dispensing at the door-way a glass of pure Clyne Lish (I think it was) to an oyster-wife who used to supply us with excellent natives at one and ninepence a dozen. "You won't want any water?" said I, and the lady ejaculated "Na! Na!" with a smile worthy of Ocean itself.

I do not know when the standard bottle or "reputed" quart actually existing—one-sixth of a gallon or rather over twenty-six ounces—was evolved. But everybody knows that pints and quarts themselves were, till lately, very "movable" feast-companions. Not to mention the ancient Scots pint, which was two English quarts, there still is, for chemical use, the "Winchester quart," which is five pints and is a stately vessel. I never saw wine bottled in it, but I have often used it as a receiver for spirits drawn from the cask. The gradations of the standard bottle—its multiples and fractions—are, as generally accepted, the rehoboam, or imperial, 8 bots.; the jeroboam, 6; the double magnum, 4; the tappit hen, 3; the magnum, 2; the bottle itself; the imperial pint; the reputed pint; and the quarter-bottle, sometimes called "nip," "baby," and other pet names.* They look very pretty "all of a row," especially in champagne form, from double magnum to "baby": and once, when I found that a child of mine had adopted an empty set for playthings, I would, had I been a person of property, have done as Boswell did or meant to do for his Veronica, when he added to her portion because of her attention to his idol.†

---

* I decline to admit the "imperial *half*-pint" in which beer is sometimes confined. Some readers may remember Christopher North's fine indignation at Sir H. Davy's "half-a-pint per man is *not too much!*" But this was at any rate *wine. I* once heard a human creature say cheerfully that one of these wretched apologies contained just *beer* enough "for him *and his wife!*" [**not too much:** I have not found the remark, but it is alluded to by John Wilson in *Noctes Ambrosianae*, no. 40 (December 1828): "Half a pint of Madeira—a moderation of which Sir Humphrey must approve—stands within a few inches of my writing hand."—*Editor*]

† It is a pity that the practice of "lozenging" bottles, with date of vintage, initials of possessor, name of house, etc., etc., has (except perhaps in the cellars of some private persons who possess the not universal combination of money and sense) apparently gone out. For it gives the individuality, more or less, which is a great secret of enjoyment. At the same time I am bound to say that my own (I think single) experience of it was not lucky. It was in the case of some '87 Lafite, which was lozenged when I bought it; and which never justified the distinction.

I am not sure that I ever possessed, or even that I ever saw, an "imperial," but I have had several jeroboams, which used to be not uncommon vessels with Scotch merchants for dispensing single gallons of whisky. They retained more of the portliness of the older wine-bottle than is now customary, that bottle having of late elongated and "slimmed" its proportions. In the earliest nineteenth century (and one has come across examples even later) there was a tendency to widen and almost "flange" the bottom. This made the vessel stand more firmly and held the crust better: but it would have been very awkward to bin without the then usual bed of sawdust. I think this sawdust was rather a mistake. It may have, when quite dry, kept the wine at an even temperature and prevented breakages, besides giving an air of age when brought up. But it encouraged insects and fungi in the corks; and in case of leakage it made a most disastrous hotbed, which sometimes quite spoilt the wine.

Such flanged bottles had some merits in picturesqueness and individuality. Earlier still the popular form seems to have been not cylindrical but globular, or like the *bocksbeutel* flasks of Steinwein. There are at Oxford some very attractive examples of the round shape rescued from ignominious burial and enshrined in the library of All Souls College. In fact, of old days there must have been a variety of form, which still lingers in liqueur-vessels to some extent. Of those which have survived, the red-brown hock and green moselle bottles, with their tapering outline, are the most graceful. At the Palatine Restaurant in Manchester they formerly used hock bottles as water-carafes. As for the "kicked" bottom of so many French wine and brandy bottles, it is perhaps, to the eye, preferable to a flat one: but of course it makes fraud easier. If I do not mistake, it is but a few years since a French Minister of Commerce addressed a vigorous allocution to his countrymen on the subject. And I know that in measuring a bottle of brandy bottled in France against one bottled in England I have sometimes found the "kick" responsible for a deficiency of nearly a sherry-glassful in the former.*

With decanters—those half-way houses between bottle and glass—one comes to questions of pure art. They can be very lovely things indeed; they can be frightfully ugly; and it is possible to have them without any great outlay—or was possible when it was possible to have anything without a great outlay—good to look at and good to use. Body-colour, when they are not kept pure white, should be, I think, restricted to a pale green—the shade of a moselle flask. Blues and reds kill the natural hues of wine, though a not too deep yellow is permissible. The noblest decanter I ever possessed was one I saw stuck away on a high shelf at Powells' (whose departure, by the way, from Whitefriars is sad). It had been made to order for the contents of a "tappit-hen" (*v. sup.*), but rejected by the (saving his reverence) idiotic orderer, and I bought it. It was of the flattened cone shape, white, fluted, and with a little frill round its fair throat. Unfortunately I never could get an

---

* In bidding adieu to "bottles" one glance may be pardoned at the former position of the *pint*. Not only does John Thorpe count his and his friends' consumption of port by pints, and several pints, but, later, Mr. Pickwick "finishes his *second* pint of particular port"—evidently a regular function. Why not a bottle? A little later still Will Waterproof had *a* pint—though, one suspects, again without prejudice to another. At any rate, the performance had no "stint" in it. Yet the wine is better in the larger vessel, and there is less relative danger and loss from crust. [**John Thorpe:** "Now, for instance, it was reckoned a remarkable thing at the last party in my rooms, that upon an average we cleared about five pints a head" (Jane Austen, *Northanger Abbey*, ch. 9). **Mr. Pickwick:** Charles Dickens, *Pickwick Papers*, ch. 26. **Will Waterproof:** Tennyson, "Will Waterproof's Lyrical Monologue," lines 3–4: "How goes the time? 'Tis five o'clock. / Go fetch a pint of port."—*Editor*]

actual tappit hen of claret to put in it—they were not infrequent at the sale of old Scotch cellars thirty or forty years ago, but are very rare now. However, it contented itself with a magnum cheerfully enough: and I am not sure that the bouquet did not develop better for the empty space. (I need hardly say that to decant more than one bottle into the same vessel is a very risky experiment.) At any rate it used to look imposing under a seven-light brass candlestick which Mr. Benson made for me. The same admirable craftsmen, who, like all persons deserving that noun and adjective, would take just as much trouble for you if you gave them a half-guinea order as if it had been such as one of their commissions I once saw on its way to Russia—a cut-glass service worth fifteen hundred pounds—made me a set of claret jugs, two of each size—pint, bottle, and magnum—of the pilgrim bottle shape, green, fluted, but with rounded bottoms, not flat like the "henmaster." And from them, from Salviati's, and from other sources one picked up things not unworthy of their intended contents.

The one drawback of cut-glass decanters—besides their cost, but apart from the purpose recommended by Count Considine in *Charles O'Malley*—is their great weight. The beauty of them no one can well contest; though I think the material shews better in the wine-glass than in the decanter. Few kinds shew off the wine itself better than the so-called "Black Forest" type, which separates a top and a bottom mass of liquid by four slender tube-columns. My earliest recollection of it (I do not think it was at all common before the middle of the nineteenth century) was derived from mounted examples in the window of a silversmith named Sachs, who used to have a shop—the only one in a highly genteel neighbourhood—below Connaught Square, and close to that quaint chapel and burying-ground which, according to legend, saw the "resurrecting" of Sterne's body. This was as far back as the early fifties. Afterwards they multiplied, and were even sold with whisky and other things in them, so that they have become quite common. But that matters little. Of more elaborate forms, curly snaky things, circlets with a big hole in the middle and the like, I am not sure. Simplicity is a mighty Goddess in the flagon, which should aim at displaying not so much itself as the wine.

It is otherwise with the wine-*glass* for not a few reasons, one of the chief being that you naturally hold it up, and look at it, and play with it in your hands. It should never in the least obscure the colour of the wine, or the possibility of looking through that wine itself and both sides of the glass to the light—a point in which some of the more gaudy Venetian examples seem to me faulty. But short of this, the taste and fancy of the designer and the glass-worker may find very wide exercise. Here cut glass—a bevel and rim of *un*-cut being kept for the lip—is in some respects, for those who can stand its cost, the best of all. It is heavy, but not, on this scale, too heavy; while its very weight keeps it steady, and saves it from the exertions of any but the strongest handmaid.

It is true that there is nothing that some servants will not break. The *mousseline* glasses, of which in their early days Thackeray complained that they "were not only enormous, but broke by dozens," fly like chaff before them; and with the aid of the pantry tap (most handy for such a purpose) almost anything can be broken. They sometimes display a really uncanny acquaintance with the secrets of natural philosophy. I had a parlour-maid once who was evidently well up in the doctrine of transmission of forces. She arranged three decanters, partly full of wine, back to back and touching each other, on the shelf of a buffet-cupboard, so that the outermost just projected a quarter of an inch in front of the edge. The shutting of the door, even quite gently, necessarily caused, as will be seen, the destruction of all three; the door itself breaking No. 1, that cracking No. 2, and that in turn accomplishing the ruin of No. 3. It was a beautiful demonstration in physics, but I wish it had occurred somewhere else. In fact, the loss of glass is so enormous that I once made a sober calculation showing how at the time—some thirty years ago when silver was cheap—it would have paid to lay in a moderate but sufficient service in pure argent. But unfortunately glass—at least so it seems to me—is your only ware for wine. I never literally put in practice the famous Welsh saying, *Gwin o eur*—"wine from *gold*." But silver, though excellent for beer (even there it is not so good as pewter), has never pleased me for wine.

Of the shapes and sizes of glasses there were no end, if one spoke at all fully. It may be said generally that those with a swelling lip are bad; those with a pinched-in one good, especially for wines of much bouquet. "Brimmers" and "bumpers" are jovial and time-honoured, but better sung about than indulged in. And if our fathers meant by "No heel-taps" that you were always to drink the whole glassful at once, even with allowance of "skylight," I think that, for once, our fathers were wrong. Beverage wines may be drunk in that fashion, of course, but nothing choice, and very specially not port, good claret or burgundy. But I prefer to think that they only barred the keeping of a remnant when you filled, so that you did not "drink fair."

Beyond all doubt there is a certain pre-established harmony between different wines and different shapes, sizes and even colours of glasses. Claret never tastes well in a small glass; burgundy I think even worse. Port is more tolerant. The old green hock-glasses were suitable enough for the wine they were named from; but I always thought that it, and all other light white wines, tasted best in some faint straw-coloured, bell-shaped things on very tall stems, which a friend was kind enough to bring me straight from Nuremberg. I have spoken before of the Salviati cloud-white, avanturine, and blue for French red wines. They did not so well suit port—which goes best in cut glass—or any white wine. Sherry being always the most accommodating of liquors, you may drink it in glasses small or large, white or coloured, plain or fancy in shape. If it is good it will always be good in any; and if it is bad, none will save it.*

As for champagne, there is room for real controversy about that. Its vehicles to the mouth may be classed fourfold: the old tall "flutes," the modern ballet-girl-skirt inverted, which is supposed to have been one of the marks of the viciousness of the French Second Empire, but which all the world hastened to adopt; tumblers; and a nondescript group of large glasses, varying from claret to goblet shape, and sometimes enormous in size. Of these I bar, at once and without appeal, the tumbler. I do this regretfully, for many good men have given me much good wine in it; but I think it is WRONG. In the first place, the wine never tastes quite right out of tumblers: they demoralise it, and approximate Reims to Saumur. And in the second, there is no stem for the finger-tips to play with; now a wine-glass without a stem is as bad as some other "creations" without a waist—or a neck, for after all the sacque, which has no waist, is a creation of some merit.

The fault of the miscellaneous glasses, some of which, however, are not bad, is that they are not *distinctive* enough. A wine of such unique character as champagne—for after all other sparkling wines are pale copies and corrupt followings of Dom

---

* What has been admitted to be a sort of "sin" in liqueurs has a "solace," as Milton would say, in the opening they give for various and pretty glasses. For most kinds there is nothing better than white glass with gold-leaf arabesques or flowers. Green chartreuse and green curaçao, as well the red liquids, ask for plain white in colour, but with shape and cutting at discretion. Nor are the tiny crumpled Venetian tumblers to be objected to. [**Milton:** E.g., *Paradise Lost*, IX, 1044: the fallen Adam and Eve make love, "The solace of their sin, till dewie sleep."—*Editor*]

- Pérignon's great discovery—ought to have a glass to itself, peculiar in something besides mere size. This connection both the flutes and the inverted skirts duly meet: and I have never entirely or decisively made up my mind between them, using now one now
- the other "while it was day." I have always been willing to recognise an over-ruling Providence in the affairs of this world—a Providence which makes the punishment fit the crime (the thirst of the Pussyfoots in the Sixth Circle, *if they are allowed there*, will
- be ten times that of the drunkards) and adjusts the supply to the demand. And so I have sometimes thought that the flute is most suitable to sweet champagnes, and the other to dry. The former must not be too small, a fault perhaps not unknown in the days when a single bottle of champagne was made to do for a dozen people. The latter should not be too large, or you get a clumsy
- something more like a *tazza* or a fruit "comport" than a glass. Its most practical form is undoubtedly that in which the stem is pierced nearly to the foot with a thin tube, for this maintains the sparkle remarkably. On the other hand the glass has to be very heavy, and it is rather difficult to keep the shaft of the funnel quite clean. But such a glass, filled with *œil-de-perdrix* wine, the bubbles lazily ascending through the stem and diffusing themselves fountain-fashion through the upper liquor, is a beautiful sight— promising a pleasant satisfaction to other senses, and good to close a chapter with, even if one perceives no immediate chance of see-
- ing it again. *Fuit* and *fuimus*—I take leave to repeat the burden of my book in various forms—are not always mournful words to the wiser and not too pusillanimous mind.

XIII. CELLAR ARRANGEMENTS

It may seem rather absurd for a man whose command of cellar-room, and his opportunity for availing himself of it, have always been extremely limited, to write a chapter under this heading. But the book, small as it is, and so suiting its circumstances, would hardly be complete without such a chapter. And this is more especially the case because the genesis of the Cellar-Book itself was connected with the fact that once and once only, a cellar such as it was, small but fairly perfect, "did," like the sword and pistol of the heroine of "Billy Taylor," "come at my command."

Until I was nearly forty such liquids as I possessed had to endure very inferior accommodation. Up to the time of the close of the first third of the nineteenth century, I have reason to believe that London middle-class houses, as indeed others were and continued to be in the country, were not so ill provided in this respect. Port, which everybody who had even a few hundreds a year drank, and of which an ordinary family would consume its bottle often, if not daily, was, as has been pointed out earlier, quite cheap; and though few people who were not positively well to do might lay down whole pieces for future consumption, it was prob-

ably bought in good quantity for more or less immediate drinking. But as this habit fell off, and as houses began to be built,
cheaply and without thought but in immense numbers, all round
London, the cellar lost its importance. The house, at Southampton, which I first knew, and which was, I suppose, built early in
the nineteenth century, had, if I am not mistaken, a good one.
But those in London just north of Kensington Gardens, where I
passed most of my life between five years old and twenty-three,
had, I think, nothing but a cupboard under the kitchen stairs—
an arrangement which secured (not to mention the proximity, not
immediate but too close, of the kitchen fire) constant shaking from
trampling of servants up and down. Nor were things much better in others where I kept house independently later, as far as
Guernsey and London were concerned, though in Elgin, where
my abode was a *ci-devant* hotel converted into a school-house, Bacchus was better accommodated.

In the early eighties, however, I moved into one of the new regions west of Kensington, and took, somewhat rashly, a 7–14–21
years' lease of a house never previously occupied, indeed not quite
ready for occupation, and the first of its pretty long row of neighbours to be inhabited. As in such cases I believe is not (or was not)
uncommon, the builders were extremely liberal in decoration and
internal arrangement, the house, while in process of completion,
serving as a sort of advertisement to the rest of the row. They let
me choose my papers; they furnished me with a bath of extraordinary elaborateness, where you could float on an upward douche
like a cork in one of the shop-fountains, subject yourself to what
was called a "wave" (it was more ingenious than exhilarating), and
by turning various cocks and levers in the hood, administer show-
ers of most interesting variety. But what was even more to my taste
was that they let me adjust, and charged me nothing for adjust-
ing, an apartment in the basement which had, I think, been meant

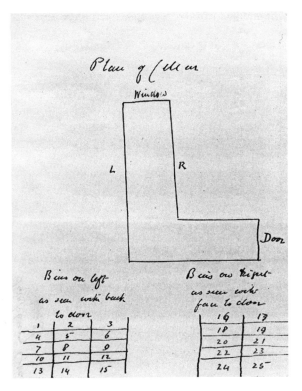

FIGURE 25. Saintsbury's plan of his cellar in Kensington, from the cellar book (Michael Broadbent, *Saintsbury the Progenitor* [London: privately printed, 1993]).

for a larder, to the purposes not of eating but of drink. It was not entirely subterranean, as the garden on which its window opened was much lower than the road; but its greatest length backed on solid earth, and there were no pipes or stoves too near. I never found it very much above or below the sacred 50'–55'. As for room, I had it spaced into 25 stone bins, 15 on one side and 10 on the other, graded, so that, without their being very deep, the lowest accommodated from 12 to 15 dozen, and the uppermost perhaps three. Unless you have large quantities of single wines, deep bins are a nuisance.

This, though no Domdaniel, seemed sufficiently like a real cellar to deserve a cellar-book, and accordingly that which forms the text of the present notes was started. But Fate is notoriously capricious, and though I am happy to say that the grim Eastern proverb as to Who "comes in at the window when the house is finished" was not fulfilled, I was only allowed a very short possession. Scarcely four times* had one of the big bins been filled and refilled with light claret, as formerly mentioned, when I had to move my household into the country for the health's sake of one of its members, and content myself with chambers in town for the working days of the week. *There* a cupboard and an iron wine-bin sufficed; in the two country houses which I successively occupied there were cellars, but rather small ones, and I left off keeping the book regularly.

My cellar near Cambridge had one awkward peculiarity. It was approached through another of slightly lower level, and this outer cellar, at certain times of the year, used to be filled about a foot deep with the most pellucid water, apparently rising from the earth. This remained some time, and disappeared as it came. While it was there it necessitated the erection of a plank bridge to get to the wine, and incidentally made the house above rather damp. So a kind friend proposed to pump it out, and actually brought a garden-engine for the purpose. I had, while expressing

---

* Let me in gratitude name the fillers, Messrs. Harvey's "Red Seal" Medoc, and Châteaux Bonneval, Laujac and Citran. [Château Laujac, in the Bas-Médoc, is a Cru Bourgeois; Château Bonneval is in the Côtes du Frontonnais (now Fronton), near Toulouse; for Château Citran, see my note to p. 113.—*Editor*]

due gratitude, to point out to him that in that case we should be pumping against the springs of half Cambridgeshire and an unknown proportion of Essex and Suffolk, so that on the general principle of water finding its level, the operation would take some time, and it might be difficult to know what to do with what we pumped. I believe new waterworks, for Cambridge itself, have since accomplished this piece of engineering more satisfactorily. Had I been longer there the damp would, no doubt, have worked wreckage. The butler at a house in Hampshire, which, though situated high up, must have had springs near it, told me that it was there hardly safe to leave wine, without actual recorking, for more than seven years. But in this instance I had small supplies, and moved in half that time, so no harm was done.

When, in 1895, I moved once more from another place in the south of England to Edinburgh, I inhabited, for the first four years, a large house somewhat to the west of the city, and dating from the early eighteenth century. Cellars of such houses in Scotland are generally ample; I know one in which even Mr. Crotchet's "thousand dozen of wine" could be accommodated with the greatest ease, and leave room for at least another thousand, with casks to match. But though my abode had a large cellarage, it had evidently not—recently at least—been much used for the noblest purpose of such structures. There was an enormous coal-cellar, which one could and of course did—in the good days when colliers, *pace* Mr. Smillie, were quite happy with their moderate wages, and when coal merchants charged no more than twelve shillings a ton in summer—fill for a whole year's consumption on the rather extravagant Northern scale. There was an intermediate apartment, hardly at all binned, but where you could put cases, casks, and iron wine bins if you chose. And then there was the innermost recess, which was prepared—after a fashion but not very amply—for wine storage.

It was greatly infested with rats, and for a time I was puzzled by having to add thermometers to the already considerable list of rat-foods. But before very long I found out the mystery. In looking to see that the cellar was not too cold (there was not much danger of its being too hot) one sloped the candle towards the instrument, and the grease dropped on the wood. It hung just above the top of an iron wine bin, and the ingenious beasts evidently climbed up without displacing the bottles. They, to do them justice, never lost me a drop that way, though they seem to have had designs, for we once discovered a sherry glass half-way down a rat hole. But their enemy, my Scotch terrier Bounce (whose pedigree I used to keep in the same drawer with my commission as Regius Professor) was more clumsy. He followed me one day without my knowledge, saw a rat, dashed at the bin, and I immediately found him yelling with fear and struggling with the *débris* and froth of two magnums of champagne. If he had got the rat it would have been some consolation for a rather expensive kind of sport.

The last stage, the longest, and (till it ended as all things end) the most abundantly furnished in wine, was not quite so abundantly furnished with room. The cellar of my house in Edinburgh itself was not so commodious as that which I organised in London, and it was partly under stairs. But since Craig-Leith stone does not transmit vibration as deal planks do, the resting place was steady enough. It was never too cold (I was able to meet that danger by a gas-jet put low down, for one at the usual height will simply mull your top-bins), and only in the hottest Septembers (which are Edinburgh's hottest months) did it verge on undue heat. It consisted of four very large and deep stone bins on the right as you entered, and of a narrow but longer angle-piece admitting some twenty small wooden partitions, one bottle deep, on one side, and a stool and shelf for jars, etc., on the other. There was also room for an iron champagne bin at one end, and a small decanting table with shelves beneath at the other. The great and rich might have scorned it; and their butlers certainly would. But by taking advantage of corners, etc., I found it capable of accommodating all the wine I wanted, in a fashion more conveniently accessible than far more stately magazines could boast. The deep bins I utilized at the back for storing wines too young to drink, and in front as homes for the small store-casks above spoken of; while the number of the shallow ones, which would hold three or four dozen apiece, admitted of separating different liquids so as to be got at at once.

Well! a cellar is an interesting place to fill, to contemplate when filled, and to empty in the proper way. Nor, if you have to part with it, is its memory other than agreeable. The doctrine of *ut conviva satur* will not always hold; but it will here.*

---

* A talk of cellars would hardly seem complete without something about that plague of the cellar-owner, "corking." I am happy to say that I do not, as such, know very much about it. I remember being told by a famous Fellow of a more famous College, at which I was dining, that they had at one time been tried in this way to an alarming extent, without being able to determine whether it was the fault of the corks (I thought of Warton's

> Rode for a stomach, and inspected
> At annual bottlings, corks selected)

or that of the butler, or something like the biblical plague of house-leprosy in the cellar itself. None of my cellar*ets*, for they were little more, was thus cursed. Certainly I have seen, but only in the case of some bottles bought at sales, corks in a quite Gehazi-like condition from tip to wax. Such cases are no doubt hopeless. In milder ones the wine may sometimes be made not undrinkable by standing the decanter (which should have been specially bright and dry) with the stopper out before a fire (but of course not too near) for a time, which the restoration of the bouquet, if it *be* restorable, will show. It should perhaps be said that this fungus-growth, or whatever it is, which attacks other wines, does not seem to be responsible for that so-called "corking" of champagne, in reference to which there is a sharp division between two races of wine-merchants. The one protests, truly enough, that he can't help it; but if you send back the peccant bottle he will give you a fresh one. The other simply observes that he sends the cases as he receives them, and has no more to do with it. The worst nuisance of *this* corking is that a single bottle at a dinner-party will, by the filling up of half-empty glasses, infect a much larger quantity of wine. It gave me, however, once, an amusing moment. A physician of distinction, who had made himself rather conspicuous by frequent tirades in print against alcohol, positively disturbed his neighbours at a public dinner by outcries against the corking of some, as it seemed to me, quite innocent champagne. It may perhaps be well to warn "absent-minded beggars" that the "cure by heat" above suggested is *not* intended to be applied to the liquid, of which Panard sang pleasantly, "De ce vin gris Que je chéris L'écume!" (Besides the information about Artemisias, I owe my friend Sir W. T. Thiselton-Dyer the name of the "corked wine" fungus, *Merulius lacrymans*, which is much too lovely to leave out, though it reached me a little late for the text. I hope that it will suggest to others, as it did to me, the famous "Il en rougit, le traître!" with *pleure* instead of *rougit!*) [**"corks selected"**: Thomas Warton, the Younger, "The Progress of Discontent," lines 118–19:

> At annual bottlings, corks selected,
> And dined untax'd, untroubled.

"absent-minded beggars": See Kipling's "The Absent-Minded Beggar" (1899), written to raise money to supply amenities for the troops in the Boer War. **"je chéris L'écume!"**: "that grey [i.e. pinkish] wine whose foam I cherish." *Merulius lacrymans:* The main cause of cork taint is now identified as a chemical called trichloranisole (TCA), but there are other causes as well. **"Il en rougit, le traître!"**: Théophile de Viau, *Pyrâme et Thisbé* (1621): "he blushes for it, the traitor!"; in Saintsbury's suggested adaptation, "he [the peccant fungus] weeps for it."—*Editor*]

CONCLUSIO AD DIVERSOS
(With a Few Barmecide Invitations)

•

The excuse for a proem to these few pages may seem to want repetition and emphasising in the case of a "Post-face"; but it is perhaps not a mere paradox to say that the smaller the book the greater the need for such a thing. Among the various groups to whom an *Envoi* may not be superfluous I shall not omit, though I recognise the almost hopelessness of their admission, the Prohibitionists, open and concealed. It would, I fear, be utterly useless to content oneself with the good-humoured request of Dorat to the French *philosophes:*

•

> Mais, pour Dieu, soyez bonnes gens,
> Et, si vous pouvez, plus modestes!

For if there were any possibility of their being *bonnes gens,* they could hardly be what they are.

In my journalist days I was once complimented by an editor on possessing an unusual variety of "jackets"; literary, political, historical, philosophical, culinary, and even theological, not to mention others. In donning the theological one I had not neglected (nor I hope in the other cases) to qualify myself to some extent for the wearing. I think few theologians will disagree with me when I say that thanklessness towards God and malice towards men constitute about as awkward a "soul-*diathesis*" as can be imagined.* Nor, moving the calculus, will the preference of questionable "scientific" theories to age-long practical experience come out much better. When the doctors and the Reverends (self-dubbed and other) and the occasional magistrates who cackle about the mischiefs of alcohol, condescend to face facts,† there may be something more to say to them. But no more at present, except to urge the most strenuous opposition to the subdolous and impertinent foreign interference which they are calling to their aid; and to express regret that Archbishops and Bishops, if they do not definitely set themselves against the advice of St. Paul and the practice of Christ, should join movements, the clear effect, and in some cases the hardly disguised object, of which is to make the adoption of that advice and the imitation of that practice impossible.

Turning to the sheep after leaving these goats (though I have always thought it a little hard on the goat, which is generally a

---

* Prohibitionists disclaim the "malice," of course. But so, with much more reason, would Torquemada have done. The "thanklessness" speaks for itself.

† Here is one for which I have more than once vouched in print, and which I defy anyone to invalidate. Six years' experience (1868–1874) of the island of Guernsey, where you could get blind drunk for sixpence; a population of between 30,000 and 40,000; a garrison frequently renewed; sailors from many parts of the world dropping in; scarcely any police; *no* serious crime; hardly any minor disorder; and a splendid bill of health. When a man commits a crime under what is miscalled the "influence" of drink, he should, where possible, be punished double—once for the bad act, and once for the misuse of the good thing, by forcing it to reveal his true nature.

good-looking and sometimes an agreeable animal) I have to apol-
ogise to greater experts than myself for any over-positiveness of
statement and any deficiency of information. I am only an amateur, of course; only a man who has made the study and enjoyment of wine and its fellows (their kinds, their merits and their
innumerable and world-ranging associations, in life and literature,
in history and society) one of the amusements, relaxations, and
auxiliaries of a rather unusually hard-working life.* As one looks
back over such a life there are many things that one regards with
thankfulness. It is good to have walked by oneself five hundred
miles in twenty days and one pair of boots (never needing the cobbler till the very last day) without any training and with a fairly

---

* I should not be dealing candidly with my reader, if I did not warn
him that Pussyfoot scientists call the state of perceived well-being and
capability for well-doing, which alcohol induces, "toxic euphoria."
Toxic euphoria as a phrase is good; it is even better than "mobled queen";
it is delicious. It brings a fresh pang at the approaching *dys*thanasia of
its language which some people (including pretty surely the Pussyfoot
scientists themselves) are trying to bring about. But as they use it, it carries a vain and fallacious meaning, fondly if not fraudulently invented.
As real men of science (who cannot be too carefully distinguished from
"scientists") have pointed out before now, alcohol is auto-antidotic, its
narcotic quality tending to dispel its other tendency, as Mr. Gargery so
delicately put it, to "over-stim*i*late." The toxicity, as all bad things unfortunately do not *yet* do, whatever Apocatastasis may bring about (if
they want Greek they can have plenty) vanishes; the euphoria, as all good
things do, and always will do, remains. [**"mobled queen"**: "That's good,
'mobled queen' is good," as Polonius says: *Hamlet*, II, ii, 526. **dys-
thanasia**: The antonym of *euthanasia*: not an easy but a bad death.
"over-stim*i*late": Charles Dickens, *Great Expectations*, vol. 2, ch. 8:
"wot a pipe and a pint of beer do give refreshment to the working-man,
Sir, and do not over stimilate." **Apocatastasis**: Return to a previous condition.—*Editor*]

heavy knapsack.* It is good to have seen something on this and many other occasions, sometimes alone, sometimes in company, of the secret of the sea and the lessons of the land from Scilly to Skye; from the Land's End to Dover; from the Nore to the Moray Firth; from Dartmoor to Lochaber; and from the Weald of Sussex to those Northumbrian lakes that lie, lonely and rather uncanny, under the Roman Wall. It is good to have attended evening chapel at Oxford, then gone up to town and danced all night (the maximum of dances with the minimum of partners), returning next morning and attending chapel again. It is good to have prevented an editor, some time before Pigott caught the *Times*, from engaging in negotiations with that ingenious person as he had intended to do; and to have actually silenced a Radical canvasser.† It is good to have been always like-minded with the old and not

---

* I do not mention this as anything wonderful in itself, though Lord Roberts did once tell me (with his usual amiability, and perhaps thinking mainly of the boots) that a general, everyone of whose men could do as much, would be uncommonly lucky. I only say it is good to have done it. [**Lord Roberts:** Field Marshal Frederick Sleigh Roberts (1832–1914), first Earl Roberts, the leading British soldier of his day, commanded in India and South Africa.—*Editor*]

† He wanted my vote, and when I told him that I was "over the way" he politely requested leave to put some reasons on his side before me. I said, "My good sir, I have been a political journalist for twenty years, and a student of politics and history for about thirty. I can tell you beforehand everything you are going to say, and everything I am going to answer; and your replies and so on. We are, I suppose, both busy men; can't we as well leave it where it is?" He must have been better than his creed; for he smiled and said, "Perhaps so, sir," and went. I should have liked to offer him something to drink—whence the relevance here—but this would have offended the Nonconformist Conscience and might even have been construed into a Corrupt Practice.

the modern law of England, to the effect that "collective bargaining" can never be anything but collective bullying. It is good to have read Walz's *Rhetores Graeci*, and the *Grand Cyrus*, and nearly all the English poets that anybody has ever heard of; also to find *The Earthly Paradise*, at a twentieth reading in 1920, as delightful as it was at a first in 1868. It is good to have heard Sims Reeves flood St. James's Hall with "Adelaida," till you felt as if you were being drowned, not in a bath but in an ocean of musical malmsey; and to have descanted on the beauties of your first Burne-Jones, without knowing that a half-puzzled, half-amused don stood behind you. Many other things past, and some present, have been and are—for anything, once more, that has been is—good.

But I do not feel the slightest shame in ranking as good likewise and very good, those voyages to the Oracle of the Bottle and those obediences to its utterance, taken literally as well as allegorically, which are partially chronicled here. If I subjoin a few examples of *menus*, and some wine-lists, it is chiefly for the purpose of illustrating the doctrines laid down and the practices recommended in this book.* They are all records of meals and wines discussed in my own houses, and mostly devised by ourselves. Some great authorities have pronounced such things not bad reading, Barmecidal as they are. I know that I found them comfortable in the days of rationing, when there were other calls, even on the absurd modicum of meat that was allotted to one in common with babies, dead men and vegetarians, and when one had to be content with sprats and spaghetti. I wish I could imitate the Barmecide himself in following up these ghostly banquets with real ones. But I hope that all good men and all fair ladies who

---

* I do not enter into any controversy as to some points in these *menus*, such as the mixture of English and French titles, and the omission of the definite article in the latter. I do as I like, and others may do as they like.

read me will accept the assurance that I would if I could minister unto them, even as I was privileged to do to others of their kind from fifty to five years ago, when "we drank it as the Fates ordained it," and took, as cheerfully as we drank it, what else the Fates ordained.

Let us begin with two specimens of a kind of dinner which I now think over-elaborated. Two *entrées* are quite enough. But the fact was that at the time when they and others like them were given (the opening years of the Cellar-Book, 1884–6), both my wife and I were rather fascinated by a French *chef* named Grégoire, who in those days both sent out and superintended dishes, less impossibly than poor Rosa Timmins's volunteer assistant, and very admirably. Alas! he died. His soufflés were sublime.*

---

* By one of these may hang a little tale. At a dinner of the usual "sonnet" or "fourteener" number, the lady on my left refused it; the man next her, who was busy talking to his other neighbour, did ditto; so did his accomplice; and what a seventeenth-century Puritan pamphleteer, picturesquely anticipating later slang, calls "a rot among the Bishops," set in. My wife might have stopped it, but didn't: and the dish came back to me virgin. I helped myself, observed gravely "I'm sorry to keep you all waiting," and ate. Thereupon my lady said "It looks very good: may I change my mind?" And the man next her changed *his* mind; and his damsel followed; and they all followed—the whole dozen of them (omitting my wife, who is sometimes *propositi tenax*). I said nothing aloud: but murmured to myself and the *soufflé*, "Sheep!" [***propositi tenax:*** "Holding fast to his principle": Horace, *Odes*, III, iii, 1.—*Editor*]

I.

Montilla.	Consommé aux Pointes
—	d'Asperges.
	—
Johannisberg.	John Dory.
Claus Auslese, 1874.	Sauce Livournaise.
—	—
Ch. Grillet, 1865.	Filets de Saumon à la gelée.
—	—
Champagne.	Côtelettes à la Joncourt.
Jeroboam.* Dagonet, 1874.	—
	Plovers' Eggs.
—	—
Romanée Conti, 1858.	Aspic de Volaille à la Reine.—
—	Haunch of Mutton.
Ch. Margaux, 1868.	—
—	Mayonnaise de Homard.
Port, 1853.	—
	Soufflé glacé au Marasquin.
—	—
Pedro Ximénès.	Canapés de Crevettes.

* We used to wreath the jeroboams as centre-pieces, and a poetical guest once besought leave to crown my wife with the circlet of primroses and violets.

II.

Sherry.	Consommé.
"Margarita."	—
	Filets de Sole à la
—	Venitienne.
Ch. Grillet, 1865.	—
	Bastions d'Anguilles.
—	—
Champagne.	Vol au vent à la Financière.
St. Marceaux, 1880.	—
	Filets de Pigeons à la
—	Pompadour.
Ch. Latour, 1870.	—
	Braised Fillet of Beef.
—	—
Romanée Conti, 1858.	Roast Pheasants.
—	—
	Soufflé glacé aux Pistaches.
Hermitage, 1846.*	—
	Œufs à l'Annécy.

* The last bottle of that spoken of in Chap. I.

III.

As a contrast of simplicity take the following, long afterwards (some twenty years) constructed as an endeavour to carry out, for a single guest, the admirable combination of *ordre et largeur* in Foker's prescription, "a bottle of sherry, a bottle of sham, a bottle of port, and a shass-caffy."

Sherry.	Clear Soup.
"Titania."	—
	Fried Trout.
—	—
Champagne.	Filets de Bœuf à la
Moët, 1893.	St. Aubyn.
	—
—	Roast Duckling.
	—
Port.	Apricots à la Rosebery.
Cockburn's 1881.	—
	Sardines
—	Dieu-sait-Comment.*
	—
Green Chartreuse.	Coffee.

* A prescription of my wife's, named by me.

IV.*

White Dry Paxarette.	Consommé.
—	—
White Hermitage, 1865.	Filets de Soles en Crêpes.
—	—
Champagne.	Pain de Volaille.
Perrier-Jouet, 1884.	—
—	Savoury Aspic.
Ch. Latour, 1878.	—
—	Haunch of Mutton.
Port, 1858.	—
—	Pintades au Cresson.
Sherry.	—
Caveza.	Surprise Pudding.
	Italian Cream.
	—
	Royans à la Bordelaise.

* The dinner referred to at the end of Chap II. Date, 1894.

V.

(A dinner without champagne.)

Montilla.	Oysters.
—	—
	Consommé.
Ch. Yquem, 1870.	—
—	Grilled Red Mullet.
	—
Ch. Margaux, 1870	Cutlets à l'Américaine.
(Magnum).	—
—	Grouse.
Port.	—
Cockburn's, 1851	Macaroni Pudding.
(Magnum).	—
	Shrimp Toast.

VI.

*(A June-Eating.)**

Margarita Sherry.	Oxtail Soup.
—	Whitebait.
Champagne. St. Marceaux, 1874.	Mutton Cutlets.
—	Chicken Salad.
Ch. Mouton-Rothschild, 1875 (Magnum).	Iced Gooseberry Fool. — Olives au Nid.

* This was the dinner at which M. Beljame was present (see Chap. IV.). I arranged it with nothing French except the wine and the "savoury," on the principles of an excellent retort which my friend Mowbray Morris told me against himself. He was entertaining the famous caricaturist, Pellegrini, and half in jest (they were in London) asked if he would have some macaroni. Pellegrini shook his finger in front of his face and said: "Mor*riss!*—my friend!—when I ask you to dinner at Naples I will not give you a beef-steak!" [**Mowbray Morris:** Morris (1848–1911) was editor of *Macmillan's Magazine*. **Pelligrini:** Carlo Pellegrini (1839–89), the artist of the long series of caricatures of notable people in *Vanity Fair* under the signature "Ape."—*Editor*]

VII.*

Sherry.	Clear Soup.
Margarita.†	—
—	Fillets of Whiting.
Ch. Carbonnieux, 1899.	Dutch Sauce.
—	—
Champagne.	Chicken Rissoles.
Vve. Clicquot, 1899.	—
—	Saddle of Mutton.
Ch. Montrose, 1893.	—
—	Raspberry Sponge.
Port.	—
Dow's 1890.	Celery Cream.

* Another yoking (again many years later, for the Beljame feast was in 1886, and this in 1908) of plain home food and good foreign wine.

† I have said in the text that this admirable pale dry sherry was one of my greatest stand-bys all through, which will account for its frequent appearance, even in this selection.

*VIII.**

Tio Pepe.	Consommé.
—	—
Meursault, 1870.	Grilse.
	—
—	Filets de Soles Ravigotte.
Champagne.	—
Pommery.	Côtelettes de Mouton
Extra Sec, 1876.	Soubise.
	—
—	Chaudfroid de Volaille.
Still Red Verzenay, 1868.	—
	Vol-au-vent Financière.
—	—
Gold Dry Sherry.	Virginian Quails.
	—
—	Soufflé glacé au Chocolat.
Ch. Lafite, 1862.	—
	Canapés d'Anchois au Fromage.

* An early (1884), and I think not bad dinner, particularly as regards the wine, though the Claret might have been better. Perhaps the chaud-froid (or chau*ffroix*, if any one prefers it), and the vol-au-vent come, in both senses, too close together. But I remember how good the still red Verzenay was with the Virginian Quails. I have spoken of the Tio Pepe and the Meursault in the text, but not, I think, of the "Gold Dry." It was one of Messrs. Harvey's wines, and "of a noble race," like Shenkin. [**chau*ffroix*:** The *OED* does not recognize this variant, nor does *Robert*. **"of a noble race," like Shenkin:** The stock Welsh character in English stage comedy, along with Teague the Irishman and Sawney the Scots-man.—*Editor*]

*IX.**

Pale Sherry.	Clear Soup.
—	—
Graves, 1893.	Filleted Sole.
—	—
Champagne.	Dutch Sweet-breads.
Perrier Jouet, 1893.	—
—	Mutton Cutlets à la
Ch. Léoville-Poyferré,	Oporto.
1896.	—
—	Beans and Bacon.
Ch. Latour, 1893.	—
—	Beehive Pudding.
Port.	—
Warre's 1884.	Cheese Trifles.

* 1904. Another contrast.

X.*

Vino de Pasto.	Clear Soup.
	—
—	Boiled Salmon.
	—
Champagne.	Pollo con Arroz.
St. Marceaux, 1880.	—
	Lobster au Gratin.
—	—
	Forequarter of Lamb.
Ch. Léoville Barton,	—
1874.	Cherry Tart. Meringues.
	—
	Schabzieger Toast.

* A country dinner in 1888. The savoury substituted from another of the same class and time. We were very fond of Schabzieger (or -züger, for there are opposing theories), and were seldom without it. "I hold in my soul," as the Spanish folk-song says, two *stories* about it. In very early days my dear mother, to whose house I had brought some, implored me to "put it out of the window." And later, when I was buying it at Fortnum and Mason's, the aged shopman looked at me doubtfully and said, "Excuse me, Sir, but are you acquainted with this cheese?" I assured him that this cheese and I were on the best terms. "Oh! well, Sir," he added, "then I hope you'll pardon me. But only yesterday a lady came here and threw it on the counter and said, 'Young man [N.B. He must have been at least 80], what do you mean by selling stuff like this?' So I said, 'Please, ma'am, how did you eat it?' and *she* said, 'Why of course like any other cheese; we cut it in pieces and *tried* to eat it!!!'" The elect need not be informed that it should be grated, mixed with butter, and spread, not too lavishly, on toast. As for its odour, some Cypriote cheese, which the arbitrary but beneficent Jubal Webb (known formerly to all dwellers in or near Kensington) let me have as a favour, could give it twenty in fifty and beat it. This was a light on some mentions of cheese in Greek literature:

In coming to some specimens, few out of many, of dinners given in that most hospitable of places, Edinburgh, there is a touch of sadness in the sifting. Naturally enough, our hosts to begin with, and guests afterwards, were, as a rule, older people than in earlier days: and in looking over the lists jotted on the backs of the cards (not, as some cynic puts it, to signify "paid off," but to prevent repetition of just the same company another time), I have sometimes found that all except ourselves have joined the majority. The last dinner (XV.) is that at which our Finnish Venus (*v. sup.* p. 96) drank and liked the '74 Sauterne. Shortly after this, domestic reasons made us give up going out to dinner, and entertaining, except on a small scale, and very rarely on a larger, at home.

---

though I was never man enough to try it with Greek *wine*, not being, as above observed, Hercules. I should like to draw attention to the "Pollo con Arroz," an excellent Spanish dish which I found in one of the 96 cookery books I once possessed, and never saw elsewhere till the other day at the Old University Club in Suffolk Street, where a good friend (not for the first time by many) guested me. [**Schabzieger:** Hard green cheese, flavored with melilot (sweet clover) and used in cooking: *sapsago* is a corrupt form of the name. **Jubal Webb:** Wholesale cheesemonger, English and foreign provision merchant, 73 High Street, Kensington: his telegraphic address was "Gorgonzola" (*Post Office London Directory*, 1894).—*Editor*]

XI.

White Dry Paxarette.

—

Montrachet.

—

Champagne.
Dagonet.
Brut, 1887.

—

Port, 1858.

—

Romanée, 1887.

—

Ch. Léoville, 1878.

—

Golden Sherry.

Consommé.

—

Cod. Green Dutch Sauce.

—

Centres de Limandes.

—

Mutton Cutlets aux
Pastèques.

—

Chicken Salad.

—

Ecrevisses à la Crême.

—

Boiled Turkey.

—

Haunch of Venison.

—

Pears with Apple Sauce.

—

Plum Pudding.
Chocolate Cream.

—

Saumon Panaché.

XII.

Amontillado.	Consommé.
—	—
Hock.	Soles à la Stamford.
Deidesheimer, 1886.	—
	Escalopes de Veau.
	Sauce Génoise.
—	—
Champagne.	Canapés Tria-juncta.*
Moët, 1889.	—
	Saddle of Mutton.
—	—
Romanée, 1887.	Capercailzie with
	Cranberry Sauce.
—	—
	Macédoine au Champagne.
Ch. Léoville, 1878.†	—
	Chocolate Meringues.
—	—
	Salmagundy.
Port, 1873;	—
bott. 1882.	Ices.

* This was a device of my own, I believe, but I forget what the three things were.

† I have never drunk a bad Léoville (Barton at least, for though Lascases and Poyferré—see Menu IX., one of the few good wines of its year—can be excellent, they are less immutable), just as I have never smoked a bad Flor de Cuba; but I do not say that I have never drunk a better wine than the one or smoked a better cigar than the other.

XIII.

Clear Soup.

—

Sherry.
Dos Cortados, 1873.

Fillets of Whiting.

—

—

Calf's Head à la Terrapin.

Ch. La Frette, 1865.

—

Oysters en caisses.

—

—

Champagne.
Giesler, 1889.

Aspic of Tunny.

—

—

Braised Beef.

Ch. Margaux, 1870.

—

Roast Guinea Fowls.

—

—

Burgundy.
La Tâche, 1886.

Apricots in Jelly.

—

—

Velvet Cream.

Port, 1870.

—

Anchois Zadioff.

—

Ices.

XIV.

Sherry.	Clear Soup.
"Isabel," 1868.	—
	Beignets of Halibut.
—	—
	Vol-au-vent de Homard.
Scharzhofberger, 1893.	—
	Reform Cutlets.
—	—
Champagne.	Boiled Turkey.
Irroy, 1893.	—
	Blackcock.*
—	—
	Viennese Pudding.
Ch. de Beychevelle, 1878.	—
(magnum)	Meringue Anonyme.
	—
—	Sardines à la Titania.
Port, 1872.	—
	Ices.

* On seeing this in print my wife said (and I agree with her) that we might have improved the combination of turkey and blackcock.

XV.

Golden Sherry.	Clear Soup.
—	—
Sauterne, 1874.	Zootje of Sole.
—	—
Champagne.	Mutton Cutlets.
Perrier-Jouet, 1893.	—
	Eggs in Cream Sauce.
—	—
Ch. Lafite-Carruades,	Boiled Chicken.
1878.	—
	Ham and Peas.
—	—
Port.	Easter Pudding.
Graham's 1881.	—
	Risotto en caisses.

POSTSCRIPTS

(1) Unconfessed injustice is only worthy of a teetotaller. I see I have omitted that most excellent creature, shandygaff, one of the rare cases of thoroughly successful coalition. And, in a certain limitation (p. 69) of my praise of Feuerheerd's Port, I had forgotten that the admirable late-bottled '73, which I have celebrated in the context, was, almost certainly, that shipper's. Another omission, though not one involving injustice, was in the list of bottle-sizes—that of the imperial *quart*. It is uncommon but useful, and I once had some champagne (Giesler) in it.

(2) The Budget has just paid a fresh and flattering, if inconvenient, compliment to the patriotism of good drinkers.

(3) I cannot help quoting, as a colophon to this little book, some memorable words of Professor H. E. Armstrong's in a recent letter to the *Times* about synthetic and natural indigo. He closed with a parallel. Alcohol as alcohol could be obtained, he said, from all sorts of things; not so "a vintage wine, one of the most perfect of nature's products—to those who can appreciate perfection." And it is so. On those who would deprive us of it, let the curse of Nature rest.

G. S.,
1 Royal Crescent, Bath,
St. George's Day, 1920.

APPENDIX

—◄—◄∃◊∃►—►—

OTHER WRITINGS ON WINE AND SPIRITS
BY SAINTSBURY

A SENTIMENTAL CELLAR

The Yellow Book, *April 1894*

Editor's note: It would appear from the reference to a "Queen" that the following piece was written in or with a view to the reign of Queen Anne, though an anachronism or two (such as a reference to the '45 and a quotation from Adam Smith) may be noted. On the other hand, an occasional mixture of "you" and "thou" seems to argue a date before Johnson. It must at any rate have been composed for, or in imitation of the style of, one or other of the eighteenth-century collections of Essays.

It chanced the other day that I had a mind to visit my old friend Falernianus. The maid who opened the door to me showed me into his study, and apologised for her master's absence by saying that he was in the cellar. He soon appeared, and I rallied him a little on the gravity of his occupation. Falernianus, I must tell you, is neither a drunkard nor a man of fortune. But he has a pretty taste in wine, indulges it rather in collection than in consumption, and arranges his cellar (or, as he sometimes calls it, "cellaret") himself, having no butler or other man-servant. He took my pleasantry very good-humouredly; and when I asked him further if I might behold this temple of his devotions he complied at once.

"'Tis rather a chantry than a temple, Eugenius," said he, "but you are very welcome to see it if you please; and if you are minded to hear a sermon, perhaps I can preach one different from what you may expect at an Oracle of the Bottle."

We soon reached the cavern, which, indeed, was much less magnificent than that over which Bacbuc presided; and I perused, not without interest (for I had often tasted the contents), the various bins in which bottles of different shapes and sizes were stowed away with a modest neatness. Falernianus amused himself, and did not go so far as to weary me, with some tales of luck or disappointment in his purchases, of the singular improvement of this vintage, and the mortifying conduct of that. For these wine-lovers are curious in their phrase; and it is not disgusting to hear them say regretfully that the claret of such and such a year "has not spoken yet"; or that another was long "under the curse of the seventies." This last phrase, indeed, had a grandiloquent and romantic turn which half surprised me from my friend, a humourist with a special horror of fine speech or writing, and turning sharply I saw a smile on his lips.

"But," said I, "my Falernianus, your sermon? For I scarce think that this wine-chat would be dignified by you with such a name."

"You are right, Eugenius," answered he, "but I do not quite know whether I am wise to disclose even to you the ruling fancy under which I have formed this little liquid museum, or Baccheum if you prefer it."

"I think you may," said I, "for in the first place we are old enough friends for such confidences, and in the second I know you to be too much given to laugh at your own foibles to be greatly afraid of another's ridicule."

"You say well," he said, "so mark! For if my sermon inflicts what our toasts call ennui upon you, remember that in the words of their favourite Molière, 'You have willed it.'"

"I do not, Eugenius, pretend to be indifferent to good wine in itself. But when I called this little cellar of mine just now a museum I did no dishonour to the daughters of Mnemosyne. For you will observe that wine, by the fact of its keeping powers and by the other fact of its date being known, is a sort of calendar made to the hand of whoso would commemorate, with a festive solemnity, the things that are, as Mr. Dryden says,

"Hid in the sacred treasure of the past."

•

If not the mere juice of the grape (for the merit of the strongest wine after fifty or sixty years is mostly but itself a memory), strong waters brewed on the day of a man's birth will keep their fire and gain ever fresh mellowness though he were to outlive the longest lifetime; and in these little flasks here, my Eugenius, you will find a cup of Nantz that was born with me, and that will keep • its virtues long after thou and I have gone to solve the great enigma. Again, thou seest those pints of red port which nestle together? Within a few days, Eugenius, of the time when that must was foaming round the Douro peasants, I made mine entrance to the University. You can imagine with what a mixture of tender and humorous feelings I quaff them now and then. When their juice was tunned, what amiable visions, what boyish hopes floated before my eyes! I was to carry off all that Cam or Isis had of honours or profit, all that either could give of learning. I was to have my choice of learned retirement on the one hand, or of ardent struggle at the hoarse bar on the other, with the prizes of the senate beyond. They were scarce throwing down their crust when that dream faded; they had scarce become drinkable by a hasty toper before I saw clearly that metaphysical aid was wanting, and that a very different fate must be mine. I make no moan over it, Eugenius, and I puff away like a worse than prostitute as she is, the demon Envy when she whispers in my ear the names of Titius or Seius, and adds, "Had they better parts, or only better stars than you?" But as they fable that the wine itself throbs with the early movement of the sap in the vines, so, Eugenius, when I sip that cordial (and truth 'tis a noble vintage) the old hopes, the old follies, the old dreams waken in me, and I am once more eighteen.

"Look yonder again at those cobwebbed vessels of various shapes that lie side by side, although of different vineyards, in the peaceful bins. They all date from a year in which the wheel of fortune brought honest men to the top in England; and if only for a brief space, as, I am told, they sing in North Britain, 'the de'il went hame wi' a' the Whigs before him.' (I must tell you, Mr.____, that Falernianus, though a loyal subject to our good Queen, is a most malignant Tory, and indeed I have heard him impeached of Jacobitism by ill-willers). But no more of politics." He paused a moment and then went on: "I think I see you smile again, Eugenius, and say to yourself, 'These are but dry-lipped subjects for so flowing a calendar.' And to tell the truth, my friend, the main part of my ephemerides of this kind has been filled by the aid of the goddess who was ever nearest and kindest to Bacchus. In yonder bin lie phials of the mightiest port that Lusitanian summers ever blackened, and flasks of sack from the more southern parts of that peninsula, which our Ben or his son Herrick would have loved. In the same year which saw the pressing of these generous juices the earth was made more fair by the birth of Bellamira and Candiope. The blackest purple of the Lusitanian grape is not so black as the tresses of Candiope's hair, nor doth the golden glow of the sherris approach in flame the lock of Bellamira; but if I let the sunlight play through both, Love, with fantastic triumph, shows me, as the bright motes flicker and flee through the sack, the tawny eyes of Candiope, and the stain, no longer black or purple, but rosy red, that floats from the Oportian juice on the white napery, recalls the velvet blush of Bellamira's cheek."

"And this!" I said, pointing to a bin of Bordeaux near me. "Thou shalt try it this very day," said Falernianus with a laugh, which I thought carried off some feelings a little overstrained; "'tis a right pleasant wine, and they made it in the year when I first saw the lips of Damaris. The flavour is not unlike theirs, and if it should fluster thine head a little, and cause thee what men call heartburn, I will not say that the effects are wholly dissimilar." It is not like Falernianus even to jest at women, and I turned to another. His face cleared. "Many a year has passed," he said, "since the grape that bore that juice was gathered, and even as it was ripening it chanced that I met Lalage and won her. The wine was always good and the love likewise; but in neither in their early years was there half the pleasure that there is now. But I weary you, Eugenius, and perhaps the philosopher speaks truly in saying that these things are not matters of sympathy or, as the Scripture saith, a stranger is not partaker of them. Suffice it to say that these imprisoned rubies and topazes, amethysts and jacinths, never flash in the glass, nor collect their deeper body of colour in the flagon, without bringing a memory with them, that my lips seldom kiss them without recalling other kisses, my eye never beholds them without seeing other colours and other forms in 'the sessions of sweet silent thought.' At the refining of this elixir I assumed the virile gown; when that nectar was fit for drinking I made my first appearance in the field of letters; and this again recalls the death of dear friends and the waning of idle hopes. When I am dead, or if any reverse of fortune makes me part with this cabinet of quintessence, it will pass to heirs or purchasers as so much good wine and nothing more. To me it is that and much more—a casket of magic liquors, a museum, as I have called it, of glasses like

·   that of Dr. Dee, in which I see again the smile of beauty and the hope of youth, in which I live over again in the recesses of fantasy the vanished life of the past.

"But it is not often that I preach in this fashion. Let us take a turn in the garden while they get dinner ready, that you may taste," and he smiled, "that you may taste—if you dare—the wine that I have likened to the lips of Damaris."

THE BOUNTIES OF BACCHUS

Athenæum, *21 November 1919*

Editor's note: This is a review of André Simon, Wine and Spirits: The Connoisseur's Text-Book, *in* Athenæum *(21 November 1919): 1224–25, the first of Simon's many books to be published as a regular trade book.*

A merry and wise book on a subject intimately connected with both mirth and wisdom is no small godsend in days when we are rather apt to oscillate between the silly serious and the silly sarcastic. Perhaps Mr. Simon should not quite have called it a "connoisseur's text-book," for it is hardly that. It is an excellent primer; and if Mr. Fisher really wants to earn the praises lavished on him as a great instaurator of education, he should have it cheaply and succinctly reprinted and furnished to his favourite "continuation schools." Right principles would then be greatly strengthened throughout the land; and the wrath of the U.K.A. and the C.E.T.S. would be a joy to see.

It is very difficult in writing about wine, to avoid a certain amount of bookmaking, and a man who, in discussing sherry, said nothing of Falstaff would be "either a god or a beast." But Mr.

Simon does not give us very much of this, and he propitiates the sternest martinets of "true history" by gently observing that Shakespeare did a little anticipate in this matter. Most of his book is strictly to the point as regards the localities, making, character, etc., of the chief alcoholic beverages (he includes beer and cider in his subject, though not in his title) at present times. Indeed, he has a chapter on Water—not merely as a constituent of such beverages, but as drunk simple of itself at mineral springs. Perhaps he misses the opportunity of pointing out how grateful we ought to be for it, as without it we could not have beer, or whisky, or grog, or punch, or pegs of any kind. But one must not expect everything at once. There are useful appendices: the classic list of claret growths; one less classic, but very useful, of the shippers of vintage port under the head of each good year for the last half-century; and some general notes on vintages at large. There is a moderate but very cogent final chapter rebuking the strange modern heresy of enforced abstinence; and just before it there is the most valuable practical chapter in the book on the Care of Wine—including buying, keeping, decanting and serving. The last three heads are indeed within the competence of any butler, and many good wine-lists contain them for the instruction of the unbutlered; but the principles of wine-buying have very rarely been given to the novice in sound detail. Even the late Sir Henry Thompson, if we remember rightly, recommended not merely the possessors of great cellars and ancestral houses (who, of course, should do what he taught), but persons of ordinary means and opportunities, to "lay down a little piece" of well-reputed vintages. Now listen to Mr. Simon: "there is no expert, in the wine trade of any country, who can tell with certainty what any new wine will become with age." A sentence like that inspires confidence.

Having thus spoken, and done justice to the book as a whole, one may, without impairing the value of the judgment, mention a few points of difference. For there never were any two real wine-lovers who merely said ditto to each other; and this difference is one of the attractive and stimulating points of wine talk. Perhaps Mr. Simon, though he knows and says that "bad wine will never improve with age," is a little prone to that infirmity of noble minds which allows too much goodness in the *mere* age of things themselves good. Thus he says that "the first-growth clarets of 1871 *are* excellent." Certainly, though the vintage was never much known, they *were* excellent thirty years ago, and a comfortable stand-by between '64 (Anthony Trollope justly called '64 Léoville, which is only a second growth, "nectar") and '74. But it is almost impossible to believe that the wine, which was never a heavy one, can be drinkable now. Mr. Simon says practically nothing about Manzanilla, Paxarette, or any of the lighter and more distinctly "beverage" wines of the sherry class, though it is evident from other things in his book that he cannot disapprove them. Mere omission, however, is never to be urged too sternly; for it may be due to simple oversight. Not quite eight lines are devoted at the end of the Claret chapter to white Bordeaux, stating that "the dry wines come from Graves, and some inimitable sweet ones from Sauternes"; but no vineyard being mentioned except Château Yquem. This is doing the work somewhat negligently. It is, however, clear that Mr. Simon (and who shall find fault with him?) would echo the song as to "a bumper of Burgundy" most cheerfully. His chapter on that glorious, but rather formidable liquor is the best of all those devoted to different wines, and the most exhaustive. One would like to pledge him in the bumper itself when he falters out, "The name of *Musigny* is ever on the lips and in the heart of all who value fine wine." For the fact is that, though others may be better known to the vulgar, there *is* something particularly engaging about Musigny. And though at first one may imagine that he merely falls in with "the ancient and worldwide popularity of Clos de Vougeot," he restores himself on the next page by describing Romanée Conti as "the only vineyard which *takes precedence* of the Clos." It would indeed be interesting to know of any vineyard in the whole world of which Romanée Conti, at its best, does *not* take precedence.

The champagne chapter, as was to be expected, is chiefly occupied by the manufacture and by a history of prices, but it ends with a war-item which one would like to have confirmed. According to Mr. Simon, the order to evacuate Rheims was actually given in writing; but the men refused to obey, swearing that as long as the champagne stocks held out so would they. So they drank, and fought, and conquered at the cost of the emptying of many bottles. It is a beautiful story, whether true or not; and Mr. Simon's moral, "Wonder not therefore, and grumble not, if your champagne costs you more"—or, one might add, "if you have to give it up"—is very appropriate. "Oh! how good it is to *drink* and *fight!*" might be another addition, slightly altered from the saying which Macaulay quotes as to that "Protestant Hero" Frederic II.

It is curious that our author, who is more than usually historical on Madeira, and who does say that it is "one of the finest dessert wines and now seldom met with," does *not* say anything about the oïdium and the practical destruction of the wine in mid-nineteenth century. And he is more enthusiastic about Marsala than one would have expected from a lover of Burgundy. It is true that at the present topsy-turvy moment there appear to be people who are prepared to give more money for the Sicilian wine than they might spend on perfectly sound sherry. But then some people will do anything.

Of the spirit sections the "Brandy" is the best, and is particularly good. One is glad to see a note on, and in favour of, "Armagnac" brandy, an excellent liquor almost unknown in England by its name, though no doubt largely consumed as Cognac. There

are perhaps no two more curious instances of *populus vult decipi* in
relation to this subject than the refusal to recognize any brandy
except cognac, and the fact (vouched for by respectable merchants
at the time of the champagne riots some time ago) that it would
be impossible to sell sparkling wines of the outlying part of their
province under their own special place-names. On whisky Mr.
Simon (perhaps for reasons easily conjecturable) is not so sound;
for he does not like distillery whiskies, advocates "blends," and
thinks silent spirit a blessing. Well! well! once more, one cannot
expect everything of everybody. But if Mr. Simon, who would be
horrified at a blend of Burgundy manufactured out of Romanée
and Beaujolais to suit "what the public require," could be artisti-
cally indoctrinated in the differences and the merits of Smith's
Glenlivet, Glen Grant, Clyne Lish, Talisker, Lagavulin, Ardbeg
and others, he might perhaps be brought to a more wholesome
state of mind. Under "Rum" he exposes what is perhaps not too
commonly known—the reason of the great difference and infe-
riority of the modern spirit as compared with what used to be
made; this latter being distilled from actual mashed sugar-cane
juice, the other from molasses.

But enough of these scrap notes, though Mr. Simon would give
pleasant and useful texts on Punch and Beer; on Liqueurs (did he
leave out Chartreuse on the great Roman principle?) and Cider.
Let us end as we began with a blessing. The book is not only good
for instruction of the ignorant: it raises many pleasant shades of
memory in those who have known. More particularly, it suggests
the frightful impoverishment of human existence that would take
place if the enemies of alcohol had their way, putting aside altogether the actual inebriating qualities of that "dangerous drug,"
as they call it. (By the way, if C_2H_2OH is a "drug" why is not
H_2O?) Most persons of sense are agreed that variety of interest
is the salt of life; and as even this scanty notice of a book which

is itself anything but exhaustive will show, the variety of interest in the drinking of good (and even of bad) liquor is endless. It is doubtful whether anyone ever lived who had drunk all the wines of the world that are worth drinking and had learned to shun those that are not. In this, as in other ways, one can do but what one can. But also in this, as in others, "the unending endless quest" may fitly occupy part, and will notably enlighten and enliven the other parts, of life, both active and contemplative.

"WHITE"

A Scrap Book, *1922*

"White."—How many people know this charming verse from *The Loyal Garland* (seventeenth century)?—

> Her lips are two bumpers of clary,
> Who drinks of them sure he'll miscarry—*
> Her breasts of delight
> Are two bottles of white,
> And her eyes are two cups of canary!

Here, independently of the pure delight in conjoining things delightful, there are two points to note. One is the selection of *gold*-brown for the lady's eyes—an admirable but by no means common one. The other concerns a problem which has often puzzled oenophilists: what, exactly, *was* the "white" or "white wine" which is often mentioned by seventeenth- and early eighteenth-century writers? As everybody knows, the term was later, and is still,

---

* Slight clumsiness of rhythm in original smoothed out. *It* runs, I think, "Which made me first to Miscarry," and anybody who likes rough verse may have it so.

greatly enlarged. *We* call yellow wines—even when the yellow darkens to the deepest brown, as in sherry—"white": in fact, in modern times, "white" wine simply means wine that isn't *red*. Obviously our very agreeable bard did not understand the term in that way, or he would hardly have written "of delight." Of course there is the usual licence of comparing transparent or water- to opaque or milk-*white*; but that is nothing. A "bottle of white" may have been something like the very lightest produce of French, Italian, or Spanish vineyards. It cannot have been sherry, hardly even hock.

"OBRIAN"
A Scrap Book, *1922*

"Obrian."—In my *Notes on a Cellar-Book* there was noticed and quoted Pepys's reference, under the name of "Ho Bryen," to a certain claret, still famous and delectable under its proper style of Haut Brion. But the writer had forgotten another more or less contemporary mention which he had noted years before from the *Roxburghe Ballads* (v. 4):

> With flood of *Obrian* we'll fill up each vein.

Now what made this wine so popular in the latter half of the seventeenth century? As a matter of fact, individual vineyards are very seldom mentioned in English literature before the nineteenth,* though there are a few exceptions, which do not, so far as I remember, include one other claret now in consumption. It has occurred to me that Saint-Evremond may have had something to do with it. He was, of course, himself a Norman; but he had

---

* Even then Scott somewhere calls "Margaux" "Margout," and to this day people will double *t* "Lafite."

been much in Gascony with the Duc de Candale of whom he has left such a double-edged account; and he was not merely an Epicurean, but an epicure of the first water. During his forty years in our wilderness he would have had plenty of time to provide for the special tastes he had formed earlier in the society of Les Côteaux, and as he was familiar with men of letters as well as with the court, to communicate them widely.*

* It is true that in one of his best known passages, while he blasphemes Burgundy (he repented later) and glorifies champagne—*not*, it must be remembered, sparkling champagne, which was only invented ten years before his almost centenarian life ceased—he does not mention any Bordeaux. But I have not seen the fullest—there is, I believe, no actually *complete*—edition of him for many years.—By the way, I have been rebuked in friendliest fashion for speaking of "Gascony" and not of "Guienne" in reference to claret. But "the *Gascon* wine" is too classical a phrase to be neglected. [**does not mention any Bordeaux:** The passage in question occurs in Saint-Évremonde's letter to the Comte d'Olonne, in 1674, advising, among other things, on the choice of wines: "Spare no cost to get Champagne Wines, tho' you were two hundred leagues from Paris. Those of Burgundy have lost all their credit with the men of good taste, and scarce do they preserve a small remainder of their old Reputation with the Citizens" (John Hayward, ed., *The Letters of Saint Evremond* [London: George Routledge, 1930], pp. 152–53). Saint-Évremonde is credited with introducing Champagne, his favorite wine, to the English.—*Editor*]

LE TEMPS JADIS: WALLET II

A Second Scrap Book, *1923*

Editor's note: Saintsbury explains that wallet *alludes to the speech of Ulysses in Shakespeare's* Troilus and Cressida: *"Time hath, my Lord, a wallet at his back / Wherein he puts alms for Oblivion"* (A Second Scrap Book *[London: Macmillan, 1923], p. 157n).*

There is yet another wallet or "poke" whence perhaps we may rescue, if only for the moment, some alms of Time from their destined devourer. Two of them might have found a place in the earliest division of this booklet, and one has indeed been more than once referred to there. It is the great ballad-epic of bonfire, *A Lay written about the Year of the College DCI.*, supplemented by a Latin parody (much altered in subject) of Ovid—the work of a *vates*, to be justly called *sacer*—indeed I should say *sacerrimus*, if the superlative had not (I never could make out why) a habit of confining itself to the bad sense of the positive. I forget how many copies of this were printed "for private circulation only," but I have never seen one catalogued for sale. It is one of the best of the innumerable *pastiches* of Macaulay's Lays.

The other Mertonian document is quite unprinted, and has, I

suppose, never been seen by more than a very few pairs of eyes. But it is certainly curious, and to anybody interested in the great subject of Wine, very curious indeed. It is a letter,* dated February 3, 1871, from the late Mr. Wilkins—then a somewhat senior Fellow of Merton and a Harrovian, and, though a good scholar, an odd person in some ways—to the late Bishop Creighton, then not a Bishop at all, of course, and only a fellow of some four or five years' standing.

Whether at the moment Creighton had anything to do with the important business of "Domestic Bursar" I do not know, but the first words of the letter—written on a round dozen pages of large quarto letter-paper, in a pretty good hand—show that the Common-room was very seriously concerned about two certainly important subjects, Champagne and Claret.† It is really a fine exordium: "My dear Creighton—The question what champagne, what claret to buy is so closely allied to the question *where* to buy it, that I should not like to venture a suggestion, were it not that I have not only no relation, but not even a friend, in the wine

---

* Mrs. Creighton most kindly gave me this a dozen or so years ago, and with equal kindness authorises my comment on it now. But I am not sure that I ought not to bequeath it to the College itself. [**bequeath it to the College itself:** Merton has no record of Saintsbury's giving this letter to the college: information from the Fellow Librarian.—*Editor*]

† As I have remarked above, I dined two or three times and wined more frequently in that sacred chamber only a few years before this. But champagne would not appear at wines, and did not, as far as I remember, at dinner—it was still, in the 'sixties, an exceptional wine. I remember nothing *against* the claret, but nothing as distinctly in its favour as in that of the wonderful brown sherry. It was a gracious ceremony, and thoroughly emollient to the morals and manners, when the butler stopped you at the Hall door after dinner with "Mr. So-and-so's compliments, sir, and he would be glad if you would take wine with him."

trade." That, I think, is worthy of anybody in Enfield's *Speaker*, if not of Mr. Burke himself.

We then learn that "Wulks" (as, *more undergraduatorum*, he used to be called) thinks the College "will find it easier to overtake the effects of the bad system pursued for ten years in champagne than in the case of claret," and (I myself read this with unaffected sorrow) that "we have gone on the hand-to-mouth principle, and have often bought champagne without enquiry either as to the vintage or the grower. *Indeed we have sometimes been afflicted with champagne at 6s. 6d. a bottle, with a fancy brand, a sign that the grower is ashamed to own it!*"

"Grower" is, of course, not the right word for champagne, and brands, other than the shipper's usual one, are not always contemptible; but Mr. Wilkins's indignation is not itself contemptible at all. I fear some "hot young men," as they used to say, will cry at this moment, "What did he expect to get for 6s. 6d.?" Let them wait a little. He proceeds, "Of course you can easily ascertain from Randolph* what sum the College will invest in buying champagne for present and future use," following this up with what he would do himself.

Here compression and abstraction become necessary. He relies chiefly, and wisely on the famous house of Christopher in Pall

---

* An excellent example of the older type of Don—son, I believe, of that remarkable person who was successively bishop of Oxford, Bangor, and London, having previously been four times professor of Poetry, Greek, Moral Philosophy, and Divinity. What an ideal life in its own line! And what can men know better, for this life and the next, than the four subjects of the Chairs? [**that remarkable person:** This was John Randolph (1749–1813); Saintsbury's remark that Randolph had been "four times" professor of poetry, Greek, moral philosophy, and divinity seems to mean that he had once held each of those four chairs (as he had); but not "four times" each.—*Editor*]

• Mall East, who, it seems, at that happy time sold dry Bollinger of '61 (*i.e.*, as he accurately puts it, 9 1/2 years old) at 72s. But the same house would, it seems, also supply a cheaper quality at 60s.

He has a very knowledgeable comparison of recent vintages; and, to my delight (for I had independently come to the conclusion some three years after him, but more than thirty before I ever read

• his letter), ranks '65 as the finest year of the century. Later, too, he says, "Above all, lay in a stock of Perrier-Jouet *extra cuvée* '65, the finest wine, in Christopher's opinion," of that finest vintage. So "we all three saw" it—the expert, the scholar, and the strug-

• gling schoolmaster—like Esau and Kate and the other in the song.

But the most interesting thing in this letter is a definition of what champagne ought to be, which is distinctly of *le temps jadis*. Wilkins's ten-year-old Bollinger was, he says, "*delicately* dry" (remember that in 1871 dry champagne was still to some extent a wine militant), but "with the true pineapple flavour and bouquet" and "sufficiently powerful." Now that is exactly the kind of champagne which it is now and has for long been nearly impossible to get, the "brandy and soda" variety* having almost completely ousted it. I remember one of my own early mentors—whether it was the same Mr. Thomson of Pall Mall or Mr. John Harvey of Bristol, I am not sure—telling me that '65 was not only the best, but almost the last perfect specimen, of this make of wine. I should not myself have called the flavour exactly "pineapple," and it was not in the least like the "muscatel" (true or faked, grape or elder-flower) flavour of Moselle. But it was emphatically "*winy*," as Thackeray says of champagne.

After making a note, interesting as a *point de repère*, that

• "Christopher has a great name for claret, Tanqueray for cham-

* My friend Mr. Andrew Thomson of Pall Mall's phrase. See *Notes on a Cellar-Book* [p. 90 and note].

pagne," and that he himself likes the former best for both, Wilkins passes to Bordeaux itself, on which he is, in general, sound and rather full, but I fancy not so enthusiastic, and not *quite* so well informed in detail, as on the North-Eastern wine. Still he seems to have relied on "the princely merchants Barton and Guestier," and he could not do much better than that. They tell him that "the more a wine deposits, the better they think of it," and he is rather gloomy about "moved" claret. Moreover, he points out, very shrewdly, that as "merchants add every year to the price of claret kept in their cellars," the College has lost both ways in not beginning ten years ago to lay down '57,* '58, '61, '64, and '65. He

---

* '57 *champagne* was, of course, magnificent, but was '57 claret much good? I never drank it (to my distinct remembrance, though I see, in looking back, that it figures in the list of the "Harmony," recorded before, p. 161), nor '61. Some '62 was good certainly, and some '65, though a good deal of this was disappointing. Of '58 and '64 one need not speak. But the excellent "Wulks" doesn't seem fully aware that laying down *claret* early is rather a risky business, much more so than laying down port or champagne. Even experts, unless I am wrongly informed, get caught sometimes. '65 was, I think, a special case of this. [**'57 claret much good?**: '57 was the first crop produced after the oidium blight had been controlled. André Simon calls the vintage "fair" (*Vintagewise* [London: Michael Joseph, 1945], p. 61). **recorded before, p. 161:** In *A Second Scrap Book*; this was a dinner in 1886 featuring a set of "Harmonies of Bordeaux," that is, several vintages of the same châteaux. Lafite of 1857 was included. **nor '61:** The crop was severely reduced by frost, the little wine produced very good and very expensive (Michael Broadbent, *The Great Vintage Wine Book* [New York: Knopf, 1980], p. 37). Simon calls it "irregular" (*Vintagewise*, p. 64), Edmund Penning-Rowsell "moderate" (*The Wines of Bordeaux* [London: Michael Joseph, 1969], p. 267). **some '65:** "There were some most delightful '65's" (Simon, *Vintagewise*, p. 65). Simon says that Saintsbury ignored the 1865s completely, as he certainly does in *Notes on a Cellar-Book*; this reference, however, shows that Saintsbury was aware

- recommends Coningham of Regent Street, (whom I know not) for claret, especially what he calls "the light, pleasantly flavoured claret called *Pichon*," marked 48s. on his list, and Christopher again for "St. Julien and Larose," the latter being also obtainable from Tanqueray, and the prices running from 54s. to 60s. He ranks Léoville above Larose, and Mouton above Léoville, if not also above Lafite, telling the story of the damage done to the premier
- vineyards by the cupidity of Samuel Scott, and (quite properly) praising the restoration in quality—in its case and Mouton's—
- by the Rothschilds.

  All this is so good that one wonders at two things in it. Surely Wilkins must have known that to put "St. Julien" on terms with "Pichon" and "Larose" was what, in the other scholarship he possessed, would be called a false concord of the most glaring kind. Why, both Léoville and Larose *are* St. Juliens! And to speak of Pichon, especially if he means Pichon-Longueville (I am not sure that I ever drank the other—Lalande), as "light and pleasant," is rather like calling a marquis "possessor of a very decent rank in the English peerage." But let us not cavil. The document shows a most creditable attempt to check a venerable institution in some slight errors of its ways, and argues very sound principles as regards the particular subject, if no other, in its author. Also it reveals a state of things old now, but how good! Ten-year-old Bollinger, dry but full-flavoured, for 6s. a bottle! and Larose of the same age at 54s. a dozen. Why, Thackeray, a decade before, had given us the price
- of *his*, or at least Mr. Pendennis's, Larose as 72s.!

---

of their possibilities. Penning-Rowsell says of the 1865s that they were "prolific and the quality good but they took some time to come around" (*Wines of Bordeaux*, p. 267).—*Editor*]

THE ORDER OF DRINKS

A Second Scrap Book, *1923*

The Order of Drinks.—There is, I think, no doubt that "Te(a) *ve-nient die*" is more than a joke or a jingle. I do not, like most people, drink it *before* breakfast; but I have never discovered anything to equal it *at* that meal. Coffee, though nice enough, is not sufficiently thirst-quenching; chocolate still less so; the cocoas made-up with flour or what not, least of all. Clear cocoa-*nib* infusion, though by no means easy to make, does quench thirst when well made; but it has not the peculiar *clean*-ness of tea, when well made like-wise, not too strong, not over-milked, and, above all, kept free from cream. A worse *mésalliance* than tea (except green tea which is all the better for it) and cream I hardly know, though there are few commoner. Of the irreplaceableness of tea I can speak with better justification than most people, for twice in my life, during considerable periods, I have been "ordered off" it. The cocoa-nib cocoa above mentioned was the presecribed succedaneum in the first stage; but one got dreadfully tired of it. In the second, claret and water was suggested; and I think if anything could have made me hate claret this would. Beer, tea's predecessor, is not fully satisfactory *with* breakfast, though some strongish beer just *after* it is *probatum* of many choice scholars, good sportsmen, and, "in the best sense of the term," *men*. But for regular breakfast drink there is nothing like tea.

Between breakfast and luncheon the choice lies, of course, between beer and "pegs," but, except when one is taking much exercise or for special reasons, I think drinking between meals should be avoided. That it is recommended by the modern "test-tube" doctor is an additional but unnecessary reason for this. Old tradition and common sense are against it, though of course not to the extent of prohibition. A whisky and soda or potash, a mug of cider (for those who can drink it) or shandygaff, a tankard of sound plain beer, will hurt no one now and then, and perhaps are at no time more enjoyable.

At luncheon the choice is large, but I should say that beer is decidedly the most appropriate of many not inappropriate liquors, without prejudice, of course, to a glass of sherry or port after it.* If wine is insisted on, it had better be white, not red, and *I* should say, without wishing to dictate, still rather than sparkling. Champagne at a populous lunch always reminds me of that dismallest (except when it was your own) of all feasts, the wedding breakfast of yore. But when you are hand to fist *en fête* either with your own

* With fish or soup, equally of course the sherry may come before. But I think fish is better at breakfast and dinner than in the middle of the day; and I have seldom been a great soup-eater. There is, however, no better lunch than the old (Birch's) kind of turtle-soup; but with that you naturally drink Madeira. And it is not economical. My own humble substitute for some years was a bowl of *pea*-soup, bread and cheese, and a pint of "College" ale. [**the old (Birch's) kind of turtle-soup:** Birch's was an eating-house on Cornhill, London, famous for its turtle soup. "A queer Jacobean shop . . . at the end of Cornhill, serving really true aldermanic turtle soup" (Trevor Blakemore, "London Restaurants of Fifty Years Ago," *Wine and Food*, no. 65 [Spring 1950]: 6).—*Editor*]

wife or another (I do not say another's), "the foaming grape of Eastern France" is permitted—nay, recommended. The affection of the sex which has always, till now, groaned in servitude (and made others groan in another kind of ditto) for champagne, is interesting. If Dom Perignon had lived at the proper time, and (as a good "Dom" doubtless would) had tried to outmanoeuvre Satan by offering a glass of it instead of the apple (you *can't* drink champagne *with* apples), I feel sure that our ancestress would have accepted the beaker. Is it not recorded at a later date that "for champagne and lobster salad in the way of honour" the divine Miss Fotheringay "would have gone anywhere"? And do I not know a singular corroboration of this statement of Thackeray's? A vast number of years ago an actress, of considerable repute at the time, was staying with her husband "on tour" in the same lodging-house with us. According to what I have been told is a habit of the profession, they lived with doors open, and once we heard the star speak. "You'll give us a drop of fizz, won't you?" it said plaintively, and I hope it got it.

The afternoon is as the morning, though (with the same licences) even less should be required if the luncheon has been, and the dinner is going to be, duly *arrosé*. If people will have afternoon tea, they must; but I can greatly extol the practice of a late distinguished physician with whom we used to stay, and who, when one came in to that intrusive pseudo-meal from walking or driving, used to say, "I'm sure you'd rather have an antiphlogistic," and to provide the materials thereof in the shape of whisky and "cyphon," as old French hotel-bills pleasantly spell it.

And now I come to a less pleasant part of this prattle. One or two of the very kind reviewers of my *Cellar-Book* expressed surprise at the absence of detail (there was a mention of the thing) about cocktails. The simple fact is that I detest, abominate, and in the extremest Rabelaisian variety and floridity condemn the "cocktail habit." Of course the mixtures are agreeable in themselves, and particularly so because they never need be "as before." But they undergo, in a complicated and intensified degree if used too frequently, the strictures I had to pass in the *Cellar-Book* itself on "Liqueurs" and on "Mixed Liquors." And there is one thing about them which is worst of all: it was by the way of cocktails, more than by any other, that Prohibition made *its* way in the United States of America; and anything that helps the invasion of that Blatant Beast (by Tyranny out of Folly) should be avoided at any price.*

As for dinner itself, anything may be drunk at it according to taste, except tea (which converts it into something not dinner) and milk, which is nasty and fulsome *with* food; while coffee, of course, comes after, not with.† Even mere water is less unwholesome at dinner, in the intervals of wine, than at other times; while of course it—plain or aerated—combines with wine and spirits *as* at other times. And the liberty continues more or less till bed-time. I never, indeed, could approve the French habit of drinking beer more or less immediately *after* wine. The general "Order of the Day" (as far as alcoholic liquors are concerned) should be Beer—Wine—Spirits. But so much depends on the occupations of the evening that no general rules can be laid down. Nothing is so good to dance on as beer; champagne is unpleasantly provocative of heat and perspiration, so are cups. And though you often, in Victorian days, had to make private interest with servants to procure it in houses where you were not very familiar, I always found that the pretti-

---

* I was young at the height of the sherry-and-bitters-before-dinner mania, and of course have often gone through that ritual, chiefly for manners' sake. But my principle is "No liquid immediately before eating." After your first spoon- or fork-ful, what you please.

† It seems to me that coffee *and* food are incompatible.

est and nicest and best-dancing girls liked nothing so much. And when, hours after dinner, you come home, theatre-wearied, how welcome is the voice of the Bass as it poppeth and poppleth, with the surging of the Guinness to meet it!

As for the conclusion of an ordinary home evening, any of the four spirits with "mineral" or hot water will do, always remembering that rum and *brown* brandy are not good with soda or potash, though they go well enough with lemonade as a sort of minor punch. Of the major kinds of that great liquor I have spoken elsewhere.

THE QUALITIES OF WINE

Morning Post, *22 May 1923; reprinted in*
George Saintsbury: The Memorial Volume, *1945*

Now since there is here much to be written on wine, let us discuss briefly some points of special interest after the manner of Aristotle. And these points shall be: (1) The colour of wine; (2) the bigness and smallness of wine, and their respective excellences; (3) the times most proper for drinking wine.

As to this it is to be feared that some great ones have been too hasty and somewhat uncatholic in preference of red wine over white. (References to the famous Persian poet and philosopher to his great translator and to others are for a fuller margin.) For we should always follow Nature, and Nature has made grapes red and white; though it follow not invariably that the wines made thereof be of the same colour.

Also the goodness of some white wines is so great that it were impious to regard them as in any way inferior. Yet further, there is more bad red wine in the world than there is bad white; and this more than in proportion to the total quantity of both produced.

Nevertheless, it must be admitted that somehow or other redness does accompany the general idea of wine more often than whiteness and that of the greatest wines—claret, burgundy, and port—claret is always red (white claret for Graves and Sauternes being a mere misnomer) and port always ought to be, while though some white burgundies are great they are scarcely so great in quality as the reds and far fewer in number and variety. Therefore, let us conclude that wine is not exclusively or pre-eminently red; but that as other creatures were created male and female, so wine was created red and white.

Once upon a time there was an author who though not a vintner wrote about wine, and some of the experts found (though not very sternly) fault with him as with one who leant too much to "bigness," "stoutness," and the like in that matter. But this was surely excessive, in that he had extolled above all others claret, which, for many years has, except relatively and within its own range, not been a "big" wine at all. And here as elsewhere he had endeavoured to achieve the utmost possible catholicity.

There is a time for all wine except bad wine, and perhaps there is a time even for that, as for it to be poured into drains, administered to criminals who have been accustomed to good, or even in extreme cases used to make Dukes of Clarence out of Pussyfoot leaders.

Certainly there is a time for light wines and a time for heavy. But even as it was said above, that wine was created red and white, so also was it created light and heavy; and to cleave to one only or even to prefer (conditions and time adjusted) one to the other is irregular.

Thus, where a large, fresh-tasting, and comparatively weak drink is required, a man should not drink port. And it has been felt by some who are unable to share the admiration expressed by others for a certain great novelist not long defunct, that they understood their inability better when they heard that he at least once drank port out and to the extent of a pewter pot.

Again, if his partisans urged that this was after a walking to

Dover no less memorable than the riding thither so famous in law
and verse—and that strengthening was required by the strong,
through the strong, in the strong—it would be replied that the
condition of throat and palate precluded any possible appreciation of the flavour of the port. Whereas even a pewter—though
better a glass—tankard of Graves or Moselle, of light Hock,
Rioja, or even Manzanilla, would have been wholly in place. Nay,
putting volume for brute thirst aside, and coming to the finest
flavours, who shall say that Hermitage is "better" than burgundy,
or burgundy than claret?

Here, as else- and every-where in criticism, not only the hardest thing to attain but also the hardest thing to get recognized
when attained, is the appreciation of difference without insisting
on superiority. "Give me," the wise man will say, "red wine or
white, big wine or little, wine to be drunk (as the tale says) in
"moogs," and wine to be drunk in Tokay glasses—always provided, with an indispensable provision, that it is good wine."

Some things said under both the foregoing heads will lead up
not improperly to this third. It has been held by some that wine is
to be drunk at all times of the day and night. Tom Brown the Elder,
though not a proper moral man, was a very clever one, and has
the special merit of at once indicating the mystery of names and
the utter absurdity of Spelling Reform, by his personal and literary contrast with his contemporary, Sir Thomas Browne. Also he
wrote a poem, "Wine, wine in the morning," which is as a poem
good, and was much admired both for form and matter by Lockhart, still the most sadly under-valued of English critics.

Southey, one of the best of men and prose-men, and very far
from the worst of poets, used to breakfast at Oxford on bread and
cheese and red wine negus; and Thackeray has expressed himself
in the same sense as Tom Brown and Lockhart, deploring the
pusillanimity which prevents men from obeying their precepts.

Yet a man albeit he has a sneaking kindness for Tom and the most unhesitating admiration for the other three, may hesitate about agreeing with them here.

There was once one who was ordered by the leeches to drop tea and coffee at breakfast and substitute either cocoa (which he loathed) or claret (diluted or not) which in the abstract and in the undiluted form he loved very much. But it never seemed right to him.

Beer at breakfast *is* all right: the common expressions of surprise at Queen Elizabeth's maids of honour are futile. But it seems to some of us that with Bacchus, as with some less divine heroes of Romance, his virtues and his values grow with the hours of the waking day and do not reach full perfection till those of his brother Apollo begin to pale.

And so let it be concluded that there shall be no "class distinctions," as men say now, between red and white or between big and little. But the conclusion shall not be so absolute in the case of the hours, and if any would follow Tom, and Robert, and John Gibson, and William Makepeace let him. Yet the present writer would rather drink wine at lunch than at breakfast, and rather at dinner than at lunch, nay, even rather after dinner than at it. And it may be pointed out that the opportunities lost or refused at the earlier meals can by the healthy and fortunate be easily made up at and after the latest—which was the manner of our fathers that were before us: the men who gained good things for us to throw away.

THE CELLAR

The Book of the Queen's Dolls' House, *1924*

Editor's note: The elaborate and expensive book The Queen's Dolls' House *(A. C. Benson and Sir Lawrence Weaver, eds. [London: Methuen, 1924]) was produced to accompany the gift to Queen Mary of a dolls' house for her collection of dolls. The furnishings of the house, all in miniature, are finished to the last detail. Saintsbury contributed the chapter devoted to the house's wine cellar. The house—and the contents of the cellar—is still on view at Windsor Castle.*

Great as must have been the consideration required by other apartments of this House, reasons might be put forward for doubting whether any demanded so much as the cellar. And this is said on no idle "there-is-nothing-like-leather" principle. For he who says it has, in a long and hard-working life, had to give consideration to many things besides cellars—things political, things literary, things educational, things of all sorts, or almost all.

Let us hope that the necessity of a cellar—perhaps not a universal apartment or compartment in Dolls' Houses—was never in actual question. It is not possible to conceive that to persons of such taste and judgment as the original devisers of this edifice there could have been present any doubt of the propriety of such a compartment *ab initio* or of its positive necessity on subsidiary considerations. Resident Dolls would probably—indeed certainly—get married, and would it be even decent for them to have to "send out" for champagne and probably get wine of the description modestly described in advertisements as "light and pleasant: suitable for weddings, picnics and other parties"? The Doll of the moment might have influenza—the modern "English disease," as "spleen" used to be called. The one medicine for influenza is Burgundy: and the one wine which it is most difficult to be sure of, in casual buying, is Burgundy likewise. I turn to that enlarged copy of the Dolls' Cellar Book with which I have been kindly entrusted, and I find that this fortunate repository has been supplied with five dozen each of 1906 Veuve Clicquot, Pommery 1915, L. Roederer 1911, and G. H. Mumm of the same year, together with two dozen Magnums of the last-named shipper's Cordon Rouge for that year likewise. Although a critic of full fifty years' standing in literature, of more than forty in politics, and of nearly as long practice in wine, I cannot better the list; and the notes on the order of use are of the soundest. But will not the butler be offended by the suggestion that he requires them?

Then let us turn to the Burgundy. There is only one entry, and I think properly so; but if I had been consulted, the word which appears at the page-top would have been *my* word—Romanée. They do not add "Conti" or "Saint-Vivant," or any other minor localisation, but never mind. With Romanée 1904—two dozen of it—in our cellar we may bid "flu" fly!

I am not sure, however, that if my profane lips were permitted actually to taste one and one only of the liquors here inscribed, I should not ask for some of the Duke of Penaranda's gift sherry—vintage or solera not dated, but "shipped by Garvey" as "Amontillado Duque d'Alba." Despising sherry was one of the foolishest consequences or instances of that undervaluation of Victorian tastes which seems now to be happily passing; and I have myself recently drunk samples of very admirable quality. But "Amontillado, Duque d'Alba" is a title that appeals at once to one's palate and to one's historical and literary memories. I daresay the wine with which the Marquis of Steyne resuscitated Mr. Arthur Pendennis was very like this. And whenever I read a newspaper report of that prettiest of all games, polo, wherein the other Duke—the giver—so often figures, I shall imagine the flavour of his gift.

We cannot, of course, go in quite this fashion through all the wines, spirits, liqueurs and malt liquors—for these are most rightly not neglected—which stock this most agreeable apartment. The doll—most fortunate in ever so many sorts of ways—has Montrachet of 1889—the best of all White Burgundies, as I hold Romanée to be of red: while this notable cellar has been supplied with no less than six varieties of Port, including Cockburn's '74 and Taylor's '96, with Warre and Fonseca of various days, and two dozen *magnums* of 1912 Dow! This is particularly satisfactory, for I once knew a young lady of great beauty, intelligence and charm who after illness was restored to the possession and exercise of all three by the administration of a magnum of Cockburn's '51—not in a single dose, it is true—but ingeniously decanted and distributed down to the last drop. Bordeaux supplies Lafite of '75 (I wonder what it is like), Haut-Brion of '88 in magnums (ditto); Margaux (the best of the '99's), and a six-year-old Le Prieuré. One other, however, of the bins deserves a kind of mention which ought to interest even some who regard ordinary wine-talk with indifference if not contempt—for it comes under the head of archæology as well as oenology. This is Bin 12, containing two dozen of 1820 Madeira—"Finest Bual." Wine of 1820 will, of course, never come again in any case; but wine of the same kind and as good as that of 1820 has, it is believed, actually come in the case of Port, and may have done so in others. Wine, as good as this was at its best, never has recently come from Madeira: and we may say without much rashness never will. Most, if not all, good judges agree that though the vines newly planted after the devastation caused by oïdium three-quarters of a century ago have had that time to make good their footing and flavour, they have never done it with complete success and never will. Only Burke could justly commemorate this addition to the *cimelia* of Windsor Castle from this point of view.

It is impossible also not to spare a special mention to the Château Yquem '94 with which this miniature temple of the Dive Bouteille and its fortunate priestess or priestesses have been endowed: but we must pass to the less dignified but hardly less grateful and comforting contents thereof. Of these the most stately, beyond all doubt, are the certain casks of whisky and of beer— for there is a "cut-and-come-againness," a "sure stronghold" feeling about a cask which the mere bottle can hardly attain. It is difficult to resist that perhaps deadliest of all deadly sins—envy— when one learns that the deputy-mistress or mistresses to whom Her Majesty may from time to time confide the not at all monstrous regiment of this abode, will have at her disposal two quarter-casks. One is filled with a Scotch whisky—Smith's Glenlivet, which knows no superior if any equal in its own country, and the other with John Jameson—fondly known as "J. J."—which corresponds for Irish. Not, of course, that any prejudice or disrespect is intended to other kinds furnished. But the cellar has been, as it were, armed as the entrance of a fortress is guarded by two big guns, with two other vessels. Nor are the remaining spirits neglected except Hollands, the absence of which I regret for a reason to be stated presently. Liqueur brandy of '54 no doubt looks down on two excellent but less ancient representatives of Cognac: and neither rum nor gin fails, while the chief suppliers have con-

sulted what is pretty certain to be the Dolls' chief taste by putting in Chartreuse and Benedictine, Kümmel and Crême de
Menthe, with our own two home-made liqueurs Sloe Gin and
Cherry Brandy in decent profusion. And we may close the in-
spiring catalogue by mentioning that there is no lack of that glorious liquor if not *liqueur* which gives Scotland and Ireland no
room for triumph over England in the narrowest sense—BASS!
Bass in casks and bottles. Nor is the cellar unfurnished with plant
as well as material—thermometers and funnels and cans; bottle-
baskets and candlesticks, corkscrews, hampers and case-openers.

Mais c'est artistement complet—not in the melancholy sense in
which poor Gautier used that phrase towards the curiously unlucky close of his life

Many ranges of reflection open out from the point at which
we have now arrived. How pleasant it would be to draw up wine-
lists from these ample stores to accompany, of course, suitable
menus—so that there should be no temptation or excuse for the
Doll to entertain her friends, as is the deplorable modern fashion, elsewhere than in her own house. How often, one hopes,
would she come down and inspect the double-bayed treasury with
its bins below and its shelves above! And what a beautiful picture
she would make as she gathered up her dress with one hand and
reached down as the whim pleased her an emerald flask of Crême
de Menthe or a straight ruby bottle of Cherry Brandy with the
other! But this sweet picture suggests a reflection of a different
kind, severely practical at first, but ending in very artistic matters.
"How," some businesslike person may say, and be excused for saying, "how on earth, or under the earth, are you going to get all
these things—these casks and cans and baskets—these twenty
dozen of Champagne, sixteen of Port, twelve of Claret, and at
least twenty or thirty more of oddments in a space measuring what
this does?"

Obviously by some process of proportional reduction: and among the results of this process are some of the prettiest things I have ever seen, and not merely prettiest. On taking the liberty to put one of those magnums of Dow's port above mentioned—a beautiful vessel a full inch long and about five-sixteenths across the body—beside one of my own few most cherished possessions—a "tappit-hen" (three-bottle flask) of Sandeman's 1904, visions and thought came into my mind far too mystical—nothing could be too *great*—for this occasion. Had I been at Oxford in mid-thirteenth instead of mid-nineteenth century I should have written on this text a treatise—folio when printed later—*De Magnis et Parvis*, and Merton College would have counted on its records one more Doctor Profundus!

From this other ruby—actually lighted up by an obliging sunbeam as I write, and so setting off the proper splash of white-wash which marks its position when binned, let us turn to the emerald— really in shape as well as size a fitting eardrop for a doll's mistress though not for a doll herself. It is, of course, filled with Cusenier's *Crème de Menthe*, and with the light showing through its little body hardly emerald so much as aquamarine—real sea-green aquamarine, not the watery blue, almost white, which is allowed nowadays to usurp the name. And a straw-coloured "Apricot Liqueur," though not exactly the same shape, would make a not all bad Harlequin pendant. It was partly because of the effectiveness of these out-shapes that I lamented the absence of Hollands. A "square-face" reduced to scale and showing its blackness among these brightened colours would be very agreeable.

Another thing to draw attention to is the scrupulousness with which all that would naturally have elaborate descriptive labels are furnished with miniatures thereof. The Haut Brion Magnum— the colour of which again comes out beautifully with a touch of sun—carries its Château boldly depicted: as do all the other Bordeaux bottles: while the '54 Fine Champagne, delicately pale with age in itself, bears a map of the Cognac district with a bright red spot of special location. Lastly, a superbly miniatured bottle of Louis Roederer—gold cap, red collar and white apron all complete—leaves in a rather unusual legibility, requiring no magnifying glass, the famous name of that respectable Die-Hard who is said to have declared that as long as *he* lived no bottle of *dry* champagne should leave his cellars with his name on it. For such are the anecdotes that diversify the serious study of the history of wine.

One curious particular may be added. I do not think that many people would guess what was the greatest difficulty in completing this miniature fleet of receptacles for the gifts of Bacchus. I am told that it was neither making nor labelling, nor corking— they are all honestly corked—nor anything but the actual filling of them. A moment's thought will, of course, suggest that if you poured the stuff in after any ordinary fashion the air inside would resist re-issue through such tiny throats. I should, however, have imagined that if the bottles had been plunged, keeping them upright, in a sufficient volume of the wine, the air would have escaped of itself in however tiny bubbles. But the method actually adopted, I understand, was based on a sort of syphon-reversed principle, a still smaller tube being introduced through the gullet of the bottle and the liquor rising from below and expelling the air.

Tantae molis erat ("Such a bother it was" to translate for the benefit of some folk) in this and a hundred other ways to found this admirably representative miniature of a pattern cellar for the present day. The apartment has a vaulted roof—as all cellars ought to have—though I regret to say that none of my own ever possessed one. I do not know whether there will be imitation rats or cobwebs or attempts at the ghastly roof curtaining which comes in so vividly in *No Thoroughfare*. I hope and should suppose not.

For the whole principle on which Mr. F. L. Berry, the chief cellarer on this occasion, and his compeers appear to have gone is not imitation or sham, but honest miniaturing—the wines, etc., being the actual wines, and everything genuine though tiny.

No better form or material could, I think, have been employed in providing this little but Joyous Gard of Her Majesty's with one of the most important if not *the* most important department for the promotion of Joyousness itself; and the writer of these humble notes has enjoyed doing them even more than he would have enjoyed partaking of the very liquors they describe.

LE TEMPS JADIS; WALLET V.,
90'S AND LATER
A Last Scrap Book, *1924*

Editor's note: I omit the earlier pages, which review letters from several correspondents on various topics before turning to the letter from Sala that forms the rest of the item.

... Here are some interesting wine-prices "from a Paris Guide published in 1803," but apparently copied in translation from the actual wine-list of a restaurant in Paris itself:

Red Wines

	l. sl.
Wine of Macon	1 10
Ordinary Burgundy	1 10
Ordinary Wine of Beaune	2 0
Wine of Migraine	2 10
" " La Chenette	2 10
" " Beaune, first quality	3 0
" " Volnay	4 0

Wine of Pomard	4 0
" " Nuits	4 0
" " St. George	5 0
" " Chambertin	5 0
" " Richebour	5 0
" " Vougeos	5 0
" " Bordeaux medoc, prime quality	7 0
" " Bordeaux (claret)	7 0
" " Romanée Conti	6 0
" " Hermitage	5 0
" " Bordeaux Aubrion	4 0
" " Bordeaux Lafite	5 0
" " Red Champagne	6 0
Good Old Port	5 0

White Wines

Wine of Chably	2 0
" " Pouly	2 0
" " Mulseaux	4 0
" " Morachée	5 0
" " Hermitage	5 0
" " Grave	5 0
" " Sauterne	5 0
" " Barnac	5 0
" " Small Champagne	3 10
" " Rose-colour champaigne	5 10
" " Sparkling Champaigne	5 10
" " Sillery Champaigne	6 0

• These come from a letter of George Augustus Sala, *à propos* of the old discussion of the equivalence of "claret" and "cl*ai*ret." The mis-spellings (which that great authority, M. André Simon, has declared, I think, to be not uncommon even in France to-day, and which have always been prevalent in England, but which, of course, were not Mr. Sala's own) are sometimes curiously phonetic, as in "Aubrion."* "Lafite," for a wonder, is right, and the omission of the *g* in "Richebour" and the substitution of *s* in "Vougeos"
• not surprising. But what is, or was, "La Chenette"? And though
• I cannot say I have never drunk "Wine of Migraine," I shouldn't have expected it to be so frankly advertised as such. In the white list, "Bar*n*ac" is probably a mere clerical error, and "Chably" and "Pouly" phoneticisms as before. "Morachée" for "Montrachet" looks as if it had been taken down from the lips of a hurried and not too clear-spoken waiter; but "Mulseaux" for "Meursault" suggests a slight indulgence in the excellent liquid itself. These white Burgundies are *very* treacherous. Perhaps it is just, if only just, desirable to add that "l" = *livres* and "sl" "*sols*" or "*sous.*"

---

* I have had occasion before now to "scrap" various mis-handlings of this great wine's name. And we have also had to notice, before, the comparative modernness of Champagne as *exclusively* "sparkling." Here, it will be observed, only one kind out of four is announced as such.

NOTES

INTRODUCTION

4 **"had a hand as editor"**: Walter Leuba, *George Saintsbury* (New York: Twayne, 1967), p. 120.

5 **he was, to Ray, a "bully"**: Cyril Ray, *Bollinger: Tradition of a Champagne Family*, 2nd ed. (London: Heinemann/Peter Davies, 1982), p. 49.

6 **an effect on Saintsbury's decision:** Dorothy Jones, who has written the fullest study of Saintsbury, says that he "preserved his notes from fifty years of study and enjoyment of wines and other spirits *[sic]*" (*King of Critics: George Saintsbury, 1845–1933, Critic, Journalist, Historian, Professor* [Ann Arbor: University of Michigan Press, 1992], p. 276).

then the magazine expired: The editor was T. Earle Welby (1881–1933), a journalist and essayist with a keen interest in wine and a high admiration for Saintsbury. He would later (in 1931) be one of the founders of the Saintsbury Club, that small band of enthusiasts who still meet twice yearly to celebrate the memory of Saintsbury in good food and wine. It was said of Welby that "one of his proudest boasts" was that "he brought about the publication of *Notes from a Cellar-Book [sic]*" (Edward Shanks, "Biographical Introduction" to Welby's *Second Impressions* [London: Methuen, 1933], p. xvi).

8 **"we shall be very pleased . . . if there ever is any"**: 20 November 1919, Macmillan Papers, British Library, London.

"I reworked . . . may amuse people": 21 November 1919, 10 January 1920, Macmillan Papers, British Library, London.

9 **"Many have ascribed . . . serious about wine"**: *Woman of Taste: Memoirs from the Wine World* (London: John Murray, 1990), p. 45.

"Trinc!": The word comes from Saintsbury's favorite, Rabelais; it is the oracle of the Holy Bottle delivered to Panurge and Pantagruel (*Gargantua and Pantagruel*, bk. 5, ch. 44).

"Pussyfoot": The name is taken from the nickname given to the American William E. Johnson, then prominent in the councils of the Anti-Saloon League.

11 **"more than once . . . matter of drinks"**: *Reminiscences of a Vintner* (London: Chapman and Hall, 1950), p. 102.

"not only the hardest . . . superiority": See "The Qualities of Wine" in the appendix.

13 **"merely called me . . . do not care to think!"**: *Something of Myself* (London: Macmillan, 1937), p. 86.

14 **"I have . . . I don't and have to hunt up"**: *A History of the French Novel* (London, 1919), 2:380n.

15 **"the most allusive writer I know"**: Later, in writing to thank A. Blyth Webster for his memoir of Saintsbury, Kipling wrote, "You say he was allusive. I made out 239 allusions that I could identify in the first 271 p.p. of *The Peace of the Augustans*" (7 January 1934, St. Andrews University Library).

16 **"what I should like . . . amplifications and memories"**: 5 July 1920, University of Sussex.

TITLE PAGE

23 *Trinc!:* The oracular word of the Holy Bottle to Panurge and Pantagruel. François Rabelais, *Gargantua and Pantagruel*, bk. 5. ch. 44.

DEDICATION

25 **To R. K.:** Rudyard Kipling. The acquaintance between Kipling and Saintsbury went back to 1890, shortly after Kipling had returned to England from India as an unknown journalist and had become almost overnight the literary star of London. Saintsbury was then assistant editor of the *Saturday Review* in London; the two men knew each other as fellow members of the Savile Club, as Kipling recalls in *Something of Myself:* "Saintsbury was a solid rock of learning and geniality whom I revered all my days; profoundly a scholar and versed in the art of good living." Kipling then went off to his years in Vermont (1892–96); when he returned to England, Saintsbury had been translated to Edinburgh as Regius Professor of English Literature. Their only opportunity to have seen much of each other, then, was confined to the two years 1890 and 1891. Kipling was an admiring reader of Saintsbury's critical writings after that, but they had no direct personal relation again until 1919. Saintsbury had by then retired and had taken up residence in an annex to Number 1, Royal Crescent, Bath. Kipling was a regular visitor to Bath in the early part of each year, when his wife came for treatment of her rheumatic disorders. In February 1919 Kipling called on Saintsbury in Bath, and from that time they remained close friends, each with a genuine admiration for the accomplishments of the other.

In his letters, Kipling saluted Saintsbury as "Honoured One" or "Most Honoured," and there was nothing ironic in these names. Saintsbury, for his part, had the highest opinion of Kipling. When he determined to dedicate *Notes on a Cellar-Book* to Kipling (the only book that Saintsbury ever dedicated), he apparently indulged in language so extravagant as to embarrass its subject. Kipling wrote to Saintsbury on 21 January 1930 thus: "I've been thinking over your dedication to the Bacchus Book. Honestly, the assertion about my helping to win the war will bring down Hell on your head!" On 1 February Kipling wrote again to say that "I think your dedication as altered is more than munificent"—as indeed it is: one can only wonder what the terms of the original dedication were. The statement in the dedication that Saintsbury had not been able to offer Kipling even one review is a mistake: he reviewed Kipling's *Many Inventions* in 1893. But it is not surprising that Saintsbury, given the huge volume of his journalistic output in those days, should have forgotten this item.

PRELIMINARY

27 **to resume it:** In the preface to the second volume of *A History of the French Novel* (London, 1919), a work that Saintsbury meant to be his last scholarly labor, he noted that he had planned only two "literary schemes" that he had never carried out. One was a "History of the English Scholastics"; the other, a "History of Wine." The latter "was actually commissioned, planned, and begun just before I was appointed to my chair at Edinburgh [that is, in 1895]." He gave it up, he adds, "not from any pusillanimity or loss of interest in the subject, but partly because I had too much else to do, and because I thought it unfair to expose that respectable institution to the venom of the most unscrupulous of all fanatics—those of teetotalism. I could take this up with pleasure, but I have lost my cellar" (p. xi). Saintsbury's undated plan for an "Unwritten History of Wine" in two volumes was in the possession of his biographer, Dorothy Richardson Jones, in 1992: see her *King of Critics* (Ann Arbor: University of Michigan Press, 1992), p. 357n25. Its present whereabouts are unknown.

even "publisherial" requests reached me: The publisher was Sir Frederick Macmillan: see pp. 6–8. Sir Frederick (1851–1936) was the son of the founder of the firm of Macmillan, which was, under Sir Frederick's direction, greatly expanded. He was for many years one of the pillars of the London publishing establishment. Saintsbury's connection with the firm went back to 1881, when Macmillan published his first book on English literature, *John Dryden*. In the years that followed, Macmillan published twelve more of Saintsbury's books, including two posthumous collections.

28 **Thackeray perhaps the greatest of them:** Thackeray's knowledge of wine, written out in detail in his novels, has not yet been given the book that the subject would require. The late Maynard Amerine, the distinguished professor in the Department of Viticulture and Enology at the University of California, Davis, began such a work but did not complete it. Saintsbury, who edited Thackeray for the Oxford University Press (17 vols., 1908), cites Thackeray more often than any other author in *Notes on a Cellar-Book*.

"Carte Blanche": The term is used on labels by more than one Champagne firm for different styles of Champagne.

Panard: Charles François Panard (or Pannard) (1694–1765), writer of satiric verse and comic operas. By tradition, he wrote in cafés on paper splashed with wine—"le cachet du génie," he called it—and composed Bacchic songs (*Dictionnaire des lettres françaises* [Paris, 1950]). Two of his poems are written in lines of varying length so as to represent a bottle and a glass. Saintsbury writes of him in part 6 of "A Frame of Miniatures" in *Miscellaneous Essays* (New York, 1892): "He lived in peace and charity with all men and women, consumed a vast quantity of more or less good wine, and yielded in his turn a vast quantity of more or less good verse" (pp. 379–80).

Tom Brown: Thomas Brown (1663–1704), English satirist; his *Letters on Several Occasions* includes one "From a Vintner in the City, to a Young Vintner in Covent Garden" full of cynical knowledge about the trade.

Peacock: Thomas Love Peacock (1785–1866), whose satirical fictions (one can hardly call them novels) were among Saintsbury's favorites. Saintsbury edited Peacock's *Works*, 5 vols. (London, 1895–97).

"streaks of the tulip": The neoclassic advice of Imlac to the artist in Samuel Johnson's *Rasselas*, ch. 10: "a poet," Imlac says, "does not number the streaks of the tulip" but seeks a general idea.

29 *Piccadilly Review:* The editor of the *Piccadilly Review* was T. Earle Welby (see my note to p. 6). The journal ran for only five issues, from 23 October to 20 November 1919; contributors included A. P.

Herbert, Ford Madox Ford, and Rose Macaulay. Saintsbury's contributions, under the heading of "Notes on a Cellar Book," appeared in the issues of 23 October and 12 November. They are slightly abbreviated versions of chapters 1 and 2 of *Notes on a Cellar-Book.*

29 *bobolitionist:* A term of abuse used to mock abolitionists before the Civil War. Saintsbury presumably means to mock the prohibitionist.

30 **"grudge my horse corn":** "Autour de Mon Chapeau," in *Roundabout Papers* (1861–63).

incalculable: Saintsbury means the Representation of the People Act of 1918, by which the franchise, including women's suffrage, was extended by more than preceding acts put together had done. At the time, no one could do more than guess at the numbers to be added to the list of voters—hence Saintsbury's "incalculable."

31 **Temperance party:** The "temperance" movement in England was dominated by the United Kingdom Alliance (the resonant full title was the United Kingdom Alliance for the Total and Immediate Suppression of the Liquor Traffic) and the Church of England Temperance Reformation Society; their activity was particularly strenuous and noisy at this time. It is useful to keep in mind that Saintsbury was writing just at the moment that Prohibition began in the United States and is thus more than usually conscious of the bluenose and the teetotaler. The Eighteenth Amendment to the American Constitution, prohibiting the trade in alcoholic drink, had been ratified in 1919 and went into force on 16 January 1920. It was thus impending through the months that Saintsbury was engaged in the writing of *Notes on a Cellar-Book.*

The American experiment had, of course, the effect of greatly stimulating the hopes of the dry element in Great Britain, hopes that had already been raised by the various official restrictions on the sale of drink imposed during the war years (the notorious restrictions on hours of opening in British pubs, currently still in the process of being relaxed, are a legacy of the war). Britain now saw a flurry of prohibitionist activity. An American prohibitionist, the much-publicized William E. "Pussyfoot" Johnson (see my note to

p. 36), had been agitating in Great Britain since 1918. A Scottish Temperance Act, allowing local option and Sunday closing, had already been passed, and a similar bill for Wales was introduced into Parliament in February 1920. At the same time, the American Anti-Saloon League was organizing a "World League against Alcoholism," with England as the first target of its campaign.

31 **A.M.D.G.:** Ad Majorem Gloriam Dei ("to the greater glory of God"), the motto of, among other organizations, the Jesuits. I suppose that Saintsbury means that the religious claim is always dishonest, and that the arguments for it are invariably "jesuitical."

Mucklewrath: The fanatical preacher in Sir Walter Scott's *Old Mortality* (1816).

34 *abusus non tollit usum:* Proverbial: "Abuse is no argument against use."

35 **"duplicate horn":** The phrase occurs in Poe's "Ulalume," lines 36 and 38, in allusion to the crescent moon. But Saintsbury means the twin peaks of Parnassus.

NOTE TO THIRD EDITION

36 **as Mr. Kipling has it:** "Et Dona Ferentes," line 26: "and the same was merry war."

Pussyfoot: The archfiend in Saintsbury's demonology, "Pussyfoot" stands for the rigid prohibitionist: "Pussyfoot" and "Pussyfootism" make one of the leading leitmotifs of the book. The nickname, much in the news at the time of *Notes on a Cellar-Book*, belonged to the American prohibitionist William E. Johnson (1862–1945). He had acquired the nickname Pussyfoot from his activities as an agent employed to suppress the liquor trade on American Indian reservations. His method was to operate at night, and by surprise. Since 1912 he had been an officer of the Anti-Saloon League, the most potent force in the drive for national prohibition in the United States. The League's work, following its American success, was now extended worldwide, and Johnson was one of the League's star turns. In November 1919, he lost the sight of one eye when a formal debate at Essex Hall, London, was broken up by rioting students from the University of London. Johnson had an important part in producing the *Standard Encyclopedia of the Alcohol Problem* (ed. Ernest Hurst Cherrington, 6 vols. [Westerville, OH: American Issue Publishing, 1925–30]), a monument to its own labors produced by the Anti-Saloon League. It would, I think, please Saintsbury to know that I have found the *Standard Encyclopedia* a most helpful reference in annotating *Notes on a Cellar-Book*, a use that Pussyfoot could not have foreseen.

36 *sbirri:* Bodyguards; hired bravos.

37 **"you could get blind drunk in Guernsey for sixpence":** Not from the same (unidentified) reviewer just mentioned but from a review by Philip Guedalla, reprinted as "Mr. George Saintsbury," in *Masters and Men* (New York: Putnam, 1923), pp. 113–16: "He resided for six years on the island of Guernsey, 'where,' as he tells in a mood of gentle regret which would melt the intrepid Mr. Johnson ['Pussyfoot'] himself, 'you could get blind drunk for sixpence.'"

Burton's: See p. 154.

George Borrow himself: George Borrow, *The Bible in Spain* (London, 1843): "Villa Viciosa, a small, dirty town. . . . It is sometimes called La Capitál de las Avellanas, or the Capital of the Filberts, from the immense quantity of this fruit which is grown in the neighbourhood" (ch. 34).

39 **"honey and fire":** "'What wine this is!' 'True Syrian—fire and honey; fourteen years old next vintage, my Raphael!'" (ch. 2).

40 **meyny:** Company, fellowship.

Aristides: Aelius Aristides (117–89 C.E.), Greek rhetorician. *Paraphthegmata* is a rhetorical term meaning an added qualification, or, as a secondary meaning, a fault in statement: Saintsbury's "things I ought not to have said."

42 **"speak no more of my matters":** Cf. 2 Samuel 19:29: "Why speakest thou any more of thy matters?"

"beeswing": "The second crust, consisting of shining filmy scales of tartar, formed in port and some other wines after long keeping"

(OED). Other authorities state that its origin is wholly vegetable rather than mineral, and that it is particularly—perhaps uniquely—associated with prephylloxera ports: see Sarah Bradford, *The Englishman's Wine* (London: Macmillan, 1969), p. 9. It is, in any case, a sign of bottle age.

I. ORIGINS

43 **"the Past":** J. R. Planché (1796–1880), fertile writer for the London stage, authority on historical dress and heraldry, and theatrical manager. He was Somerset Herald from 1866, by which time he had quit the theater. I cannot find these verses either in Planché's *Songs and Poems from 1819 to 1879* (London, 1881), or in his *Recollections and Reflections* (London, 1872).

"Nessun maggior dolore": Dante, *Inferno*, V, 121: "There is no greater sorrow" (than to remember past happiness in present grief).

"happier things": Tennyson, "Locksley Hall," line 76.

"Non tamen irritum": Horace, *Odes*, III, xxix ("irritum" for "inritum" is a typographical error that was not corrected in later printings of the book): "Nothing he does can undo what has been done."

"I have had my hour": Dryden, translation of Horace in *Sylvae* (1685): "But what has been . . ." The slight misquotation is of interest only as evidence that Saintsbury is quoting without book, as he does throughout.

44 **not imposing:** The cellar book, which records the cellars that Saintsbury kept in West Kensington (1884–86) and Edinburgh (1895–1915), has passed through several sales. According to H. W. Yoxall ("Preface to the Second Reissue," *Notes on a Cellar-Book* [London: Macmillan, 1978], p. xi), the book "was sold some twenty years ago at Christie's for £300, resold by the purchaser, an antiquarian bookseller, to an enthusiastic *amateur*, and in the autumn of 1977, now handsomely cased in leather, was offered again at auction and fetched £1,550."

the year 1878: The year 1878 was the last of a great sequence of

Bordeaux vintages in the 1870s before the phylloxera plague. For other excellences belonging to this year, see pp. 51–52.

44 **firm . . . Pall Mall:** Messrs. Bell, Rannie, and Co., 49 Pall Mall *(Post Office London Directory)*. The "old Scotsman" who managed it was Andrew Thomson, according to Saintsbury (see p. 226 in the appendix). André Simon identifies him as Thomas Laing, but I do not know on what authority *(Vintagewise* [London: Michael Joseph, 1945], p. 128).

45 **compurgators:** A compurgator is "one who vouches for or clears of any charge" *(OED)*.

46 **just before I was born:** That is, just before 23 October 1845.

Crusaders: Hermitage is made from the Syrah grape, whose name is a variant of Shiraz, the ancient Persian city sometimes identified as the place where the grapevine itself originated. The actual origin of the vine called Syrah, as is true of most of the great varieties, is not known. One of the several traditions regarding Hermitage is that it originated with the thirteenth-century knight Henri-Gaspard de Stérimberg, who settled as a hermit on the site after the crusade against the Albigensians (Robert W. Mayberry, *Wines of the Rhone Valley* [Totowa, NJ: Rowman and Littlefield, 1987], p. 176). As Frank Schoonmaker points out, Stérimberg had not been within a thousand miles of Persia, and the vineyards of Hermitage probably existed already in Roman days *(Encyclopedia of Wine,* 6th ed. [New York: Hastings House, 1975], s.v. "Hermitage").

better drink it: Chapter 20, "An Aged and a Great Wine," in Meredith's *The Egoist,* presents a ninety-year-old port, an "ancestral wine." It may be mentioned that Meredith, after meeting Saintsbury, wrote to Robert Louis Stevenson that "Saintsbury is in this matter of Burgundy, so profound, of such high Bacchic smack of discernment, that upon my word we cannot exclude him" (17 March 1883, C. L. Cline, ed., *The Letters of George Meredith,* 3 vols. [Oxford: Clarendon Press, 1970], 2:692).

47 **pre-oïdium and pre-phylloxera wine:** Oidium *(Uncinula necator),* or powdery mildew, is a fungus disease brought from the New World

to the Old in the 1840s. It virtually destroyed the wine industry in Madeira and did much damage in the European winegrowing countries. It is controlled by sulfur dusting. Phylloxera *(Dactylosphaera vitifoliae)*, an aphid native to North America, destroys vines by attacking their roots; it was accidentally brought to Europe in the 1860s and thereafter spread throughout the continent with devastating effect. The remedy adopted was to graft vines of European origin, which are without resistance to the pest, to rootstocks of native American vines, some of which are resistant (or "tolerant," as the plant pathologists say). The postphylloxera era of winemaking in Europe (and in the rest of the world with but very few exceptions) rests, then, upon vines that have been compounded. This fact has generated endless argument as to whether postphylloxera wines could ever be so good as prephylloxera wines were or were reputed to be. The question is not one of the sort that can be settled.

47 **"fearful joy"**: Thomas Gray, "Ode on a Distant Prospect of Eton College," line 40.

48 **Salviati's:** Salviati and Co., glass manufacturers, 213 Regent Street *(Post Office London Directory)*.ooo
avanturine: Brownish glass flecked with gold-colored spangles.

49 **my father:** Saintsbury's father, also named George, was secretary to the Southampton Dock Company at the time of his son's birth; in 1850 he became secretary of the East India and China Association in London, a post at which he remained until his death in 1859, when the younger George was fourteen.
"the other shop": Thackeray, *Pendennis*, ch. 18: "I would advise you to employ an honest and respectable house in London for your small stock of wine, rather than to have recourse to the Oxbridge tradesmen, whose liquor, if I remember rightly, was both deleterious in quality and exorbitant in price."
Guy & Gammon's: Founded in 1751 as Leadbetter and Company, Cornmarket, Oxford.
Manchester: Saintsbury, on leaving Oxford, taught for six months in the Manchester Grammar School, 1868.

49 **Guernsey:** From September 1868 to September 1874, Saintsbury was senior classical master at Elizabeth College, Guernsey.

agreeable . . . as in all others: Saintsbury describes the amenities of life on Guernsey as he knew it in *A History of the French Novel* (London, 1919), 2:118–20, including the drink available. "When I was there you could buy not undrinkable or poisonous Hollands at four shillings a gallon, and brandy—not, of course, exactly cognac or *fine champagne*, but deserving the same epithets—for six. If you were a luxurious person, you paid half-a-crown a bottle for the genuine produce of the Charente, little or not at all inferior to Martell or Hennessy, and a florin for excellent Scotch or Irish whiskey."

51 **Elgin . . . 1874–6:** To be headmaster of the newly founded and short-lived Elgin Educational Institute, a boarding school.

Professor Masson: David Masson (1822–1907), a Scotsman trained at Aberdeen and Edinburgh, led a busy life as a journalist, author, and editor. He started and edited *Macmillan's Magazine* and was professor of English literature at the University of Edinburgh, 1865–95, when Saintsbury succeeded him in the chair. Among his many scholarly works, *The Life of Milton* (6 vols., 1859–80), long the standard authority, is now best remembered.

Lamb's on tobacco: Charles Lamb, "A Farewell to Tobacco," 1805.

Dryden: *John Dryden,* English Men of Letters Series (London, 1881).

Ducru-Beaucaillou: As explained in the introduction, I do not identify châteaux, such as Ducru-Beaucaillou, that figure in the classified list of Bordeaux growths of 1855. The vintage of 1864 was among the most celebrated of the nineteenth century, described, for example, by Edmund Penning-Rowsell as a "classic vintage, . . . plentiful as well as of the highest quality" (*The Wines of Bordeaux* [London: Michael Joseph, 1969], p. 267).

'65 Krug: Krug and Co., Reims, founded in 1843. Simon called the '65 vintage "the best year of the decade" (*Vintagewise,* p. 124). He notes (p. 125), as does Saintsbury (see p. 90) that most Champagne then would have been sweet, or at least not dry with the dryness of "brut." For an account of the shift from sweet to dry in Champagne for the English trade, see Patrick Forbes, *Champagne: The Wine, the Land, and the People* (New York; Reynal and Co., [1967]), pp. 161–64.

51 **reasons . . . cellar:** The school did not prosper, and Saintsbury left it a poorer man than when he arrived; it was closed in 1879 (Dorothy Jones, *King of Critics* [Ann Arbor: University of Michigan Press, 1992], p. 43).

"fled *to* the Press": Saintsbury's pun on Chaucer, *Balade de Bon Conseyl*, line 1: "Flee fro the prees, and dwelle with sothfastnesse." On leaving his unsatisfactory post at Elgin, Saintsbury migrated to West Kensington to begin life as a journalist in London (Jones, *King of Critics*, p. 45). He continued in this work until his appointment to Edinburgh in 1895. For many of those years, he was assistant editor of the *Saturday Review*, but that accounted for only a little of the work that flowed copiously from his pen as editor, critic, reviewer, essayist, translator, and scholar. Saintsbury estimated that the anonymous journalism alone of all that he wrote in this period would fill more than a hundred volumes (Jones, *King of Critics*, p. 92).

Poems and Ballads: Algernon Swinburne, *Poems and Ballads: Second Series* (1878).

52 **Anthony Trollope . . . thereof:** Trollope called Léoville Barton '64 "the most divine of nectars" (*Ayala's Angel* [1881], ch. 5).

But when I knew not — You: Presumably the lines are Saintsbury's. Lord Macaulay used to attribute his comic verses to the "Judicious Poet," and I suppose that Saintsbury, finding the name in Trevelyan's *Life and Letters of Macaulay* (1876), adopted it as the source of his own. But there are other possibilities.

II. SHERRY AND MADEIRA

53 *pure* "sherry": Thackeray, *Pendennis*, final chapter: "one of the most necessary articles to her husband's comfort is *pure sherry.*" The chevalier had just gone into the wine business. Saintsbury has cor-

rected this passage from the first edition, in which he wrote "*good sherry.*"

53 **"Vino de Pasto":** Ordinary or everyday wine but also in use by the English trade for a mediocre grade of sherry, "pale and not too dry" (Oscar A. Mendelsohn, *The Dictionary of Drink and Drinking* [New York: Hawthorn Books, 1965]).

54 **Xérès and San Lucar:** San Lúcar de Barrameda, with Jerez (or Xérès, as Saintsbury spells it after the French fashion) and Puerto de Santa María, is one of the three towns that are the sites of sherry production. San Lúcar is the source of the light sherry type called Manzanilla.

Thackeray's sanction: "His Highness (at a supper of oysters and champagne) was brought to consent" (*Barry Lyndon*, ch. 11).

Paxarettes: After the tower of Paxarete, near Jerez. Originally a sweet wine, *paxarete* or *pajarete* is now a wine or must blended with *arrope*, concentrated grape juice, and used as a coloring and sweetening agent. Even if Saintsbury is thinking of the older Paxarete, it is hard to see how any Paxarete could be light. The name evidently had a different meaning for him.

Sir Telegraph in "Melincourt": Sir Telegraph Paxarett in Peacock's *Melincourt* (1817): "I am a moderate man: one bottle of Madeira and another of claret are enough for me at any time" (ch. 4).

"dry" America . . . butts: Wine and other alcoholic drinks could be exported from the United States between the passage of the Eighteenth Amendment in January 1919 and January 1920, when the Volstead Act enforcing national prohibition would come into operation. After that, no such traffic would be allowed. There was naturally a scramble to unload, in Europe and elsewhere, the stocks held in America. I do not know what particular episode Saintsbury has in mind.

supernacular: From *supernaculum:* a wine to be drunk to the last drop, excellent. The word translates the German *auf den nagel*, referring to the "practice of turning up the emptied cup or glass on one's left thumb-nail, to show that all the liquor has been drunk" *(OED).*

54 **"Tio Pepe":** The name (roughly equivalent to "Uncle Joe") of a fino sherry, the property of the firm of Gonzalez, Byass, and Co.; it is named for Don José de la Peña, who originally developed it.

55 **Wisdom's:** The firm of Wisdom and Warter, established in Jerez in 1854.

"Nectar de Xérès": The firm of Gonzalez, Byass has a cream sherry labeled "Nectar": it is possible that Saintsbury means this, though he calls it a "class" of wine.

56 **"Carte d'Or" . . . champagne:** A label belonging to the Champagne firm of De St. Marceaux, particularly popular in England in Saintsbury's day. "The brand of the house most appreciated in this country is its Carte d'Or, a very dry wine which, in conjunction with the firm's Extra Quality, secured the first place at a recent champagne competition in England" (Henry Vizetelly, *Facts about Champagne* [London, 1879], p. 100).

"Solera" . . . sherry: Not a kind of wine but a method of fractional blending especially identified with the production of sherry. The method, which is intended to provide a consistent product, requires several rows of casks, usually one atop the other. A part of the oldest wine, from the bottom row, is drawn off for bottling; the bottom casks are then refilled from the row of casks above, and that row from the row above, until the top row, with the youngest wine, is reached. More young wine is added so that the sequence can begin anew. In this manner a steady process of blending of newer with older wines is established. As a rule, less than half of the wine in the bottom row is drawn off in the course of a year. A solera is frequently dated from the time of its first establishment, but after a few years of operation the proportion of wine left from the date of origin is very small indeed.

57 **"Emilia" . . . "Isabel" . . . "Maria":** This was particularly the fashion for Manzanilla sherries: "La Pastora," "La Victoria," "Eva": see Jan Read, *Sherry and the Sherry Bodegas* (London: Sotheby's Publications, 1988), p. 32.

fantastries: "Fantastic display or show" *(OED).*

57 **Amontillado:** Literally, "from Montilla," or, by extension, "in the style of Montilla." The wine of Montilla (not a sherry) is unfortified and dry. The sherry called Amontillado is now the most popular style, though the name is often applied to wine that is not genuine Amontillado. A real Amontillado is an aged fino and, therefore, inevitably expensive. Most "Amontillados" now are not that at all but blends, often rather sweet. Evidently that was the case in Saintsbury's day too.

"sack" . . . sugar: One of the suggested etymologies for the wine Shakespeare called "sack" is the Spanish "secco" (dry), though this is not accepted by today's lexicographers. "Sack and sugar" occurs twice in Shakespeare: Poins calls Falstaff "Sir John Sack and Sugar" (*I Henry IV,* I, ii, 113), and Falstaff confesses that "if sack and sugar be a fault, God help the wicked!" (*I Henry IV,* II, iv, 470).

fuss about sugar and jam: At the end of 1919, when sugar was still under wartime regulation, a world shortage threatened to drive prices out of control. The British authorities in response to this prospect cut the sugar ration for both domestic and commercial use for 1920. All restrictions on sugar were lifted at the end of February 1921. Saintsbury's guess seems to have been confirmed: the British are among the leading consumers of sugar in the world.

59 **Pedro Ximénès:** More usually Pedro Ximénez, one of the traditional grapes of the sherry region (and of Malaga, Valencia, and Montilla), particularly favored for sweet wines.

John Harvey: The second John Harvey (1832?–1900) of the famous firm of wine merchants on Denmark Street in Bristol. He was senior partner of the firm from 1878 to 1893 and chairman from 1893 to 1900.

West Indian friends: The West Indies (and the American South) were traditionally the leading markets for Madeira. Under the British Navigation Acts, the wine of Madeira could be shipped directly to the American colonies, while all European wine had to pass through England. The island of Madeira had also the advantage of lying on the outward-bound track of sailing ships from Europe.

These two conditions gave Madeira an unchallengeable position in the colonial market.

59 **"Gladstone" claret:** In 1861, as chancellor of the exchequer, W. E. Gladstone succeeded in lowering the English duties on French wine to one shilling a gallon for table wines, and combined this measure with a new liberality in granting off-licenses for the sale of wines: "He opened the wine trade to grocers, drapers, stores and all and sundry traders" (André Simon, *Vintagewise* [London: Michael Joseph, 1945], p. 16). Gladstone's motive was not so much the cause of temperance as that of free trade and the prosperity it was thought to bring. French wines had, of course, long been discriminated against by English tariffs. The greatly augmented importation of light French wines inevitably provoked snobbish remarks about "Gladstone" claret or "grocer's" claret: "We've got sherry, and port wine, and Gladstone," the young man says in Trollope's *Ralph the Heir* (1871), ch. 3. But it need not have been always "contemptible."

"Sir, I drink no memories": Recorded by Dr. Patrick Delany, *Observations upon Lord Orrery's Remarks etc. of Swift* (London, 1754), and cited by Thackeray in "Swift," in *The English Humourists of the Eighteenth Century* (1851).

pre-oïdium wines were exhausted: The island of Madeira was particularly hard-hit by the ravages of oidium in the 1850s. It could not supply its markets, and its wines have never regained anything like the esteem that they once enjoyed, particularly in America. The devastation of oidium was then, from 1873, compounded by the ravages of phylloxera. In consequence, most of the traditional varieties of grape from which Madeira was made disappeared (see my note to p. 60). André Simon repeats an established view when he says that "none of the wines which were made after the oidium scourge of the '50's ever came up to the standard of excellence of their elders" (*Notes on the Late J. Pierpont Morgan's Cellar Book, 1906* [London: Curwen Press, privately printed, 1944], p. 3). On the other hand, Michael Broadbent (*The Great Vintage Wine Book* [New York:

Knopf, 1980], 399–401) lists a number of distinguished vintages from 1860 on.

59 **"London Particular"** . . . **West:** "London Particular" was Madeira especially imported for the London market; "the West" may mean Bristol, long the leading city in the West India trade. It is also said that London Particular was Madeira wine that, beginning in the reign of Queen Anne, was "additionally fortified by British merchants with seven liters of brandy per pipe" (McGrew and Montgomery, *American Wine Society Journal* 19 [Winter 1987]: 114).

60 **"liming" sack:** Lime was sometimes added to wine verging on vinegar in order to reduce the acidity.

Bual or Sercial: Types of Madeira, named for the grapes from which they derive. Sercial is dry, Bual somewhat sweeter. After the devastation of the vineyards by phylloxera, such traditional grapes were replaced by inferior varieties, principally the Tinta Negra Mole, and by American hybrids, now illegal. Though the old varietal names were retained for the wines, grapes of these traditional varieties have only slowly returned to the Madeira vineyards. The European Economic Community now forbids the use of the classic varietal names—Sercial, Verdelho, Bual, Malmsey—on Madeira wines sold in the Community unless they consist of at least 85 percent of the variety named. In consequence most Madeira wines have had to be renamed.

in perfection: Madeira is the longest-lived of wines (in part because it is, in the course of its production, thoroughly oxidized). Broadbent records drinking 1789 Madeira in 1980 (*Great Vintage Wine Book*, p. 397), and every fancier of Madeira will have at least a remotely comparable story to tell.

"Sherry cobbler": Any "cobbler" is a long drink with ice and fruit or sugar, usually but not necessarily made with wine. It is said to be originally American. There is no general agreement as to ingredients or proportions.

"Father" Stanton: The Reverend Arthur Henry Stanton (1839–

1913), curate of Saint Albans, Holborn, universally known as "Father" Stanton. Stanton was an ultrahigh churchman whose "ritualistic" practices offended the church establishment, which cut him off from all preferment. He spent his life as an unbeneficed clergyman devoted to the care of his slum parish, where he had gone even before the (very expensive) parish church was built in 1862. His sermons have been called a blend of "ritualist teaching and Methodist fervour" (*The Times,* 29 March 1913). Stanton was a graduate of Trinity College, Oxford.

62   **sherry "pegs" . . . little satisfaction:** Whiskey was made scarce during the war; *peg* is Anglo-Indian slang for a long drink, most often brandy and soda.

"Caveza": This wine is listed at the end of the menu given on p. 190.

III. PORT

64   **Cockburn's:** Cockburn, Smithes and Co., founded by the Scotsman Robert Cockburn, a brother of the distinguished lawyer Henry, Lord Cockburn, in 1815; 1851 was, by common consent, a great year. According to H. Warner Allen (*The Wines of Portugal* [London: George Rainbird in association with Michael Joseph, 1963], p. 100), it was not until the vintage of 1851 that shippers' names became commonly associated with port sold in England. André Simon calls Cockburn's 1851 "a real aristocrat" (*Vintagewise* [London: Michael Joseph, 1945], p. 35).

Mr. Powell: Walter Powell (1842–81), of Chippenham, Wiltshire, member of Parliament for Malmesbury, was carried out to sea from Bridport in a one-man balloon, *Saladin,* on 10 December 1881, and never seen again: see *The Times,* 13 December 1881, pp. 6, 9.

1820: "Generally regarded as a classic" (Wyndham Fletcher, *Port: An Introduction to Its History and Delights* [London: Sotheby, Parke Bernet, 1978], p. 43).

64 **'34 . . . '47:** Fletcher calls 1834 "a very fine year" (*Port*, p. 43), and Michael Broadbent calls it "a great classic vintage" (*The Great Vintage Wine Book* [New York: Knopf, 1980], p. 368). André Simon describes 1847 as "a very remarkable vintage, the wines so rich and well-balanced that they are still beautiful today, provided they have been well bottled and kept in a good cellar" (*Port* [London: Constable, 1934], p. 74). See also his account of '47 ports in *Vintagewise*, pp. 32–33: "Surely there never was another Port like the '47's." Saintsbury writes in *A Second Scrap Book* that the last occasion on which he had '47 port "in decent condition" was a dinner in 1896 at Pembroke College, Oxford, in honor of Dr. Johnson ([London: Macmillan, 1923], p. 226).

65 **he never did:** Simon does not go quite so far as Saintsbury in praise of '51, but affirms that the wines "were very fine, indeed, finer than any Port of the present century, and they lasted remarkably well" (*Vintagewise*, pp. 34–35). Broadbent calls a Stibbart's 1851 "the most magnificent old port I have ever drunk" (*Great Vintage Wine Book*, p. 368).

'54: "A very fair vintage, in spite of the first inroads of the oïdium" (Simon, *Vintagewise*, p. 34). It was "declared" by only four shippers.

'58: "A very good vintage . . . but not great" (Simon, *Vintagewise*, pp. 34, 36).

'61: According to Simon, "fair but not fine; wines rather too light" (*Vintagewise*, p. 56).

'63: "Magnificent, rich and well-balanced" (Fletcher, *Port*, p. 43); "the best since 1853. . . . Have lasted to this [1934] day" (Simon, *Port*, p. 75).

'68: "A very fine, classic year" (Fletcher, *Port*, p. 43); a hot summer shriveled the grapes till a timely rain fell: "the shrivelled grapes . . . were bursting with sugar and only wanted this gift from heaven to swell out and bring forth a wonderful wine" (Simon, *Vintagewise*, p. 38). Every shipper but Crofts declared a vintage in this year (Jan Read, *The Wines of Portugal*, rev. ed. [London: Faber and Faber, 1987], p. 36).

'70: "Fine with good body" (Fletcher, *Port*, p. 43); this was Saintsbury's favorite (see p. 74).

'72: "Fine year" (Fletcher, *Port*, p. 43); "a fairly good vintage" (Simon, *Vintagewise*, p. 39).

'75: "Fine quality, elegant but light and dry" (Fletcher, *Port*, p. 44).

'78: "A very fine vintage" (Simon, *Port*, p. 76); "the finest vintage of the decade" (Simon, *Vintagewise*, p. 39).

65 **Dow's:** Founded in the nineteenth century, it merged with Silva and Cosens in 1877; it is now part of the Symington family's group of port firms.

Cambridgeshire village: Fulbourn, where Saintsbury lived from 1887 to 1891. He kept rooms in London and saw his family on weekends.

"piece": A "pièce" is a measure in the Burgundy trade, a barrel holding about 228 liters. Port is usually quoted in measures of "pipes," barrels of varying size but typically of more than 500 liters' capacity.

Sandeman's: The firm was founded in London by the Scotsman George Sandeman in 1790; by 1792 he was shipping port. It was for several generations a family-owned firm; it is now owned by Seagram's. Simon rates '81 port as "fair to fine" and as the best of a decade in which "no outstanding vintage wine was made" (*Vintagewise*, pp. 41–42).

Rebello Valente: Founded in the eighteenth century; taken over from Viscount Valente Allen by Robertson Brothers in 1881. They in turn sold it to Sandeman in 1953. The year 1865 was "a moderate vintage" (Simon, *Vintagewise*, p. 36).

67 **"black-strap":** An eighteenth-century term for very dark and viscous port.

'73: Regarded as a "good" year (H. Warner Allen, *Sherry and Port* [London: Constable, 1952], p. 199); Fletcher says "fine" (*Port*, p. 43); Simon (*Port*, p. 75) says "very good." Saintsbury adds (see the "Postscripts," p. 203) that this wine was "almost certainly" one of Feuerheerd's.

Maurice: Oliver Maurice, of London Street, Reading, was an M.D.,

Heidelberg, and M.R.C.S. (*Medical Directory,* 1890). He disappears from the *Medical Directory* between 1912 and 1915. Saintsbury resided in Reading from 1891 until 1895, when he moved to Edinburgh.

67 **Beulah:** Isaiah 62:4, and Bunyan, *Pilgrim's Progress:* the land beyond Death and Despair.

68 **followed from '96:** A great classic year, shipped by all houses (Fletcher, *Port,* p. 45); they were "at the top of their form" in 1934 (Simon, *Port,* p. 87).

'08: "A great classic . . . may still [1978] be consumed with great pleasure" (Fletcher, *Port,* p. 46); Simon calls them "the best since 1896" (*Port,* p. 90).

'11: Declared by only three shippers. Most of the vintage was ruined by rain, but Sandeman, Martinez, and Rebello Valente had bought such wines as had been made already and succeeded with them. Allen declared that "Sandeman 1911 may not be the greatest Port I have ever tasted, but it has given me more enjoyment than any other Douro wine" (*Sherry and Port,* p. 155).

to see the '90's: Generally offered; this was another of Saintsbury's favorites (p. 74); "a very fair vintage: wines somewhat light but shipped as a vintage" (Simon, *Port,* p. 76).

'87's: "Jubilee": this vintage generated mixed remarks; it marked the beginning of the recovery from phylloxera and so received enthusiastic judgments. But it was not yet a full recovery, and so it suffered from comparisons to the prephylloxera vintages. It was, no doubt, as Simon calls it, "the best vintage since 1878" (*Port,* p. 76).

'97: Reported as excellent but overshadowed by the neighboring '96.

69 **Smith Woodhouse:** Founded in 1784 by Christopher Smith; the Woodhouse brothers joined in 1818. It is now owned by the Symington family.

Graham: Founded by the brothers William and John Graham, it was originally a textile firm but had engaged in shipping port since the early nineteenth century. It is now owned by the Symington family.

Warre: Founded in the late seventeenth century (the company gives the date as 1670), it is perhaps the oldest of the British port shippers, though the Warre family did not join until 1729; it is now a Symington property.

69 **Croft:** Founded in 1678, one of the oldest and most famous of shippers, now owned by the Fladgate Partnership.

Martinez: Martinez Gassiot was founded in 1797 by a Spaniard trading in London; Martinez was joined in 1822 by the Huguenot Gassiot. The firm was bought by Harvey's in 1962.

Offley: Founded in 1737; its head in the mid-nineteenth century, Joseph James, Baron de Forrester (1809–62), was one of the great men of the trade.

Taylor: The firm of Taylor, Fladgate and Yeatman goes back to the seventeenth century, but Taylor did not appear until 1816, Fladgate until 1837, and Yeatman until 1844. The firm is still in family ownership.

Feuerheerd's: Established by a German from Hamburg, Diedrich Feuerheerd, in 1815; it remained a family firm until 1929. "Zimbro" is the Quinta de Zimbro in the Alto Douro.

Kopke's: Founded by Christian Kopke, consul-general for the Hanseatic League, in 1638; it was sold to English interests in 1870 and is now a part of Barros Almeida and Co. In the nineteenth century it shipped the wines of the Quinta de Roriz.

70 **"three in the wood":** Richard Harris Barham, "The Wedding Day, or, The Buccaneer's Curse," *The Ingoldsby Legends*, at the end. This passage is altered from the first edition, in which Saintsbury wrote: "There is, I think, no evidence whether Barham was thinking of Port or of claret when he wrote the memorable lines."

71 **"Ventozello":** Port from the Quinta de Ventozello on the Douro, shipped by Sandeman.

the '04's: "Very pleasing[,] . . . a wine that promised to mature rapidly—and did mature well" (Simon, *Port*, p. 90).

"past as the shadows on glasses": "More frail than the shadows on glasses," Swinburne, "Dedication 1865," line 35: what Saintsbury has compounded this with I do not know.

72 **Silva & Cosens:** Founded in 1862; it incorporated Dow in 1877.
Tuke Holdsworth: A brand then owned by the firm of Hunt Roope and Co.; established in 1735, it is now owned by Ferreira.

73 **Gould Campbell:** Gould, James Campbell, Jones and Co., established in the early nineteenth century; property of the English wine merchants Clode and Baker from 1853. It is now a Symington property.
Burmester: Founded in 1730 by H. Burmester, a German.
Messrs Silva's hands: He was informed correctly.
"morigerant": "well mannered."

74 *some '67:* A vintage not yet mentioned: Simon says of it only that it was a "very fair vintage" (*Vintagewise*, p. 36).
Tarragona: Catalonian wine from the district around the old Roman coastal city of Tarragona, especially the sweet red fortified wine long known as "the poor man's port." The grape varieties used were largely Grenache and Carignane.
wired-up eyes . . . purgation: See Dante, *Purgatorio*, XIII, where, in the second circle of purgatory, the envious are denied heaven's light by this method.
Methuen treaty: The commercial treaty between England and Portugal (1703), granting preferential English duty to the wines of Portugal over the wines of France (£7 vs. £55 per tun). This measure, aimed at injuring the trade of a hostile France, was the foundation of the success of Portuguese wines generally, and, ultimately, of port in particular, in England.
White Port: Port made from white grape varieties, fermented as a sweet white wine before fortification; it is a minor but long-established part of the port wine trade. In recent years a dry style has been made as an aperitif, but Saintsbury would not have known this wine.
with **his dinner:** "What? You won't have any port? Don't like port with your dinner? . . . And this worthy man found himself not the less attached to Pendennis because the latter disliked port wine at dinner." Later, however, Pendennis takes port with his dinner when he sees Warrington do so (Thackeray, *Pendennis*, ch. 29).

IV. CLARET AND BURGUNDY

77 **Claret:** For Saintsbury, *claret* appears to mean almost exclusively the wine of the Médoc and a few wines from the Graves: Saint-Emilion and Pomerol are not included in the meaning of the word.

great '58's: Edmund Penning-Rowsell says that what has been called the "golden age" of claret began with the 1858s: "a succession of vintages not only remarkable in themselves but in many cases with exceptional staying power" (*The Wines of Bordeaux* [London: Michael Joseph, 1969], p. 266). André Simon records drinking in 1935 a '58 claret in Bordeaux that was "a perfect bottle of the most perfect wine imaginable" (*Vintagewise* [London: Michael Joseph, 1945], p. 62).

Thackeray . . . and Fate had answered "No": "Three years since, when the comet was blazing In the autumnal sky, I stood on the château-steps of a great claret proprietor. 'Boirai-je de ton vin, ô comête'" (*Lovel the Widower*, ch. 4). Thackeray died in 1862, too soon after the vintage to enjoy the '58s.

'64: See p. 51. "One of the finest of all claret vintages on record" (André Simon, *Notes on the Late J. Pierpont Morgan's Cellar Book, 1906* [London: Curwen Press, privately printed, 1944], p. 11).

disappointing '70's: A year of a very hot summer. Simon disagrees with Saintsbury's judgment. "There never was another claret like it. The '70's, the best of them, simply refuse to die. They were rough and somewhat harsh—but never 'dumb'—for some fifty years; then, at long last, they dropped their mask of tannin, and then we had their sweet smile" (*Notes on the Late J. Pierpont Morgan's Cellar Book*, p. 15). Ian Maxwell Campbell, however, refers to them as "pachydermatous" (*Wayward Tendrils of the Vine* [London: Chapman and Hall, 1948], p. 27).

'74's and '75's: In 1874 a bad summer was redeemed by fine weather at harvest, which gave wines of "unexpected fine quality" (Simon, *Notes on the Late J. Pierpont Morgan's Cellar Book*, p. 17). The wine of 1875 was abundant: "There were no bad '75's. They were all charming wines, so light, so sunny, so simple, so fragrant that one could not help loving them all" (Simon, *Notes on the Late J. Pierpont Morgan's Cellar Book*, p. 19). Simon affirms that they were "the finest clarets that ever left Bordeaux" (*Notes on the Late J. Pierpont Morgan's Cellar Book*, p. 13).

78 **'71 Lafite:** An "irregular" vintage with "some remarkably fine wines" according to Simon, who adds that "the few '71's that were great were nearer the perfection of Claret than any other" (*Vintagewise*, p. 72). Michael Broadbent, tasting Lafite '71 in 1972, judged it "perfect" (*The Great Vintage Wine Book* [New York: Knopf, 1980], p. 39).

Powell sale: See p. 64. The vintage of 1862 is called "fairly successful, prolific" (Penning-Rowsell, *Wines of Bordeaux*, p. 267); "fair to middling" (Simon, *Vintagewise*, p. 64); "average" (Broadbent, *Great Vintage Wine Book*, p. 37).

quite as good: Cyril Ray, in defense of Lafite, writes that "Lafite of the best years did not figure in Saintsbury's cellar-book. He was comparing the best of their kind with something not at its best" (*Lafite*, [London: Peter Davies, 1968], p. 26).

as Pepys called it: "And here [the Royal Oak Tavern, Lombard Street] drank a sort of French wine called *Ho Bryan* that hath a good and most particular taste that I never met with" (Samuel Pepys, *Diary*, 10 April 1663).

'84: A year from the depths of the phylloxera blight. Simon allows that some "fine quality wines were made south of St. Julien" (*Vintagewise*, p. 76), but he seems not to have tasted any.

equal of any claret: Note that Haut Brion, a wine of the Graves, is not for Saintsbury a claret.

Margaux of '68: Despite spring frosts and summer hail, "a moderate quantity of excellent wines [was] made in that year" (Simon, *Notes on the Late J. Pierpont Morgan's Cellar Book*, p. 12); but he says in another place that "they did not live up to the great expectations of the Bordeaux experts" (*Vintagewise*, p. 66).

M. Beljame: Alexandre Beljame (1843–1906), French scholar of English literature, professor at the University of Paris.

79 **"behind the fagots"**: *Bouteille de vin de derrière les fagots:* a wine kept hidden for special occasions.

'78's: "Excellent. . . . They have been held to the admiration of the younger generations of claret lovers as the last of the pre-phylloxera vintage" (Simon, *Notes on the Late J. Pierpont Morgan's Cellar Book,* p. 22).

already spoken of: See pp. 51–52.

Lafite-Carruades: The name given to the secondary wine of Château Lafite, usually from younger vines regarded as not yet ready to supply the highest class: "The wine was nevertheless very good, the equal of many third and fourth classed growths, and of some seconds. . . . Not made since 1966" (Frank Schoonmaker, *Encyclopedia of Wine,* 6th ed. [New York: Hastings House, 1975], s.v. "Carruades"). But beginning in 1985 the name was again applied to the second wine of Lafite.

Cahors: The wine of Cahors, on the river Lot, is made from the Malbec grape, which there gave a dark wine often referred to as "black." The style is no longer produced. Cahors was much used to color the wines of Bordeaux.

mildew and the like: Mildew had been controllable since 1885 by the application of copper sulfate, lime, and water, or "Bordeaux mixture." The great scourge in the last quarter of the century was phylloxera.

wines of '87: "Some full-bodied wines, rather harsh and lacking in charm, but quite sound" (Simon, *Notes on the Late J. Pierpont Morgan's Cellar Book,* p. 24).

'88's and '89's: The '88 was "a wine which, when young, was delightfully sweet and most attractive, too light to last, and not sound enough, but delicious" (Simon, *Notes on the Late J. Pierpont Morgan's Cellar Book,* p. 25). The '89 was "darker in colour, fuller of body, but lacking in bouquet and somewhat hard" (Simon, *Vintagewise,* p. 78). Simon finds it surprising that Saintsbury should have bracketed these two vintages together, "for they were not at all like each other" (*Vintagewise,* p. 78).

79 **'99's and '00's:** "The first two really fine clarets since the phylloxera" (Simon, *Notes on the Late J. Pierpont Morgan's Cellar Book*, p. 3).

80 **'93's:** "The vintage of 1893 was magnificent; there were not only oceans of wine to be had at a ridiculously low price, but there was no bad wine made anywhere" (Simon, *Vintagewise*, p. 79).

Pape Clément: A *cru classé* of the Graves.

Haut Brion Larrivet: A château of the Graves; its name is usually given in the form Larrivet-Haut-Brion.

81 **thirty years ago:** Information presented by Penning-Rowsell (*Wines of Bordeaux*, p. 79), shows that the prices of Bordeaux declined by 40 percent between 1873 and 1896, owing to the troubles with phylloxera and other economic causes; prices rose from 1896 but had not, by 1912, yet recovered their 1873 level.

Romanée Conti '58: As Schoonmaker says, "Traditionally the *ne plus ultra* of red wine" (*Encyclopedia of Wine*); it is the yield from a mere four and a half acres of vineyard in Vosne-Romanée.

Clos-Vougeot: *Grand cru* Burgundy from the largest vineyard in the Côte d'Or. The vineyard, long a single entity, was divided among different owners in 1889 and has since been further divided. In consequence its wines have long lost the claim to stand at "the head of all Burgundies."

"hold to the blood of its clan": "I hold by the blood of my clan": Kipling, "The Ballad of East and West," line 63.

'69 Richebourg: See p. 46. Richebourg is one of the six *grand cru* Burgundies from Vosne-Romanée.

Musigny of '77: A "fine vintage. . . . I always considered Musigny '77 the best wine of the vintage; it is indeed difficult to imagine greater intensity and delicacy of sensuous gratification" (Simon, *Notes on the Late J. Pierpont Morgan's Cellar Book*, pp. 31–32).

82 **La Tâche of '86 . . . Romanée of '87:** "Two of the finest Burgundies which I remember" (Simon, *Notes on the Late J. Pierpont Morgan's Cellar Book*, p. 32).

82 **Corton of 1881:** "Very fine vintage" (Simon, *Notes on the Late J. Pierpont Morgan's Cellar Book*, p. 31).

Pommard, Santenay, Chenas: Saintsbury is moving south from the exalted regions of the Côte de Nuits: Corton, Pommard, and Santenay mark the north, the center, and the south of the Côte de Beaune; Chenas is in the heart of the Beaujolais.

83 **Chambertin:** *Grand cru* of Gevrey-Chambertin, Côte de Nuits.

"the sweet compulsion": Milton, *Arcades*, line 68.

84 **1869:** "Full bodied, yet by no means coarse wines, dark in colour, well balanced, long lived, and one of the most admirable pre-phylloxera Clarets." Beychevelle and Kirwan were "two very fine specimens of this great vintage" (Simon, *Notes on the Late J. Pierpont Morgan's Cellar Book*, p. 13).

85 **1883:** "The vintage was late, cold, wet and miserable" (Simon, *Notes on the Late J. Pierpont Morgan's Cellar Book*, p. 24). Simon later qualified this slightly: "There must have been some good wine made at Mouton-Rothschild in 1883, since some was bottled at the Château" (*Vintagewise*, p. 77).

1891: Uneven, but regarded as an "off" year (Simon, *Vintagewise*, p. 79).

1892: Like 1891, of "no reputation" (Penning-Rowsell, *Wines of Bordeaux*, p. 272).

1895: A very hot summer produced big wines of irregular quality. Some were outstanding.

1896: Simon says that "the rain practically never stopped during the picking of the grapes" (*Vintagewise*, p. 81); Broadbent, however, says that the "weather cleared for the picking," and that the wines were "delicate" (*Great Vintage Wine Book*, p. 42). Penning-Rowsell calls them "light but agreeable" (*Wines of Bordeaux*, p. 273).

86 **caproic acid:** "Goat acid" (from its smell), a fatty acid found, for example, in butter and present in small quantities in grapes and wines.

hircine: Goatish.

87 **official list:** All the wines in question (except Pape-Clément, which is in the Graves) are Médocs, but they are not included in the official list of classified growths drawn up for the Médoc in 1855: see p. 112. Haut-Brion, of course, is an exception: though a wine of the Graves, it *is* included in the 1855 classification.

Lafite *Carruades:* Not from a neighbor but from the Lafite vineyard itself: see my note to p. 79.

Smith Haut Lafite: *Cru classé* of the Graves. Broadbent says that '88 was a year from a poor summer "saved by a brilliant September" (*Great Vintage Wine Book*, p. 41); '89 came from a hot summer and wet harvest. Simon calls it of "fair to fine quality."

"came up as a flower": Job 14:2: "he cometh forth like a flower."

"A Pretty Woman": Beginning, "That fawn-skin dappled hair of hers."

between 50 and 60: There are sixty-one châteaux in the 1855 classification of the Médoc.

88 **"Cheval Blanc":** *Premier grand cru* of Saint-Emilion. Its composition is different from that of Saintsbury's favorite Médocs: Cabernet Franc, Merlot, and a little Malbec.

half-hogsheads: A hogshead is another of those measures that vary so greatly with the thing contained that no precise value can be given: a hogshead of Bordeaux contains at least 225 liters, so let us say that Saintsbury's half-hogsheads contained no fewer than 113 liters.

"before the dear years": Sir Walter Scott, *Redgauntlet*, I, letter 11: the opening sentence of "Wandering Willie's Tale."

Saint Julien's: Commune of the Médoc containing eleven classed growths.

"facetious and rejoicing ignorance": Reportedly John Gibson Lockhart on the critics of the poet Coleridge. I have not found the source of the remark.

Saint-Estèphe: Commune of the Médoc containing five classified growths.

reason: One may add here, in order to extend a little the record of Saintsbury's knowledge of claret, this brief item from *A Second Scrap*

Book ([London: Macmillan, 1923], p. 161), in which Saintsbury is sorting through a miscellany of old letters and records:

> Then comes a *menu*, "Tuesday, April 6, 1886," most elegantly adorned with primroses and bearing nine names of guests, of whom I myself and another are now, so far as I know, the only survivors. It was the "6th Combination" of a set of "Harmonies in Bordeaux" which a dead friend of mine used to give; and the clarets vouchsafed to us were (of course not in this exact order) Beychevelle of '64 and '74, Langoa of '68, Léoville of '64 and '70, Larose of '74, Haut-Brion of '65, Pichon Longueville of '64, Latour of '64, and Lafite of '57 and '64. Just think of it!

Saintsbury identified the "dead friend" as Forster M. Alleyne, a contemporary of his at Merton, afterward a barrister.

89 **very harrowing:** "Bishop Blougram's Apology," lines 132–33. In this dramatic monologue, Blougram, an English Catholic bishop, unburdens himself to the journalist Mr. Gigadibs.

Sandeau's: Jules Sandeau (1811–83), French novelist.

V. CHAMPAGNE AND
OTHER FRENCH WHITE WINES

90 **"A man . . . dry champagne":** Patrick Forbes (*Champagne* [New York: Reynal and Co., (1967)], p. 163) says that the phrase "A man who would say he likes dry champagne" comes from the time when dry Champagne was making its way in England; those who preferred the old sweet style could retort it in reply to the dry-fanciers' taunts about "gooseberry juice" or "chorus girl's mixture." The *Punch* cartoon from 1862 reproduced on p. 92 seems to show that the argument between sweet and dry in Champagne was a new thing then, but it goes back many years earlier. George Canning (1770–1827), the English statesman, "used to say that any sane person who affected to prefer dry champagne to sweet, lied" (Abraham Hay-

ward, *The Art of Dining*, ed. Charles Sayle [1836; reprint, New York, 1899], p. 151).

90 **Sillery**: Village in the Champagne region whose wine, a *blanc de noirs*, was once famous under its own name and continued so down to the end of the nineteenth century: "Connoisseurs said it was hard to find a wine that was drier or cleaner on the palate" (Forbes, *Champagne*, p. 410). It was made both still and sparkling. The name *Sillery* is now no longer used, the wine all going into Champagne blends.

Roederer: The Champagne house of Louis Roederer, Reims, founded in 1765. Its main trade in Saintsbury's day was with Russia, and it therefore had a special interest in the taste for a sweet Champagne.

Clicquot: Wine of the house of Veuve Clicquot-Ponsardin, Reims, the firm presided over by the legendary Widow Clicquot in the nineteenth century; like Roederer, it was identified with the trade to Russia.

"Russe": The imperial Russian taste in Champagne, the *gout russe*, was for the very sweet. According to Nicholas Faith, the Russians wanted "up to 20 per cent of sweet liqueur in their champagne together with a dose of yellow Chartreuse to increase its strength" (*The Story of Champagne* [London: Hamish Hamilton, 1988], p. 70).

Pommery: The firm of Pommery and Greno, Reims, founded in 1836. Its dry Champagne was "a dominant force in Victorian Britain" (Faith, *Story of Champagne*, p. 236). Henry Vizetelly notes that "Pommery Sec" was "highly appreciated by connoisseurs" (*Facts about Champagne* [London, 1879], p. 98). Forbes says that the first of the dry Pommery Champagnes in England was that of 1874 (*Champagne*, p. 462).

"bra-a-andy and sod-d-a!": See *"Le Temps Jadis*: Wallet II" in the appendix, where Saintsbury returns to this subject.

91 **Heidsieck**: There are three firms bearing the name Heidsieck: the one owning the brand "Monopole" has, since 1923, been officially named Heidsieck and Co. Monopole. Its roots go back to the original firm of Heidsieck and Co., 1785.

91 **Perrier Jouet's:** Champagne house of Épernay, founded in 1811. **Dagonet's:** Dagonet et fils, Châlons. "The heavy amber-coloured, indeed almost amber-scented champagne—Dagonet 1880, I think, was your favourite wine?" (Oscar Wilde to Lord Alfred Douglas [January–March 1897], Rupert Hart-Davis, ed., *The Letters of Oscar Wilde* [London: Hart-Davis, 1962], p. 507).

calumba: A bitter substance from the calumba root (*Jateorhiza palmate*) used in tonics and stomachics, including vermouth.

Thackeray describes it: Saintsbury elsewhere says that he regarded '65 as "the finest year of the century": see "*Le Temps Jadis:* Wallet II" in the appendix.

Krug's Private Cuvée: André Simon calls the 1906s "a very great success, the last of the great Champagne vintages" (*Vintagewise* [London: Michael Joseph, 1945], p. 137).

1857: The vintage is given five stars in Michael Broadbent, *The Great Vintage Wine Book* (New York: Knopf, 1980).

92 **ullaged:** In bottled wines, the ullage is the air-filled gap between the top of the liquid and the bottom of the cork. If this space should grow owing to evaporation or leakage, the bottle is said to be "ullaged." In storage casks the air space is regularly filled with wine to prevent oxidation, and it is from this treatment that the word, by a sort of inversion, derives (*ouillage* = "refilling").

93 **'74:** "The vintage of '74 was a magnificent one and the grapes were so ripe, when picked and pressed, that the wines of that year were of a distinctly darker shade of gold than those of previous vintages, with a faintly pink sheen which made it easy to tell a '74 from any other vintage" (Simon, *Vintagewise*, p. 127). Broadbent calls it the "most renowned vintage of the period" and gives a detailed account of its special circumstances (*Great Vintage Wine Book*).

voice that breathed o'er Eden: John Keble, "Poems: Holy Matrimony."

mutatis decenter mutandis: "Making the appropriate changes decently."

vouchsafed: A jeroboam in the Bordeaux trade is six bottles, but in

Champagne it is a double magnum, or four bottles; the term thus has at least two "proper" applications.

93 **'70's:** "Good but far from plentiful" (Simon, *Vintagewise*, p. 127). **'92 and '93:** Simon calls '92 "a very delightful wine which also lasted very well"; as for '93, that was a year of "a glut of sunshine and grapes. . . . The quantity of wine made broke all past records, and what was so wonderful was that this amazing quantity of wine was so good—and so cheap." The wine was not, however, so "aristocratic" as that of 1892, and "after a mere dozen years in bottle, the '93's took a wrong turning: they became dark, flabby, beery. They were made from over-ripe grapes; they lacked balance and they could not stay the course" (*Notes on the Late J. Pierpont Morgan's Cellar Book, 1906* [London: Curwen Press, privately printed, 1944], pp. 8–10). **'98, '99 and 1900:** Simon says that the wine of '98 was "above the average" but eclipsed by the two following: '99 was "superlative" but in short supply; "the 1900 wines were fuller than those of 1899, softer and ready sooner, but they were no better" (*Vintagewise*, p. 135). Broadbent gives them three, five, and four stars, respectively (*Great Vintage Wine Book*, p. 341). To have three successive vintage years in Champagne was unusual.

94 **Moët:** Moët et Chandon, Épernay, the biggest of the Champagne houses, founded in 1743. It is now a part of the Moët Hennessy–Louis Vuitton Group.

St. Marceaux: De St. Marceaux and Co., Reims.

"the cool champagne at dinner": "I was a little tired, but the cool champagne at dinner brought me quite round" (Arnold to his wife, 26 August 1885, *Letters of Matthew Arnold, 1848–1888*, 2 vols. [London, 1895], 2:283).

95 **Graves:** Used without modification, as here, "Graves" usually means the white wines of the Graves district of Bordeaux, despite the fact that the best-known wines of the Graves are red. White Graves is made from Sémillon and Sauvignon blanc grapes.

Barsac: Commune of the Sauternes district, whose most famous sites are those of Château Climens and Château Coutet. All Barsac may legally call itself Sauternes, but some is sold under the Barsac appellation. It is traditionally held to be lighter than Sauternes, a distinction that Saintsbury evidently accepts.

95 **Sauternes:** The most famous of French sweet wines, made from Sémillon, Sauvignon blanc, and Muscadelle grapes that have been infected by the "noble rot," *Botrytis cinerea.*

Château Yquem: Properly Château d'Yquem, by all consent greatest of Sauternes.

Montrachet: Greatest of white Burgundies, from the Côte d'Or.

white Hermitage: About a quarter of the production of Hermitage is white, from Marsanne and, to a lesser extent, Rousanne grapes.

hocks: *Hock* is the term used generically in England for German wines, especially Rhine wines. It is supposed to be derived from English mispronunciation of Hochheim, a village on the Main near its confluence with the Rhine, officially a part of the Rheingau; its use goes back to the seventeenth century.

96 **blot on his wine-record:** I do not know when Thackeray may have done this, but see *Vanity Fair,* ch. 44, where, after dinner, Becky Sharp gives Sir Pitt Crawley "a bottle of white wine" that she pretends was "picked up for nothing[,] . . . whereas the liquor was, in truth, some white Hermitage from the Marquis of Steyne's famous cellar."

Carbonnieux or Olivier: Both among the best white wines of the Graves, or, more strictly, of the new (beginning in 1987) appellation of Pessac-Léognan.

Pouilly: Saintsbury probably has in mind Pouilly-Fuissé, from the Chardonnay grape in the Mâconnais, rather than Pouilly-Fumé, from the Sauvignon blanc, grown in vineyards along the Loire in Central France.

Coutet: One of the two leading châteaux of Barsac: see my note to p. 95.

Latour Blanche: A first growth of Sauternes, usually La Tour Blanche; it is ranked just after d'Yquem in the classification of 1855.

Meursault: Burgundy village on the Côte de Beaune, celebrated for its white wines: "The finer ones are surpassed by only a few great rarities among the dry white wines of France" (Frank Schoonmaker, *Encyclopedia of Wine*, 6th ed. [New York: Hastings House, 1975]). The year 1870 is classed among the best vintages in white Burgundy in the two decades before the onset of phylloxera (Broadbent, *Great Vintage Wine Book*, p. 265).

96 **Haut Sauterne of '74:** The name "Haut Sauterne" has no legal status. André Simon, writing in 1935, says that the term "usually covers a sweet white wine which one would expect to be just a little better than wine sold merely as 'Sauternes'" (*A Dictionary of Wine* [London: Cassell, 1935]). "Haut" cannot now be used under the laws of *appellation contrôlée* unless it is a part of the *appellation* itself (e.g., Haut-Médoc). Following the repeal of Prohibition in the United States, the name was much used for any white wine that its maker might choose to put in the bottle so labeled; the practice has now disappeared. The omission of the *s* at the end of "Sauternes" was standard on U.S. labels but is remarkable on a European bottling.

97 **Freytag's best novel:** Gustav Freytag, *Soll und Haben* (1855): "'At least not your terrible white Burgundy,' cried Guido Tronko. 'My veins are still swollen like cords from our last session'" ("'Nur nicht Ihren furchtbaren weißen Burgunder' rief Guido Tronko. 'Von unserer letzten Sitzung sind mir noch heute die Adern geschwollen wie Stränge'" [bk. 2, ch. 2]). Saintsbury says that the Germans have never produced a good novel, but that *Soll und Haben* is "perhaps the nearest approach" (*A History of the French Novel* [London: Macmillan, 1919], 2:18n).

Château Grillet or Grillé: Wine from a small property, with its own *appellation contrôlée*, in the Condrieu district on the Rhone, made from the Viognier grape (note that Saintsbury identifies this as a "white Hermitage"; evidently the Rhone districts were not, from the English point of view, very clearly discriminated). Saintsbury had once called someone's spelling Château Grillet as *Grillé* "absurd"; he then found some wine actually labeled with the "absurd" spelling and recanted his judgment. So here he is careful to offer both spellings (see A. Blyth Webster, "A Biographical Memoir," in *George Saintsbury* [London: Methuen and Co., 1945], p. 49).

97 **La Frette:** Not identified.

VI. HOCK, MOSELLE AND THE REST

99 **"chorus":** Thomas Love Peacock, "The War Song of Dinas Vawr," in *The Misfortunes of Elphin*, ch. 11, concluding lines.

"Auslese": "Selected"; one of the categories of superior wine according to the German classification.

100 **"to bring a blessing with it":** Perhaps Sir Walter Scott, *Kenilworth*, ch. 7: "I hope to find a use for it which will bring a blessing on us all." But perhaps not.

Ausonius's favourite river: The Latin poet Ausonius, though born at Bordeaux, devoted his best-known poem, *Mosella* (c. 371 C.E.), to the praise of that river.

"faked" . . . grape: As early as 1874 the Cologne Chamber of Commerce complained that no natural wines were produced on the Mosel, all being both sugared and diluted (*The Times*, 15 August 1874, quoted in Christopher Fielden, *Is This the Wine You Ordered, Sir?* [London: Croom Helm, 1989], p. 80).

"Mitre": The Mitre Hotel, High Street, Oxford.

1870: That is, after the German victory in the Franco-Prussian War and the establishment of the German empire.

101 **Berncastler Doktor:** The "Doctor," as the most famous vineyard of Bernkastel is called, after one of its former proprietors, Doctor Thanisch.

Scharzhofberg: A small vineyard on the Saar, producing one of the best wines of the Mosel-Saar-Ruwer.

Piesporter to Graacher: From villages of the former Middle Moselle region, now known as the Bereich Bernkastel, where all the best of the Moselle vineyards lie.

red **Moselle?:** No.

Assmanshäuser . . . Walporzheimer, Ober-Ingelheimer: The red wine of Assmannshausen on the Rhine, around the bend down-river from Rüdesheim but officially part of the Rheingau, is the most famous of German red wines. Walporzheim is in the Ahr Valley, the one German region that specializes in red wines, and Oberingelheim (or simply Ingelheim) in the Bingen district makes mostly red wines. In all of these places, the dominant variety for red is the Pinot noir (Spätburgunder).

102 **Prosper Mérimée . . . death:** Saintsbury had studied Merimée and his work in order to edit an English translation of Merimée's *Writings* (8 vols. [New York, 1905]); but I do not find this reference there.

Red Verzenay of 1868: The production of red and white still wines (Champagne natur or, since 1974, Coteaux Champenois) has always continued beside the trade in sparkling wine in Champagne. Sillery (see chap. 5, p. 90) was the most famous of the still whites, Verzenay, along with Bouzy, of the reds. All three are on the Montagne de Reims, where the Pinot noir dominates. According to André Simon, some producers attempted to revive a taste for still white Champagne during the depression years when the sales of Champagne fell off (*Vintagewise* [London: Michael Joseph, 1945], pp. 139–40).

Côte Rôtie: The "roasted slope," near Vienne, at the northern end of the Rhone district, producing a notable red wine from the Syrah grape.

Châteauneuf du Pape: Celebrated red wine from the Rhone, this from the southern end, on the left bank north of Avignon. Officially some thirteen varieties are allowed for Châteauneuf du Pape; the most widely planted varieties are Grenache, Syrah, Mourvèdre, and Cinsault.

Châtiments . . . Contemplations: Victor Hugo, *Les Châtiments* (1853), satiric and denunciatory poems written in exile; *Les Contemplations* (1856), a collection of lyrics divided between two volumes, *Autrefois* and *Aujourd'hui*.

Saint-Péray: White wine district on the right bank of the Rhone, making both dry and sweet, still and sparkling, wines from the

Marsanne and Rousanne grapes; the sparkling wine is most in demand. The wine was in vogue in the Second Empire. The district
of production is now less than two hundred acres.

102 **fiery rain:** The seventh circle of hell, where the sodomites run per-
petually under a rain of fire (*Inferno*, XIV). Why Saintsbury should
have regarded sparkling Bordeaux as more unnatural than any other
sparkling wine I am unable to say. Perhaps because, being good in
itself, it needs no further elaboration? But the same might be said
for Burgundy.

Picardan: Here Saintsbury seems to have made a mistake. The wine
called Picardan is not from the north but the far south of France, a
sweet wine made in the Bas Languedoc from the Muscat grape called
Picardan. There was in Saintsbury's day hardly any production of
wine in the *départements* that formed the old Picardy. André Jullien
(*Topographie de tous les vignobles connus*, 5th ed. [Paris, 1866], pp. 50–
52) reports that there was still a modest production of wine, both
red and white, at Laon, Soissons, and Château Thierry in the *dé-
partement* of the Aisne, but none evidently known as "Picardan."
Wines from Picardy would have been called *vins picard* rather than
"Picardan," which, *Le Grand Robert de la langue française* says, is
formed from *piquer* and *ardent*. Whatever wine Saintsbury meant
by "Picardan," he was consistent in disliking it. In *A History of the
French Novel* ([London, 1919], 2:435), Saintsbury says of a scene in
a story by Barbey D'Aurevilly, "Un Diner d'Athées," in which a character drinks off a bumper of Picardan, that the wine is "the one wine
in all my experience which I should consider fit *only* for an atheist."

vin d'Arbois: The region of Arbois, around the town of that name
in the Jura, makes wines of all colors and styles, but is specially
known for its *vin jaune*, which, like sherry, is developed under a yeast
film, but, unlike sherry, is not fortified. Apart from red, rosé, and
white table wines, Arbois also makes a *vin de paille*, that is, a wine
from raisined grapes; both this and the *vin jaune* are rarities.

103 **Calcavellos:** Usually spelled *Carcavelos*, a fortified white wine from
vineyards at the mouth of the Tagus; they have nearly disappeared

under the westward expansion of the city of Lisbon. In 1964 only thirteen hundred gallons were made, and Carcavelos is now spoken of as virtually a historic memory.

103 **Bucellas:** Portuguese white wine, from a small region northwest of Lisbon, made from the Arinto and Esgana Cão ("dog strangler") grapes. It is sometimes said that it was introduced into England after the Peninsular Wars, but it was in fact popular before that. Very little is now made.

104 **white Rioja:** The white wines of the Rioja district, on the river Ebro, come from Malvasia, Viura, Calagraño, and Grenache grapes and were typically aged in wood.

Najara: So spelled in Froissart's *Chronicles*, now usually *Nájera;* the site of a battle in the 1367 in which the Black Prince defeated the Spanish usurper Henry of Trastamara, an episode in the Hundred Years' War. Nájera is in what is now the Rioja wine district, but the illnesses that afflicted the Black Prince's troops were suffered at Valladolid, to which they withdrew after the battle and where they endured what were "probably malaria and dysentery" (Richard Barber, *Edward Prince of Wales and Aquitaine* [New York: Scribner's, 1978], p. 205).

"Priorato": The wine long known as Priorato is a red wine from Grenache and Carignane grapes produced in the Tarragona region and named after an ancient Carthusian priory. It is typically dark and of high alcohol content (a minimum of 13.5 percent is required for the denomination). Its export prospered for a time during the phylloxera years in France. Perhaps this is what Saintsbury had? I have found no Portuguese wine of this name. In a copy of *Notes on a Cellar-Book* that apparently once belonged to Saintsbury himself and is now the property of Isaac Oelgart, a marginal note against the name "Priorato" reads: "No: Lavrachio." But what was Lavrachio? In recent years Priorato wines have enjoyed a renewed prosperity and prestige.

Tent: The anglicized form of the Spanish word *tinto*, for "dark," "deep-colored," used by extension for red wine, *vino tinto*. What the word means in its English form, *tent*, is disputed. The English use goes back to the sixteenth century or earlier and, according to the *OED*, applied to all red wines from Spain. The *Oxford Companion to Wine* widens this to include Portugal—"strong red wine from Iberia." Hugh Johnson says, however, that *tent* applied specifically to red wines from the coastal region near Cadiz, particularly those from Rota, called "tintilla" or "tinta di Rota" (*Vintage* [New York: Simon and Schuster, 1989], p. 165). William Younger agrees, but adds that tent probably came also from Alicante and Malaga (*Gods, Men, and Wine* [Cleveland: World Publishing, 1966], p. 484). Frank Schoonmaker, however, defines "tintilla di Rota" as "a sweet red wine" (*Encyclopedia of Wine*, 6th ed. [New York: Hastings House, 1975], s.v. "Tintilla"), and that is certainly not what "tent" was in general.

Jan Read affirms that the term comes from the Tinta grape as grown in Madeira, from which came "the strong red wine so liked by the Victorians" (*The Wines of Spain and Portugal* [London: Faber and Faber, 1973), p. 234). A. D. Francis, in *The Wine Trade* (New York: Barnes and Noble, 1973), allows a number of possibilities: in the time of Pepys, "tent wine . . . came from Malaga, though this red wine originally came from a small area between Rota and San Lucar. . . . The name tent came to be applied to any heavy Spanish wine" (pp. 67–68). It seems safe to say only that "tent" was certainly red, almost certainly Spanish, and likely to originate along the south coast of Spain.

104 **Alicant:** Wine from the region of the city of Alicante on the Mediterranean coast of Spain. The wines, mostly red, are both dry and sweet and come, in part, from the Grenache (sometimes called "Alicante" in France) but more from the Monastrell grape. Wines from Alicante have figured in the English wine trade since medieval days (see the connection with "tent" in the preceding note).

Ampurdam: Ampurdán, the northeastern corner of Catalonia, on the French border, now much better known as the Costa Brava. The wine of Ampurdán is mostly red or rosé from Grenache and Carignane grapes. In 1975 the region was granted Denominación de Origen status as Ampurdán (or Empordà)—Costa Brava. Some Ampurdán wine is sweet and fortified, and that is what Saintsbury seems to have in mind.

104 **"matrimony"**: A mixture of foods or drinks, not confined to wines but including them. The *OED* cites the *Examiner* (London) in 1813: "that injudicious mixing of wines, which is called matrimony."

fifty or sixty years old: The phrase stands unaltered in the third edition of the book, so presumably it is no mistake. But where could one expect to get fifty- or sixty-year-old Ampurdam?

"Iberian or Trinacrian wine": "Night after night I have seen him eating his frugal meal, consisting but of a fish, a small portion of mutton, and a small measure of Iberian or Trinacrian wine" ("On a Pear Tree," in *Roundabout Papers* [1860–63]). *Trinacrian* means "Sicilian."

Marsala: A wine invented by the British to compete in the British market with the popular fortified wines of Spain and Portugal. It was originally made in 1773 by the English merchant John Woodhouse in the town of Marsala, Sicily. A purchase of Woodhouse's Marsala for use in his fleet by Lord Nelson in 1800 is said to have had much to do with establishing the fortunes of the wine. It was far more popular in nineteenth-century England than it has been since.

105 **brown Syracuse:** An old and superior Marsala. The 1862 catalog of W. and A. Gilbey describes it as "extremely old, with rich full flavour, somewhat like the Old East India Sherry." Jefferson bought Syracuse wine during his years as president (James M. Gabler, *Passions: The Wines and Travels of Thomas Jefferson* [Baltimore: Bacchus Press, 1995], p. 202).

American: There was an export trade in American wine in the years before Prohibition, but not a large one. One relatively substantial market for American wine in England was developed by the firm of Grierson, Oldham and Co., importers of Big Tree brand of California wine, sold in brown *bocksbeutel*-style flagons with a great redwood tree–stump molded on the side of the bottle.

105 **"ventris penetralia *raspat*"**: "It grated the innards." Teofilo Folengo (1491–1544), Italian "macaronic" poet (i.e., one whose verse mixes modern words with Latin endings into Latin verse). His major work is a burlesque narrative in twenty books called *Baldus* (1517). **Tokay**: A (mostly) sweet wine, the produce of the Furmint and other grapes, from Tokaj-Hegyalja in northeastern Hungary. It was long associated with the imperial courts of Russia and Austria. There are many stories, all in the superlative mode, about its extravagant richness and its fabulous powers. Tokay Essence, most fabulous of all, is made from the free-run juice from uncrushed, botrytized grapes, expressed only by the weight of the grapes themselves: it will keep, says André Simon, longer than "any other wine in the world" (*A Dictionary of Wine* [London: Cassell, 1935]), though it would be more accurate to call it a "lightly alcoholic syrup" (*Oxford Companion to Wine*). It is not ordinarily available for sale. Tokays are made in varying degrees of sweetness, according to the proportion of grapes in the mixture that have been afflicted with "noble rot."

106 **contradiction in terms:** Tokay had not only to endure republican but communist conditions. Saintsbury was essentially right: in the markets of the West, at any rate, Tokay has been in long decline. The results of the reconstruction of the wine industry in Hungary since the reintroduction of capitalist enterprise remain to be seen. **Carlowitz:** "The only Hungarian wine which ever attained a fair measure of popularity in England during the 'sixties. It is grown on the right bank of the Danube, thirty miles north of Belgrade, within the borders of Yugoslavia" (Simon, *A Dictionary of Wine*). Now known as Sremski Karlovci, it is produced in the autonomous Serbian province of Vojvodina. **Vöslauer:** Austrian red wine from the district of Vöslau, south of Vienna in the Baden region. An 1867 wine list of Harvey's identifies it as "Austrian claret." **after eating:** Not *more* drunk, but more quickly drunk: the presence of food in the stomach has been shown to retard the rate at which alcohol is absorbed into the bloodstream.

106 **Chianti:** The best-known of all Italian wines outside of Italy; the produce of Tuscany: Florence and Siena are the centers of its exploitation. It is based on the Sangiovese grape and, in Saintsbury's day, came from a much smaller zone of production than is now legally defined.

"wersh" sparkling Asti: "Wersh" is Scottish dialect, here meaning "insipid, tasteless." Asti Spumante (now simply Asti) from the Piedmont region of Italy, being made from the white Muscat grape, is typically not tasteless but to some palates rather too much informed by the characteristic taste and aroma of Muscat.

Lacrima Cristi: Wine grown on the slopes of Mount Vesuvius, in which case it is now known as Lacryma Christi del Vesuvio. The name has been widely appropriated in Italy for a sparkling wine that cannot claim to be "del Vesuvio."

lovely . . . pleasant: Adapted from David's lament over Saul and Jonathan: 2 Samuel 1:23.

pelting of any Pussyfoot: An ungenerous remark, since the actual Pussyfoot, William E. Johnson, had been pelted and blinded in one eye less than a year before *Notes on a Cellar-Book* appeared (see my note to p. 36).

107 **"British Wines":** Generally understood to mean wines made in Great Britain from imported grape concentrate; by this method, the producer avoids the tariff on imported wines and, paying only the domestic tax, can undersell the competition, though with an admittedly inferior product. The main product is fortified wine, sold as "British sherry" or "British port." Saintsbury, as do other writers, extends the term to include such traditional native compounds as ginger and rhubarb "wines."

108 *Oxford and Cambridge Magazine:* Founded in 1856 by the group of young men of whom William Morris and Sir Edward Burne-Jones were the center: it ran for twelve issues.

Michell: Edward Blair Michell (1843–?), the son of an Oxford clergyman; B.A., Magdalen College, 1865; a barrister, appointed legal adviser to the King of Siam in 1885. He published *Boxing and Spar-*

ring (1897), *The Art and Practice of Hawking* (1900), and *A Siamese-English Dictionary* (1892).

109 **Holly Tree Inn:** The eight-year-old boy who has run away with the seven-year-old girl in order to marry her announces at the Holly Tree Inn that "Norah has always been accustomed to half a glass of currant wine at dessert. And so have I" (Charles Dickens, "The Holly Tree: Second Branch," in *Christmas Stories* [1855]).

110 **Lord Bute:** John Stuart, third Marquis of Bute (1847–1900), undertook a revival of British winegrowing by establishing a vineyard of twenty acres at Castle Coch, near Cardiff, Wales, in 1877. It produced wine, both red (from the Gamay) and white, down to the First World War; the vineyards were pulled out in 1920. Saintsbury compares it to Picardan (see my note to p. 102): "Very little above [Picardan] I should put the not wholly dissimilar liquor obtained, at great expense and trouble, by a late nobleman of high character and great ability from (it was said) an old monkish vineyard in the Isle of Britain. The monks must have exhausted the goodness of that *clos;* or else have taken the wine as penance" (*History of the French Novel*, 2:453n.).

Saumur: Sparkling wine, Saumur mousseux, made in the region around the city of Saumur on the Loire, in Anjou, based on the Chenin blanc.

Vouvray: Upriver from Saumur on the Loire, in Touraine. Like that of Saumur, the sparkling wine of Vouvray is based on the Chenin blanc grape. Also like Saumur, Vouvray produces still wines.

Swiss imitations: The sparkling wines of Neuchâtel, for instance.

111 **Constantia:** Sweet wine made from red and white Muscadel grapes from the Groot Constantia estate, near Cape Town, South Africa, the oldest vineyard of the Cape. Constantia became a sought-after wine (particularly the red), and by the early nineteenth century it had a nearly legendary reputation in England and in other European countries. Phylloxera and other misfortunes put an end to the production of the sweet Constantia. The estate, now owned by the government, still produces wine but no longer grows any Muscadelle (or Muscat), the source of the "real Constantia" to which Saintsbury refers.

111 **Bishop Creighton:** Mandell Creighton (1843–1901), historian, Bishop of Peterborough (1891–97) and of London (1897–1901). Like Saintsbury, Creighton had been a postmaster (scholar) of Merton, which he entered the year before Saintsbury; unlike Saintsbury, he was elected to a Merton fellowship, in 1866. He was Saintsbury's closest friend at Oxford (see p. 144). Creighton left Merton in 1875 for the rural parish of Embleton, Northumberland, where he remained until taking up a professorship at Cambridge in 1884. His major scholarly work was a *History of the Papacy* (1882–94).

Trevelyan . . . Richardson: This was a strange episode. Sir Walter Calverley Trevelyan (1797–1879) was a distinguished amateur scientist and, through his wife, Paulina, a member of the Pre-Raphaelite circle formed around Ruskin and Rossetti. A lifelong and ardent advocate of temperance, Trevelyan was the first president of the United Kingdom Alliance, in 1853, and of the National Temperance League, in 1856. He had inherited a great cellar at his estate of Wallington, Northumberland, where it lay untouched and only rarely visited. "Here was port laid down at the time of Culloden. Here magnums of hock acquired by the fourth baronet on Sir Walter Blackett's death in 1777. There tokay bought from Edward Wortley in 1752" (Raleigh Trevelyan, *A Pre-Raphaelite Circle* [London: Chatto and Windus, 1978], p. 124). On his death, Trevelyan left his cellar to another nondrinker, to be used for "scientific purposes" (*The Times*, 17 April 1879). This was Dr. (later Sir) Benjamin Ward Richardson (1828–96), a prominent London physician, a prolific author, and the main force among the English medical profession in the cause of total abstinence: alcohol was, in the doctor's phrase, "the devil in solution."

The press was much amused by the legacy of a great gift of wine from one teetotaler to another. If the doctor were to sell the wine at auction, as it was supposed he would do in order to raise money for "scientific purposes," would he do evil, it was asked, so that good might come? Richardson himself wrote a good-natured article, "Sir Walter Trevelyan's Wine Cellar"—"one of the most noted cellars in the whole of the kingdom." He had known Trevelyan only slightly, was embarrassed by the situation in which the legacy put him, and did not know what to do with the wine. His article concludes with the hope that someone can show him "how one total abstainer can make use of wine which another total abstainer has left him in trust, for the purposes of Science" (*Macmillan's Magazine* 41 [January 1880]: 241). I have not learned what the final disposition of the cellar was.

111 **Champagne riots:** In 1911, in protest against the inclusion of the region of the Aube in the officially defined region of Champagne production. The cellars of producers suspected of using grapes from outside the vineyards of the Marne were looted and destroyed. Years of bad harvests and hard times in the Champagne region gave the riots a special ferocity, and they were put down only with the help of a large number of troops.

112 **"as it strikes a contemporary" foreigner:** Saintsbury means the official classification of 1855. The phrase quoted is an allusion to Browning's poem "How It Strikes a Contemporary."

Mouton Rothschild: Château Mouton-Rothschild was promoted to the rank of the *premiers crus* in 1973.

"Sawedwardgeorgeeaarllyttonbulwig": From Thackeray's *The Memoirs of Mr. Charles J. Yellowplush* (1838), the chapter called "Mr. Yellowplush's Ajew," in which Sir Edward George Earle Lytton Bulwer-Lytton, the novelist and politician, is ridiculed.

> "When I asked him his name, said, in a thick gobbling kind
> of voice,—
> "Sawedwadgeorgeeaarllittnbulwig."

Later, at dinner, "Sawedwad" asks:

> "By the bye, Sir John what wemarkable good clawet this is; is
> it Lawose or Laff—? . . . this clawet is weally nectaweous."

Note that Saintsbury has not got the name quite right: again, he must be quoting without book.

clumsy Philip: Philip Firmin, told that he can't expect to afford claret if he marries without money, replies: "'We'll do without. Meantime I will take what I can get!' . . . He tosses off a pint of my

Larose, and gives a great roar of laughter, as if he had said a good thing." Philip then breaks a glass as well (Thackeray, *The Adventures of Philip*, ch. 32).

113 **Château Citran:** In the commune of Avensan, Haut-Médoc; Château Citran is now classified as a Cru Grand Bourgeois Exceptionnel.

VII. SPIRITS—HOLLANDS AND WHISKY

114 **Lantern-Land:** The land to which Pantagruel and Panurge make a pilgrimage in order to consult the Oracle of the Bottle: François Rabelais, *Gargantua and Pantagruel*, bk. 5, chs. 32–47. The message of the Oracle is the epigraph to *Notes on a Cellar-Book: "Trinc!"*

proof: The measure of alcohol in a liquid by volume. In British measure, "proof" is 57.10 percent alcohol by volume: anything higher is "over proof" (O.P.), anything lower is "under proof" (U.P.). The American proof measure is 50 percent alcohol.

"squareface" or London or Plymouth: For London and Plymouth gins, see p. 134. "Squareface" is Schiedam gin, from the square bottle in which it was sold (Eric Partridge, *Dictionary of Slang*, 8th ed.). Schiedam is the center for the production of Dutch gin ("Hollands" in England, "Jenever" in the Netherlands). Hollands is derived from a malted barley mash distilled in pot stills at a lower level of alcohol than American and English gins; it has in consequence a strong and distinctive character of its own and is meant to be drunk by itself rather than as an element in mixed drinks.

116 **J.D.K.Z.:** "Johannes DeKuyper Zoon," founded in the seventeenth century. The best-known of the Schiedam distillers; theirs were the black, square bottles that gave rise to the term *squareface* (see my note to p. 114).

Wynand Fockink: Wijnand Fockink, established in 1679 in Amsterdam, particularly known for curaçao as well as for gin.

Bols: Erven Lucas Bols, Amsterdam, founded in 1575 at Schiedam, the first of Dutch distillers.

Collings and Maingay: Not further identified.

116 **Jansen's:** Herman Jansen, gin distiller of Schiedam.

117 **man-of-war . . . Malta and Gozo:** The H.M.S. *Sultan*, a battleship of the second class, nine thousand tons, ran aground off Malta in March 1889 and was abandoned. A few days later the ship sank in a storm, but it was successfully raised in August and taken into Malta.

(rye or buckwheat?): Dutch gin was packed in cases filled with hemp husks (James Mew and John Ashton, *Drinks of the World* [New York: Scribner's, 1892], p. 139).

"midland sea": Swinburne, "The Triumph of Time," st. 41.

"Green Rhinoceros" or "Purple and Yellow": I have found no reference to these names, but perhaps by "Green Rhinoceros" Saintsbury means the blended Scotch whisky brand "Green Stripe," introduced in the 1860s by Andrew Usher, the first of the proprietary brands of blended Scotch whiskies. Such whiskies were much lighter than the traditional single-malt Scotches and were the means by which Scotch became popular outside of Scotland. But they also set off a long and unsatisfactory legal battle over the definition of "Scotch whisky."

118 **"octave":** Strictly speaking, the eighth part of a pipe, thirteen and a half gallons *(OED)*.

"anker": A Dutch or German measure, "10 old wine gallons" *(OED)*. It is still used in the Scotch whisky trade as the name of a small cask.

"Scotus . . . Iernen": Claudian, "On Stilicho's Consulship, II," 251: "totam cum Scottus Hivernen movit": in Saintsbury's adaptation, "The Scot rivals Ireland."

"Welsh" whisky: A pot-still distillery at Bala, North Wales, was built in 1887 by J. Lloyd Price and operated until the First World War: see Wynford Vaughan Thomas, "The Rise and Fall of Welsh Whisky," *Wine and Food* (Summer 1962): 80–83.

119 **"Quis separabit?":** "Who shall separate us?," the motto of, among other bodies, the Irish Guards.

number of distilleries . . . hundred: *Harper's Manual* (London,

1914) gives these figures: 149 distilleries in 1903; 153 in 1905; 132 in 1908, and 120 in 1912.

119 **"crash"** . . . **earlier:** This was not earlier than his residence in Scotland, as Saintsbury seems to say, but in 1898; the trade generally had enjoyed a boom with the growing popularity of blended whisky in the 1890s; the failure of the Edinburgh firm of whisky blenders Pattisons, Limited, in 1898, created many other failures in its wake but gave the Distillers Company, Limited, an even stronger hold on the market (Sir Robert Bruce Lockhart, *Scotch: The Whisky of Scotland in Fact and Story* [London: Putnam and Co., 1951], pp. 66–68).

120 **Clyne Lish:** Usually written *Clynelish,* from Brora, Sutherlandshire, founded in 1819 by the Duke of Sutherland; the original distillery is no longer active.

Smith's Glenlivet: From the Minmore distillery, Banffshire, founded in 1824. In 1880 John Gordon Smith, son of the founder, obtained the legal right to the exclusive use of *Glenlivet;* others who use the name must hyphenate it with some other name. The distillery is now owned by Seagram's.

Glen Grant: From the distillery at Rothes, Morayshire, founded in 1840 on the Glen Grant Burn, Speyside, by J. and J. Grant; now owned by Seagram's.

Talisker: Distilled at Carbost, Isle of Skye, since 1830; a property of United Distillers and Vintners.

Lagavulin: A distillery going back to the eighteenth century, at Lagavulin, Isle of Islay, the property of the Distillers Company, Limited.

Ardbeg: Near Lagavulin, Isle of Islay, established in 1815.

Caol Isla: Or written *Caol Ila,* Isle of Islay, founded in 1846; a property of United Distillers and Vintners.

"Long John": From the Ben Nevis distillery at Lochy Bridge, Fort William, Invernesshire, founded by Long John Macdonald in 1825.

Glendronach: Founded 1826 in the valley of the Forgue, near Huntley, Aberdeenshire; owned by Allied Distillers.

120 **"toddy":** Whisky compounded with hot water and sugar.

whisky-and-soda, or potash: "Potash-water," carbonated water with potassium bicarbonate added *(OED).*

121 **spoilt . . . terribly:** The Central Control Board, established in 1915 to regulate the liquor trade in wartime, made the dilution of spirits to 25 under proof compulsory in 1916; in the next year this was made 30. Spirits remained under wartime controls until November 1919. The Central Control Board expired in 1921.

"B.B.B.": Bed, breakfast, and bath: but why "dissenting chapels"?

122 **Jamesons, John and William:** John Jameson and Son was founded early in the nineteenth century at Dublin, devoted to pot-still whisky. Its Bow Street Distillery ceased operations in 1971, but the brand is maintained by the Irish Distillers Group, Limited. William Jameson, John's brother, operated the Marrowbone Lane Distillery, Dublin. Irish whisky today is reduced to a few brands, produced either by the Irish Distillers Group, Limited, formed in 1966, or by the firm of Cooley, established in 1987.

Roe: George Roe and Co., Thomas Street Distillery, Dublin, founded in 1757, among the largest distillers of Irish whisky in the nineteenth century.

Power: John Power and Sons, Limited, of the John's Lane Distillery, Dublin, goes back to the late eighteenth century. It was one of the three firms remaining in business that joined to form the Irish Distillers Group.

E. and J. Burke: I find nothing about them in the standard references on the subject.

Persse: The Nun's Island Distillery, Galway, had been operated by the Persse family since 1840. According to Alfred Barnard (*The Whisky Distilleries of the United Kingdom* [London, 1887], p. 397), there was no other distillery in all of Connaught then: Saintsbury's "another unnamed from Galway" must therefore have been from some earlier date or from an unlicensed still.

Coleraine: The Coleraine Distillery, Coleraine, Londonderry, founded in 1820.

122 **Comber:** There were two distilleries in Comber, County Down, the Upper Distillery and the Lower Distillery, both owned by the same firm.

Cork: Barnard, *Whisky Distilleries of the United Kingdom*, lists three distilleries at Cork in 1887: the North Mall, the Midleton, and the Glen.

Colonel Welman: Perhaps William Henry Dowling Reeves Welman, who entered the army in 1847 and retired as colonel from the Wiltshire Regiment in 1882 (*Army List*, 1883).

"J.J.": John Jameson.

123 **"And the soft wings . . . cover him round":** Abraham Cowley, trans., Virgil, *Georgics*, line 17.

Misses O'Toole: In *Ratlin the Reefer* ([1836], vol. 2, ch. 8), by Edward Howard (but often attributed to Captain Marryat), the hero, after having drifted to sea in a small boat, is towed into Cork harbor and entertained by a family of Irish peasants; then the whisky is brought out and a dance follows with the Misses O'Tooles, "really enchanting, though stockingless creatures." The hero falls asleep despite the confused uproar—"stramash"—of the dance, but dimly feels "as if some soft-rounded figure had caught me in her arms. . . . I was lapped in Elysium."

"Return of the Wild Geese": The Irish who left the country to take military service with the French were called "Wild Geese."

Canadian Club: The property of Hiram Walker and Sons. Canadian whiskey is typically a blended whiskey, mainly from corn (maize), with barley malt, rye, or wheat according to the particular formula of the distiller.

home brands: Elsewhere Saintsbury writes that "the only brand of American whisky I ever liked" was called "Mount Vernon" (*A Second Scrap Book* [London: Macmillan, 1923], p. 261). Mount Vernon was originally a straight rye whiskey. The brand still exists, but it is now a blended bourbon.

singeing . . . casks: Formerly, American bourbon was required by law to be aged in new oak barrels that had been charred inside; the barrels now need not be new. Canadian whiskey may be but is not required to be so aged.

124 **rummer:** "Rummer" has nothing to do with rum but is the German *Römer* anglicized.

specially . . . itself: Something seems to be omitted following "specially": "specially made and provided for the purpose"?

VIII. SPIRITS—BRANDY, RUM AND GIN, WITH SOME EXOTIC THINGS

125 **"feints" and "forshotts":** A "feint" (or "faint") is "the impure spirit which comes over first and last in the process of distillation" *(OED);* a "foreshot" is specifically the feint that comes over first.

126 **Cognac:** Legally, Cognac is the brandy distilled from grapes grown in certain districts of the Charente and Charente-Maritime *départements* of France. Like *Champagne,* the name has been borrowed all around the world.

"Armagnac": Armagnac is now, like Cognac, legally defined by the laws of *appellation contrôlée.* Armagnac comes from the old Armagnac region of Gascony, southwest France; it was not much exported until the middle of the nineteenth century.

"Eau de Vie de Marc": Brandy distilled from pomace, called *marc* in French. The Marc de Bourgogne was particularly prized. In Italy and California the product is called grappa.

127 **as such:** The initialisms *vsp* or *vsop* stand for "very special pale" brandy and "very special old pale" brandy. What exactly those, and brown brandy, are, I do not know.

hot brandy and water: Charles Dickens, *Pickwick Papers,* e.g., ch. 20: "I should like a glass of brandy and water warm, Sam. Where can I have it? . . . The hot brandy and water was speedily placed before him." Brandy is mentioned forty-four times in *Pickwick* (Cedric Dickens, *Drinking with Dickens* [Goring-on-Thames: Elvedon, 1983], p. 30).

Dr. Opimian: "The doctor always finished his day with a tumbler of brandy and water: soda water in summer, and hot water in Winter" (Thomas Love Peacock, *Gryll Grange*, ch. 5). Dr. Opimian's name alludes to the celebrated vintage of 121 B.C.E. in the time of the Consul Opimius.

128 **"good for de tomac"**: Captain Marryat, *Peter Simple*, vol. 2, ch. 11: the women selling coconuts containing rum rather than milk to the sailors said of it: "Dis very fine milk. Very good for de tomac."

129 **"spoken against in the Scriptures"**: Henry Fielding, *Jonathan Wild*, ch. 14: "Let us have a Bowl of Punch, a Liquor I the rather prefer, as it is nowhere spoken against in Scripture."

130 **Wallace of Kelly**: Robert Wallace (1773–1855), of Kelly, Ayrshire, member of Parliament and postal reformer. Wallace owned property in the West Indies and would thus have had the means to obtain good rum.

Dora the Detestable: "Dora" was the acronym of the Defense of the Realm Acts, under which various controls and restrictions on alcoholic drink were enacted beginning in 1914. I suppose Saintsbury means that, given the difficulty of obtaining new stocks, he drank up—or gave to others—what he already had on hand.

Wedderburn: The heaviest style of West Indian rum, originally produced in Jamaica: it is slow-fermented and pot-distilled.

gorge of the Avon: Where the city of Bristol lies, and where the firm of Harvey operated.

methods of distillation have altered: True: the darker, full-bodied rums of tradition were distilled in pot stills, by the batch method; the lighter rums are the product of continuous distillation.

the more rum the more sugar: Rum is made from molasses, which is what is left *after* sugar has been crystallized from the juice of the sugar cane.

Java and Queensland rum: Java rum (or "Batavia arrack") is a light-bodied, aromatic rum; Queensland is a center for "rum production of good quality" (Oscar A. Mendelsohn, *The Dictionary of Drink and Drinking* [New York: Hawthorne Books, 1965]).

Tantalus-case: A tantalus is a locked case for holding bottles or decanters in order to deter theft; it cannot be opened without a key but allows the containers to be seen—hence it "tantalizes." An exposition at which bottles are displayed but not sold would do the same.

132 *genièvre:* Juniper, the dominant element in the "botanical" flavoring of gin.

two hundred years ago: The neglect is illustrated by the fact that there were from six thousand to seven thousand dram shops selling gin in London by 1736; the "hasty action" was the Gin Act of 1735, which laid a tax of £1 per gallon on gin and raised the cost of a license to £50. This severe remedy failed to work, and the act was repealed in 1742.

bad name worse: With his print entitled *Gin Lane* (1751) depicting the horrors of drunkenness from cheap gin; this in contrast to the healthy good nature apparent in his print entitled *Beer Street.* Effective legislation controlling the gin trade was passed in 1751, in part through the effect of Hogarth's print.

"gin palace": The earliest use of this term recorded in the *OED* is in 1834.

upbraided Hazlitt for drinking gin: I have not found where they do this, but William Hazlitt, the essayist and critic, was a standard butt for the Noctes Ambrosianae group, especially John Wilson and John Gibson Lockhart. The "Noctes Ambrosianae" was a series of dialogues appearing in *Blackwood's Edinburgh Magazine* from 1822 to 1835.

expenses of her stay: Lucy Dormer is the girl: "Lucy inwardly had been disgusted by the gin and water, knowing nothing of its history. Her father, who had not always been punctual in paying his wine-merchant's bills, would not have touched gin and water, would not have allowed it to contaminate his table" (*Ayala's Angel* [1881], ch. 3).

134 **"refined," and not simply distilled:** There are different methods. Gin may be a compound of botanical flavorings and neutral spirits; or it may be distilled from a grain mash through the flavoring botanicals ("original distillation"); or it may be neutral spirits redistilled through the flavoring botanicals ("redistillation").

134 **as "meller" as he expected:** Tennyson, "The Northern Cobbler":
the cobbler, a reformed drunkard, keeps a square quart bottle of gin
unopened before him in his shop so that he can confront and triumph over his "enemy"; he imagines that it must, after many years,
be "fine and meller" (line 101).

"Old Tom": A style of gin sweetened with sugar. The origin of
the name is disputed: some labels show a cat, indicating one etymology; another is that "Old Tom" was a distillery employee. And
there are others. The cat theory is given with considerable cir-
cumstance by Lord Kinross, *The Kindred Spirit* (London: Newman
Neame, 1959).

"unsweetened London": The standard gin of England and the
United States: dry, flavored neutral spirit.

"Plymouth": Gin midway in character between London and Hollands, originally the product of Plymouth and traditionally the gin
for the drink called pink gin (gin colored by a dash of Angostura
bitters). Cyril Ray writes that "I have never been able to understand
how George Saintsbury could have thought [Plymouth gin] 'more
delicate in flavour'" since, Ray says, "it is more pungent" (*In a Glass
Lightly* [London: Methuen, 1967], p. 31).

Arrack: The term is generic, indicating any "local" spirit: distillates
from palm sap or rice in the East Indies, from milk in Mongolia,
from dates in the Middle East, from grain or fruit in Greece, and
from apples in Normandy have all been called "arrack" or "arak" or
"arrac" or "raki" or "rack." The word comes from the Arabic and
means "juice." What Saintsbury means is perhaps a West Indian
spirit from molasses.

Vauxhall: Vauxhall, together with Ranelagh and Cremorne, was a
pleasure garden on the banks of the Thames, a short distance upriver from London. A too-free indulgence in arrack would, of
course, have a "racking" effect the morning after. I cannot explain
the "alleged constituent."

"Aquavit": From the Scandinavian *akvavit* (*aqua vitae*, eau-de-vie,
"water of life"); again, a term almost generic, but in Scandinavia

meaning neutral spirits (from grain or potatoes) flavored with caraway and other seeds and spices. Norway is now a distant third to Sweden and Denmark in the production of aquavit.

134 *Forest Life: a Fisherman's Sketches in Norway and Sweden: Forest Life in Norway and Sweden: Being Extracts from the Journal of a Fisherman*, by the Reverend Henry Garrett Newland (London, 1858), first published as *Forest Scenes in Norway and Sweden* (1854).

"corn-brandy": Kornbranntwein is neutral spirit from grain, usually rye (Mendelsohn, *Dictionary of Drinks and Drinking*). Aquavit was originally a true brandy, or eau-de-vie, distilled from wine; it was later produced from grain and then, frequently, from potatoes. When it was distilled from grain, it would have been in fact Kornbranntwein, or simply Korn in Germany, where one may still find a spirit of that name. Kornbranntwein may also be flavored.

Russian Revolution: The imperial government prohibited vodka during the war; after the revolution the Bolsheviks attempted to make prohibition general but did not succeed.

135 **"Raki":** See my note to p. 134.

"plum spirit": Distillates from plums include the Alsatian Quetsch, the Mirabelle of Lorraine, and the Slivovitz of Bosnia and Serbia. Saintsbury evidently means the latter: see next note.

"spell itself with a *we*": Vojvodina, an "autonomous province" incorporated into Serbia as a part of Yugoslavia in 1918; it is a center of production for Slivovitz. In Dickens's *Pickwick Papers* (ch. 34), Mr. Weller, in answer to the question "Do you spell it [his name] with a 'V' or a 'W?'" answers, "I spells it with a 'V.'"

IX. LIQUEURS

138 **"Berrichonne":** The word is the adjective form of the old French province of Berry.

"Génépi des Alpes": I have not found any further information about this liqueur apart from its appearance in a list of J. L. Denman, London, 1862. *Génépi* means "gentian" *(Gentiana lutea)*, the plant whose root contributes a bitter element to many aperitifs (e.g., Campari, Suze).

139 **Chartreuse:** Made at the monastery of the Grande Chartreuse (*Chartreuse* is the French for "Carthusian"), near Grenoble, from early in the seventeenth century, though the final formula was not achieved until the middle of the eighteenth century. It is now made by a private, secular firm, under the direction of the Carthusian order. The most familiar form is green; yellow Chartreuse is sweeter and less potent; there is a third style, the original "elixir," pure white and very potent: this is sold through pharmacies. The recipe is of course a closely guarded secret, but the guessed-at ingredients make an interesting list: "The liquor is believed to be made by the maceration and distillation of balm leaves and tops as the principal ingredient, with orange-peel, dried hyssop-tops, peppermint, wormwood, angelica seed and root, cinnamon, mace, cloves, Tonkin beans, *Calamus aromaticus,* and cardomoms" (*Standard Encyclopedia of the Alcohol Problem,* vol. 2, s.v. "Chartreuse"). E. S. Dallas, in *Kettner's Book of the Table* ([1877; reprint, London: Centaur Press, 1968], s.v. "Chartreuse"), states that "it is chiefly made from a plant having the beatific name of Angelica Archangelica." Another authority contents itself with the remark that "Chartreuse contains 130 herbs" (Alec Gold, ed., *Wines and Spirits of the World* [London, Virtue, 1968], p. 622). At the time that Saintsbury wrote, the Carthusians were still in exile in Spain: see my note to p. 140.

Curaçao: Named for the Dutch island in the Caribbean. It is (or was) made from the peel of the green orange grown on the island and is the model for the many other orange-based liqueurs. The name is now generic.

Liqueurish Brentford: An allusion to the comic notion of "the two kings of Brentford," from the Duke of Buckingham's farce, *The Rehearsal* (1672).

Benedictine: Distilled at Fécamp, Normandy, not by monks but by a private company. The name is said to refer to the order of the Italian monk who originally devised the formula, which, reportedly, contains twenty-seven different dried herbs and plants, among them tea, juniper berries, balm, cloves, and nutmeg (Hurst Hannum and Robert S. Blumberg, *Brandies and Liqueurs of the World* [Garden City, NY: Doubleday and Co., 1976], p. 164).

139 **Trappistine:** Based on Armagnac and made by the Trappists at the Abbaye de Grâce de Dieu in the department of the Doubs.

140 **"Père Kermann":** A liqueur associated with Father Kermann, a French monk who worked in eighteenth-century Brazil before returning to France, where he produced herbal liqueurs at Bordeaux that were particularly popular in South America and Africa. Some labels showed a bearded monk's head.

Chartreuse or Certosa: Certosa is an Italian liqueur named after a Carthusian (Certosa) monastery near Pavia (Oscar A. Mendelsohn, *The Dictionary of Drink and Drinking* [New York: Hawthorne Books, 1965]) and is said to be red (Alexis Lichine, *Alexis Lichine's Encyclopedia of Wines and Spirits*, 5th ed. [1967; reprint, New York: Knopf, 1987]).

exiled: A wave of anticlerical feeling in France led to the passage of the Associations Act in 1901, by which many religious orders were expelled from France, the Carthusians among them. The Carthusians left their monastery and distillery in 1904 and reestablished themselves at Tarragona, Spain, where they still were at the time Saintsbury was writing.

141 **vanished Opera Colonnade:** Justerini and Brooks had been at Number 2, the Colonnade (later Pall Mall), at the bottom of the Haymarket, since 1749 and remained there until 1953. The Colonnade itself was pulled down in 1895.

"Grand Marnier": A version of curaçao devised in 1880 by Marnier-Lapostolle of Paris, notable as being based on Cognac. It comes in two strengths, "cordon rouge" and "cordon jaune."

Vanderhum: Meaning, roughly, "what's its name?," a liqueur native to South Africa, whose basis is the orange called *nartje* (there are other spellings). In another place Saintsbury, speaking of Charles-Augustin Sainte-Beuve's favorite mixture of "rum and curaçao as a liqueur," says "it is a pity that he did not know the excellent Cape liqueur called Vanderhum, which is not a mixture but a true hybrid of the two" (*A History of the French Novel* [London, 1919], 2:286n). I have not seen it elsewhere stated that Vanderhum is related to rum.

141 **Maraschino:** A liqueur made from the sour Marasca cherry (the name is derived from *amaro*, "bitter"); in Saintsbury's day it came exclusively from the town of Zara (now Zadar), in Dalmatia, then in Austrian hands. Both the fruit and the kernel are used in the product. According to Dallas, it is (or was) "fermented first with honey, then with the leaves and kernels of the fruit, and is at last distilled and sweetened with sugar" *(Kettner's Book of the Table)*. Contemporary procedure is different: the stones are distilled separately; the pulp is then fermented and pressed. The juice from the press is not used for Maraschino (it becomes the basis for a cherry brandy): rather, the pomace is added to the cherry-stone distillate, and from this compound the liqueur is distilled (Hannum and Blumberg, *Brandies and Liqueurs of the World*, pp. 194–95).

Noyau: "Colorless or slightly pink sweetened liqueur with the flavor of oil of almonds, or of peach or cherry kernels" (Lichine, *Alexis Lichine's Encyclopedia of Wines and Spirits*). The name is the French word meaning the stone or kernel of a fruit such as the peach, cherry, plum, and apricot, and the flavor is derived from amygdalin, the substance found in almonds and other fruit kernels. It is a French invention. The earliest citation in the *OED* is from 1787.

142 **maraschino punch:** Perhaps the "cherry-gin" that was "always kept in preparation" for George IV (Christopher Hibbert, *George IV: Regent and King, 1811–1830* [New York: Harper and Row, 1973], p. 322). A cherry gin punch is described by Abraham Hayward thus: "Pour half-a-pint of gin on the outer peel of a lemon, then a little lemon-juice, sugar, a glass of Maraschino, about a pint-and-a-quarter of water, and two bottles of iced soda-water" (Percy Fitzgerald, *The Life and Times of William IV* [London: Tinsley Brothers, 1884], 2:246n).

142 **Martinique can hold its own with Zara:** Zara, in Dalmatia, is where Maraschino was distilled (see my note to p. 141). According to G. Selmer Fougner (*Along the Wine Trail, II: Distilled Liquors* [New York: The Sun, 1934], p. 71), "The most celebrated Noyau comes from the island of Martinique." Another explanation may be that the finest of Noyaus was produced by the firm of Champion in Bordeaux, and that the original M. Champion came from Martinique (Peter Hallgarten, *Spirits and Liqueurs* [London: Faber, 1979], pp. 151–52). Hence Martinique can hold its own with Zara. The remark seems to refer to the appearance rather than to the quality or character of the liqueurs.

143 **Luxardo and Drioli:** The two leading distillers of Maraschino, originally operating in Zara but now in Padua and Venice, respectively.

"Water of Cherry": Kirschwasser, the cherry eau-de-vie traditionally produced in Alsace and, on the other side of the Rhine, in the Schwarzwald; hence German Kirsch may be called Schwarzwalder.

"Water of Gold": Goldwasser, traditionally distilled in Danzig and usually identified as "Danziger Goldwasser." Goldwasser is flavored with anise, caraway, cinnamon, and other spices, and its plain clarity is made interesting by the addition of gold flakes. There was also a Silver Water, lemon-flavored. Dorothy Margaret Stuart remembered Saintsbury in retirement at Bath drinking Goldwasser: "It amused him to tilt the flask to-and-fro so that I might see the flimsy lambent flakes of gold-leaf swimming inside" ("The Last Years," in *A Last Vintage* [London: Methuen, 1950], p. 22).

Kümmel: *Kümmel* is the German word for caraway (*Carum carvi*), a type of anise. It is also the German word for cumin (*Cuminum cyminum*). The plants cumin, caraway, and anise are all closely related and difficult to distinguish, as the confused reference of the word *kümmel* shows. The caraway-flavored spirit called Kümmel (Kümmelbrantwein in full) originated in Holland and was soon produced in Germany; famous Kümmels were also made in Latvia and in Russia, places with which Saintsbury evidently associates it.

144 **"ça chatouille le palais":** "That tickles the palate." Cf. La Fontaine,

"Paté d'anguille," *Contes:* "Un paté d'anguille: ce mets/Lui cha-
touillait fort le palais."

144 **"Parfait Amour":** A sweet, purplish liqueur produced in France and
Holland. Tom Moore's Fudge family were drinking it in Paris in
1818. Dallas says that it "is made of the bitter zest of limes, molli-
fied with syrup, with the spirit or roses, and with spicy odours. It is
in fact a kind of orange bitters spoilt" *(Kettner's Book of the Table).*
Rosolio: Sometimes spelled "Rossolis" or "Rosoglio" or "Rossoli."
Originating in Italy, it was popular in France so long ago as the early
seventeenth century and was a favorite of Louis XIV, though he seems
to have had a very special royal version of it. The name—from *ros
solis,* or "dew of the sun"—expresses a very enthusiastic judgment.
There is a plant of that name—the sundew—which has been supposed to be an element in the liqueur but is not. There are various
descriptions of Rosolio: for example, that it is compounded of "burnt
brandy, sugar, and the juice of sweet fruits, such as cherries and mul-
berries" (James Mew and John Ashton, *Drinks of the World* [New
York, 1892], p. 165); the *OED* adds "raisins." Lichine, in *Alexis Lichine's Encyclopedia of Wines and Spirits,* says that Rosolio has "a taste
of roses," and Harold J. Grossman (*Grossman's Guide to Wines, Spirits, and Beers,* 5th ed. [New York: Scribner's, 1974], p. 315) says that
"petals of red roses" are part of the mix. One wonders whether roses
were part of the original recipe or whether they found their way in
through confusion as to the meaning of the name? Or perhaps the
brief remark of Hallgarten is more to the point: "le rossoli," he writes,
"were liqueurs of many recipes" (*Spirits and Liqueurs,* p. 22).

Samuel Titmarsh suffered: Thackeray, *The Great Hoggarty Diamond* (London, 1841): Titmarsh's aunt, Mrs. Hoggarty, keeps an "infernal sour black-currant wine" that she calls "Rosolio" (ch. 1).

Cassis: A low-alcohol liqueur from black currants (*cassis* in French):
not to be confused with the *appellation contrôlée* white wine from the
village of Cassis in Provence, traditionally drunk with the bouilla-
baisse of Marseilles.

Anisette: Liqueur flavored with the seed of the anise plant, aromatic and carminative, a favorite principle of Mediterranean aperitifs. The most famous anisette is that of Marie Brizard of Bordeaux, and according to the *OED* the proper name is in fact Anisette de Bordeaux, which is made not with the European anise *(Pimpinella anisum)* but with the star anise *(Illicium anisatum)* native to the far east. Anisette de Bordeaux is still produced by the successors to the original eighteenth-century firm, but with European anise.

144 **Crème de Menthe:** Liqueurs may be roughly defined as "sweetened spirits," but some are sweeter than others, notably the class of "crèmes": the mint in crème de menthe is peppermint.

"**Cointreau**": A style of curaçao made in Angers since 1849 by the distillers of that name.

"**drink with His Grace and Chartres**": Alexander Pope, "Epistle to a Lady," lines 63–64: "Now deep in Taylor and the Book of Martyrs, / Now drinking citron with his Grace and Chartres." Pope's editors define "citron" here as "citron-water, brandy flavored with citron- or lemon-peel." The *OED* agrees, and calls the name "obsolete." Pope's poem is from 1735. "Chartres" is Colonel Francis Charteris (1675–1732), a notorious profligate.

Water of the Star . . . whereof many men have died: Cf. Revelation 8:11: "And the name of the star is called Wormwood: and the third part of the waters became wormwood; and many men died of the waters, because they were made bitter."

the greatest of Roman poets meant: Lucretius, *De Rerum Natura*, line 936: "foul-tasting wormwood." "Worse sense," since absinthe was held to be not merely foul-tasting but injurious to health.

146 "**went into the Church**": Thackeray, *The Newcomes*, ch. 1: "a fellow of very kind feeling, who has gone into the Church since."

star-smaragd: *Smaragd* is an old form of *emerald*.

X. BEER, CIDER, ETC.

148 **small beer:** The *OED* says this is "beer of a weak, poor, or inferior quality." It might be domestically brewed "table beer," or, if com-

mercially produced, "brewed from a second mashing after the strong wort had been drawn off the mash tun" (T. R. Gourvish and R. G. Wilson, *The British Brewing Industry, 1830–1980* [Cambridge: Cambridge University Press, 1994], p. 105). No beer is now sold under this name.

148 **Cobbett . . . *some* keeping:** In William Cobbett's *Cottage Economy*, the brewing of beer is the first subject considered: "Any beer is better than water, but it should have some strength and some weeks of age, at any rate" (para. 64). Cobbett's celebration of beer was set off by his detestation of tea drinking: tea was a "destroyer of health, an enfeebler of the frame, an engenderer of effeminacy and laziness, a debaucher of youth and a maker of misery for old age" (*Cottage Economy* [London: Peter Davies, 1926), para. 29).

lober agol: White ale, according to John Bickerdyke [Charles Henry Cook] in *The Curiosities of Ale and Beer* ([London, 1889], p. 163), was a Devonshire specialty originally made of malt, hops, flour, spices, a secret ingredient called "grout," and eggs; a later version was ordinary ale to which eggs and flour were added. A white ale in Cornwall was called "Laboragol" (p. 164). The "grout" in white ale is perhaps identified by one of the meanings listed in the *OED:* "some plant used as a flavouring for beer before the introduction of hops."

"pullet-sperm in the brewage": As Falstaff complains of the sack given him: *Merry Wives of Windsor,* III, v, 31.

149 **his second:** George Borrow, *Wild Wales,* chs. 49 and 72. On his first visit to Bala, in Wales, Borrow has an ale brewed in the inn that was "admirable, equal to the best that I had ever before drunk—rich and mellow, with scarcely any smack of the hop in it, and though so pale and delicate to the eye, nearly as strong as brandy." On his return the ale is very bad, "the last in the cask."

Bass: The product of the Bass Brewery at Burton-on-Trent, founded in 1777; for many years it specialized in bitter beer for the India trade, but after the middle of the nineteenth century it greatly expanded its domestic trade and became the largest brewery in the kingdom.

150 **Mr. Smillie and Mr. Thomas:** Leaders of two great British trade unions. Robert Smillie (1857–1940) was president of the Scottish Miners' Federation from 1894 and of the Miners' Federation of Great Britain from 1912 to 1921; he was also a founder of the Independent Labour Party. James Henry Thomas (1874–1949) was leader of the National Union of Railwaymen and directed the railway strike of 1919; he was a Labour member of Parliament from 1910. He remained loyal to Ramsay Macdonald after the formation of the coalition "National" government in 1931 and was, in consequence, expelled from and ostracized by the union to which he had devoted his life.

Younger's: William Younger, the leading Edinburgh brewer. Scottish ale was traditionally stronger and sweeter than English.

Mr. Lang: Andrew Lang (1844–1912), Saintsbury's good friend and fellow-laborer among the journalists of London. They were associated on the *Saturday Review*, among other publications, and in the Savile Club. Saintsbury published several articles on Lang after Lang's death. Like Saintsbury, Lang was a scholar and a writer of legendary copiousness and speed, who published poems, classical studies and translations, studies in religion and folklore, histories and biographies, essays and novels, and an immeasurable quantity of miscellaneous journalism. Roger Lancelyn Green estimated that "even excluding" the mass of Lang's anonymous journalism, his known work would fill three hundred volumes (*Andrew Lang: A Critical Biography* [Leicester: Edmund Ward, 1946], p. x). Where in the jungle of Lang's writing the remark about Cambridge may be found I have no idea.

151 **reinstatement there:** Saintsbury had been elected an honorary fellow of Merton in 1909.

"lay-fratre Petro": R. H. Barham, "A Lay of St. Dunstan" in *The Ingoldsby Legends* (1840). The lay-brother Peter, Dunstan's servant, orders his master's magical broom-stick to bring him beer and drowns in the resulting flood.

152 **Lord de Tabley:** John Byrne Leicester Warren (1835–95), third and

last Baron De Tabley, of Tabley House, Cheshire, a numismatist, botanist, and collector of bookplates; he published a number of books of poetry, without much response, until a selection appeared in 1893.

152 **flip:** "A mixture of beer and spirit sweetened with sugar and heated with a hot iron" *(OED)*. The heated iron was called a "flip-dog." Oscar A. Mendelsohn particularizes the eighteenth-century formula: "a quart of bitter beer spiked . . . with a gill of rum and heated with a flip-iron or loggerhead" (*The Dictionary of Drink and Drinking* [New York: Hawthorne Books, 1965]). In modern usage it has come to mean any alcoholic drink with a beaten egg added.

mum: Of this the *OED* knows only that it was "a kind of bitter beer brewed in Brunswick"—etymology uncertain. The first reference that the *OED* gives is from 1640: "I thinke you'r drunk with Lubecks beere or Brunswicks Mum." It appears to have been a wheat beer, like the modern *Weißbier* associated with Berlin. Mendelsohn, however, gives a quite different description: "an old English brewed beverage prepared from various grains and pulses together with a hotch-potch of aromatic vegetable matter" *(Dictionary of Drinks and Drinking)*. Edward Spencer says that it was a "species of unsophisticated ale, brewed from wheat, or oats, with a little bean-meal occasionally introduced" (*The Flowing Bowl* [London: Stanley Paul, 1925], p. 40). André Simon, writing in 1946, says of mum that it "is still popular in Brunswick" (though Brunswick ceased to exist in 1946: *A Concise Encyclopedia of Gastronomy* [London: Collins, 1952]). See also next note.

The Antiquary: Oldbuck, the antiquary, "despising the modern slops of tea and coffee," had with his breakfast "a glass of a sort of beverage called 'mum,' a species of fat ale brewed from wheat and bitter herbs, of which the present generation only know the name by its occurrence in acts of parliament, coupled with cider, perry, and other excisable commodities. . . . Lovel, who was seduced to taste it, with difficulty refrained from pronouncing it detestable" (Walter Scott, *The Antiquary*, ch. 11).

152 **"The Ryme of Sir Lancelot Bogle":** W. E. Aytoun and Sir Theodore Martin, "The Rhyme of Sir Lancelot Bogle, a Legend of Glasgow," in *The Book of Ballads, edited by Bon Gaultier*, new ed. (London, [1851?]): "Of Usquebaugh and rum, you will find I reckon some, / Besides the beer and mum, extra stout." In the poem, a parody of Mrs. Browning, the Glaswegians attacking Sir Lancelot's castle get drunk on the contents of the castle cellars and are themselves slaughtered.

153 **Guinness:** Strong, heavily hopped porter ("stout") brewed by the Guinness family in Dublin since 1759.

light porter: The best way to define "light porter" is, I suppose, to say that it is not "stout": see the preceding note. Porter itself is an ale brewed from a dark roasted malt, the darker the stouter. The name comes from "Porter's beer" or "Porter's ale," meaning a beer drunk by porters or "the lower class of labourers" *(OED)*.

Rotterdam: The address suggests that the beer in question may have been from the Oranjeboom brewery, founded in Rotterdam in 1671 and closed in 1990.

154 **"offended by them":** Robert Burton, *The Anatomy of Melancholy*, pt. 1, sec. 2, memb. 2, subsect. 3.

perry: Perry is to pears what cider is to apples.

155 **mead or metheglin:** Mead is fermented from a solution of honey; metheglin (Welsh, *meddyglyn*) is a spiced mead, though the term has been used for plain mead.

XI. "MIXED LIQUORS"

156 **"brandy, etc.?":** "Those juggling compositions, which, under the name of mixed liquors, slur a great deal of brandy or other poison under less and less water continually, until they come next to none, and so none at all" ("Confessions of a Drunkard," first published in 1813).

"bishop": "A sweet drink variously compounded," but typically using wine, oranges or lemons, and sugar, is the first sense given in the

OED; it then adds an alternative meaning, which is Saintsbury's "mulled and spiced port."

156 **"cups"**: A mixed drink not clearly distinguishable from other names for mixed drinks: by some definitions, "bishop" (see preceding note) is a "cup." But a cup is often a summer drink, and a cool drink: wine with fruit juice, lemonade, or soda added is a possible minimal definition; most would add spirits or liqueur and various garnishes. For one of Saintsbury's recipes, see p. 160.

"Swedish punch": A sweetened and flavored Batavian rum, sold bottled.

157 *The Three Clerks:* Trollope, *The Three Clerks*, chs. 9 and 10. The drink in question was in fact bishop, referred to as a "doctored tipple."

claret: Claret or other red wine.

point of view: The *OED* cites this passage from Saintsbury in its definition of "Pope," but adds other illustrations to support its definition as a "hot spiced drink of mull based on any of various wines"—including Tokay and Champagne.

158 **negus**: Named for its inventor, Colonel Francis Negus, in the time of Queen Anne: a mixture of wine, especially port or sherry, hot water, sugar, and flavorings (e.g., lemon and nutmeg, or a tamarind, as in the passage quoted in my note below).

Dr. Slammer's card: Charles Dickens, *Pickwick Papers*, ch. 2: "'Oh! I see.' said the stranger, half aside, 'negus too strong here—liberal landlord—very foolish—very—lemonade much better—hot rooms—elderly gentleman—suffer for it in the morning—cruel—cruel.'"

Mr. Winterblossom: Philip Winterblossom, the elderly sensualist who is "president" of the table d'hôte at the spa of St. Ronan's Well in Walter Scott's novel of that name. His after-dinner ritual goes thus:

> "And Dinah, bring the sugar—the soft East India sugar, Dinah—and a lemon, Dinah, one of those which came fresh to-day—go fetch it from the bar, Toby—and don't tumble downstairs, if you can help it. And Dinah—stay, Dinah—the nutmeg, Dinah, and the ginger, my good girl—And, Dinah—

put the cushion up behind my back—and the footstool to my foot, for my toe is something the worse of my walk with your ladyship this morning to the top of Belvedere. . . . And, Dinah," continued the president, "lift up my handkerchief— and—a bit of biscuit, Dinah—and—and I do not think that I want anything else—Look to the company, my good girl. I have the honour to drink the company's good health—will your ladyship honour me by accepting a glass of negus? I learned to make negus from old Dartineuf's son. He always used East India sugar, and added a tamarind—it improves the flavour infinitely." (*Saint Ronan's Well*, ch. 2)

158 **children's parties:** The *OED* cites this passage from Leslie Stephen, in 1874: "The difference between the stiffest of nautical grogs and the negus provided by thoughtful parents for a child's evening party." But what went into it?

("screeching hot, ye divil"): The Irish gentleman's order at the Ballinasloe inn for "some hot wather—screeching hot, you devil" (Thackeray, *Irish Sketch Book* [1843], ch. 23).

159 **before spoken of:** See p. 134.

Mr. Tudor: In *The Three Clerks:* see my note to p. 157. The scene of Alaric Tudor's sufferings was Tavistock.

162 **Mercury . . . Apollo:** Presumably Saintsbury means the languages of commerce and of poetry.

wreck of the *Carmilhan*: Longfellow, "The Musician's Tale: The Ballad of Carmilhan," from *Tales of a Wayside Inn:* but this says nothing about a golden cricket-ball or a coin-filled casket, though tradition says that the ship was laden with treasure.

163 **Dickens:** "Let's rinse our mouths with a drop of burnt sherry": *Pickwick Papers*, ch. 41. "Burnt" here means "made hot."

***Hunted Down* . . . burnt brandy:** In "Hunted Down" (1860), the villain attempts to collect a life insurance policy on a gentleman whom he supposes he has reduced to a hopeless and lethal addiction to hot brandy.

"confusion": Perhaps Leviticus 20:12? "And if a man lie with his daughter in law, both of them shall surely be put to death: they have wrought confusion; their blood *shall* be upon them."

XII. BOTTLES AND GLASSES

164 **Balclutha, desolate:** From James McPherson's *Poems of Ossian,* 1762 ff.

165 **Veronica:** James Boswell, *Life of Johnson,* 15 August 1773.

166 *bocksbeutel* **flasks of Steinwein:** The *bocksbeutel* (goat's scrotum) shape, almost circular and flat-sided, is traditionally used for the wines of the Main region of Germany. Of these, the wines from the Stein vineyard in Wurzburg are among the best-known and have given their name as a sort of generic term for the wines of the Main.

"kicked" bottom: The so-called punt, the indentation at the bottom of certain wine bottles, originally unavoidable because of the process of manufacture and still retained in some bottles, though for no utilitarian purpose except in the Champagne bottle, where it allows for extra strength in the bottom.

167 **Powells':** The Whitefriars Glass Works of James Powell and Sons, 26 Tudor Street, Whitefriars, manufacturers of lamps, lusters, chandeliers, decorative glass, etc. They were among the manufacturers used by William Morris to make glass according to his designs. Their showroom was at 11 Conduit Street.

168 **Mr. Benson:** W. A. S. Benson and Co., art metal workers, silversmiths, and electrical engineers, 83 New Bond Street.

pilgrim bottle shape: The costrel, a bottle with an ear or ears so that it could be hung from the pilgrim's waist or shoulder.

"hen-master": The decanter intended to hold the contents of a tappit-hen?

Charles O'Malley: According to the Count, one may throw a wine glass in a man's face to signify "denial and displeasure," but in response to an insult one should throw a decanter: "a cut-glass decanter, well-aimed and low, I have seen do effective service" (Charles Lever, *Charles O'Malley* [1841], ch. 7).

168 **Sterne's body:** Laurence Sterne, the writer, was buried on 22 March 1768 in a new burying ground in Paddington, near the intersection of Edgware Road and Oxford Road (now Street). The body was stolen from the grave, probably on the next night, and reappeared for dissection at the anatomy amphitheater in Cambridge. The doctor presiding, recognizing the body as Sterne's, sent it back for reburial (Arthur H. Cash, *Laurence Sterne: The Later Years* [London: Methuen, 1986], pp. 328–32).

169 **"broke by dozens":** *The Adventures of Philip*, ch. 22.

170 **"Brimmers" and "bumpers":** Not glass shapes but full glasses of any shape. E. S. Dallas, in *Kettner's Book of the Table* ([1877, reprint, London: Centaur Press, 1968], s.v. "Bumper"), says that there is a distinction between the two terms: "A brimmer is a glass so full of wine that it touches the brim. But this may happen by force of attraction—the wine climbing up to the brim, and leaving a slight hollow in the central surface. Add a few more drops of wine, and this central depression will not only be filled up, but a bump of wine will arise like a hill in the centre of the glass, which may then be described as a bumper."

"skylight": The unfilled portion at the top of the glass.

171 **approximate Reims to Saumur:** That is, Champagne to one of its imitations.

172 **Dom Pérignon's great discovery:** Pérignon (1639–1715), chief cellarer of the Benedictine Abbey of Hautvillers, by tradition called the inventor of Champagne. He did have much to do with its refinement.

"while it was day": Cf. John 9:4: "I must work the works of him that sent me, while it is day." If this passage is what Saintsbury has in mind, and if, as I suppose, he means that part of his life in which he could drink freely, it is a somewhat bold stroke to interpret Christ's injunction to mean drinking Champagne.

172 **the drunkards:** The gluttons in the sixth circle of the Inferno are submerged in mud under a stream of rain, hail, and snow, with the dog Cerberus barking over them. "Thirst" does not appear to be an element.

or a fruit "comport": *Tazza* is Italian for "cup": the word is applied to large and ornate wine cups made for ceremonial purposes. *Comport* is a corrupt form of "compote," a dessert dish raised on a stem.

Fuit and ***fuimus:*** "It has been"; "we have been" (and are no more).

XIII. CELLAR ARRANGEMENTS

173 **"come at my command":** *Billee Taylor,* by Edward Taylor and Henry Pottinger Stephens (1880), a musical comedy in which the heroine assumes the position of her worthless lover as a lieutenant in the navy (vocal score published in London, 1881).

174 **Kensington Gardens:** Saintsbury lived during his boyhood at No. 31, Pembridge Villas, between Notting Hill Gate and Westbourne Grove (Dorothy Jones, *King of Critics* [Ann Arbor: University of Michigan Press, 1992], p. 5).

west of Kensington: The house was at 75 Gunterstone Road: Saintsbury bought the lease in 1882.

176 **Domdaniel:** A great submarine hall presided over by a magician; in English literature, "Domdaniel" figures in Robert Southey's *Thalaba, the Destroyer* (1801), where it is a palace "under the roots of the sea." **"house is finished":** Death.

keeping the book regularly: The sequence of Saintsbury's residences is not quite clear but is roughly thus: from 1882 to 1887, 75 Gunterstone Road, West Kensington, the house with the cellar; 1887–91, Fulbourn, Cambridgeshire; 1891–95, Reading. These last two were the "country houses." Saintsbury's London rooms were on Great Ormond Street. In 1895 he moved to Edinburgh, first to Murrayfield House and then, in 1899, to 2 Eton Terrace.

177 **early eighteenth century:** Murrayfield House, where Saintsbury lived from 1895 to 1899.

177 **"thousand dozen of wine":** Thomas Love Peacock, *Crotchet Castle*, ch. 2: "In the cellar of my friend, Mr. Crotchet, there is the talismanic antidote of a thousand dozen of old wine."

178 **house in Edinburgh itself:** The house was at 2 Eton Terrace, where Saintsbury lived from 1899 to 1915.

179 *ut conviva satur:* Horace, *Satires*, I, 119: "like a satisfied guest" (will quit life in contentment).

CONCLUSIO AD DIVERSOS

181 **Barmecide:** The prince in the *Arabian Nights* who entertains a beggar at a dinner of imaginary dishes. When the beggar enters into the joke, he is rewarded with a real feast: see p. 185.

Dorat: Claude-Joseph Dorat (1734–80), playwright and poet.

182 **"soul-*diathesis*":** As a medical term, *diathesis* means "a constitutional predisposition or tendency" *(OED)*.

subdolous: Crafty, cunning. The reference is presumably to the American element in the British prohibition movement.

St. Paul and the practice of Christ: For Christ, no doubt the miracle at Cana is meant, as well as the Last Supper; for Paul, perhaps his injunction to "use a little wine for thy stomach's sake" (2 Timothy 5:23).

184 **Pigott caught the *Times:*** Richard Pigott sold *The Times* forged letters implicating Charles Parnell, the champion of Irish home rule, in the Phoenix Park murders, 1882, which *The Times* used in attacking Parnell. When the forgery was discovered, *The Times* had to pay heavy damages and suffered much loss of prestige. Saintsbury had prevented the *Saturday Review* from buying the letters when Pigott offered them: see *The History of "The Times," 1884–1912* (London: The Times, 1947), pp. 43–89; Saintsbury, *A Last Scrap Book* (London: Macmillan, 1924), pp. 273–76.

185 **Walz's *Rhetores Graeci:*** Ernst Christian Friedrich Walz, *Rhetores Graeci*, 9 vols. (Stuttgart and Tübingen, 1832–36).

Grand Cyrus: *Artamène ou le Grand Cyrus*, a romance in ten volumes (1649–53) by Mlle. de Scudéry, notorious for its length. Saintsbury said that "I now really know the *Grand Cyrus,* though even now I will again not say that I have read every one of its perhaps two million words, or even the whole of every one of its more than 12,000 pages" (*A History of the French Novel* [London, 1917], 1:154n.).

185 ***The Earthly Paradise:*** Twenty-four verse narratives by William Morris (1868–70).

Sims Reeves: (John) Sims Reeves (1818–1900), the leading English tenor of his day in opera, oratorio, and recital. St. James's Hall, demolished in 1905, stood on the north side of Piccadilly.

"Adelaida": Perhaps Beethoven's "Adelaide," opus 46, for soprano or tenor, is meant.

Burne-Jones: That is, a painting or drawing by the English artist Sir Edward Burne-Jones (1833–98).

records of meals and wines discussed: In the old sense of "consumed."

186 **Rosa Timmins's volunteer assistant:** Thackeray, "A Little Dinner at the Timmins's" (1848). A French chef, who has "volunteered" to construct a dinner, proposes so expensive a meal that Mrs. Timmins is obliged to send him away.

189 **"shass-caffy":** Thackeray, *Pendennis,* ch. 4.

203 **shandygaff:** Beer and ginger beer.

imperial *quart:* That is, a quarter of an imperial gallon, or a little more than a liter.

good drinkers: The budget, introduced on 19 April 1920, tripled the taxes on spirits, raised those on beer from seventy to one hundred shillings a barrel, and doubled those on wine. *The Times* called these "very heavy indeed, far heavier than was expected" (20 April).

Armstrong's: H. E. Armstrong (1848–1937), professor of chemistry, London Institution, 1871–74; Central Technical College, South Kensington, 1884–1913: "the doyen of British chemists" *(Dictionary of National Biography).* His letter appears in *The Times,* 8 April 1920.

A SENTIMENTAL CELLAR

208 **"Oracle of the Bottle":** In Rabelais: see the note on the title page. "Bacbuc" in the next sentence is the "pontiff" who presides over the Holy Bottle.

"You have willed it": "Vous l'avez voulu, Georges Dandin, vous l'avez voulu": Molière, *Georges Dandin*, I, ix.

209 **"Hid in the sacred treasure of the past":** John Dryden, *Don Sebastian*, III, i, 184.

cup of Nantz: Brandy from Nantes, on the Loire. In Smollet's *Peregrine Pickle*, ch. 13, Commodore Trunnion, having had a severe fright, is comforted with "a cup of Nantz."

210 **the top in England:** Presumably 1710, when the Tories took power under Harley and Bolingbroke.

Our Ben or his son Herrick: The poets Ben Jonson (1572–1637) and Robert Herrick (1591–1674), the latter one of the self-styled "sons of Ben."

211 **not partaker of them:** I can find nothing quite like this in scripture. Exodus 29:33? "And they shall eat those things wherewith atonement was made, to consecrate *and* to sanctify them: but a stranger shall not eat *thereof*, because they *are* holy."

"sweet silent thought": Shakespeare, Sonnet 30.

212 **Dr. Dee:** John Dee (1527–1608), Fellow of Trinity College, Cambridge, mathematician and astrologer, reputed to be a magician. Dee's *speculum*, or mirror, a piece of solid glass the size of an orange, is preserved in the British Museum. With this and other forms of glass or crystal he conducted "scrying" sessions, in which one could see the secrets of past and future.

THE BOUNTIES OF BACCHUS

213 **Mr. Fisher:** Herbert Albert Laurens Fisher (1865–1940), scholar, politician, and administrator, and president of the Board of Education since 1916. He advocated part-time education up to age

324 / NOTES TO PAGES 213-20

eighteen through "continuation schools" rather than setting the school-leaving age at fourteen.

213 **the U.K.A. and the C.E.T.S.:** The United Kingdom Alliance and the Church of England Temperance Reformation Society: see my note to p. 31.

"either a god or a beast": Aristotle, *Politics*, bk. 1, ch. 2: "either a beast or a god."

214 **Sir Henry Thompson:** Thompson (1820–1904), first baronet, surgeon, astronomer, artist, writer, and host, famous for his "octave" dinners: eight courses for eight people at eight o'clock.

215 **"nectar":** See my note to p. 55.

216 **Frederic II:** "Oh, how good it is to pray and fight," an English Protestant's remark on Frederic, quoted in Lord Macaulay's essay "Frederic the Great" (1842).

217 *populus vult decipi:* "The people wish to be deceived. [Let them be deceived]": attributed to Cardinal Caraffa.

silent spirit: A term for grain neutral spirit such as is used in blending Scotch whisky.

218 **"the unending endless quest":** Longfellow, "Dedication to G.W.G.," line 16.

"WHITE"

219 *The Loyal Garland:* "Song LIII: An Excellent Song," in *The Loyal Garland, Containing Choice Songs and Sonnets of Our Late Unhappy Revolution*, 4th ed. (1671). In the edition published by J. O. Halliwell (London, 1850), the lines Saintsbury quotes are given thus:

> For her lips two brimmers of claret,
> Where first I began to miscarry;
> Her breasts of delight
> Are two bottles of white,
> And her eyes are two cups of canary.

220 **hardly even hock:** The *OED* neither confirms nor denies Saintsbury's argument about the older meaning of "white" applied to

wine, though "wine that isn't red" does seem to be the traditional sense.

"OBRIAN"

221 **Haut Brion:** See my note to p. 78.

"fill up each vein": J. Woodfall Ebsworth, ed., *The Roxburghe Ballads* (Hertford, 1881), IV:47. The line as printed there shows a slight variation from Saintsbury's text: "With a flood of *Obrian*, we fill up each vein."

Saint-Evremond: Charles de Saint-Denis, Sieur de Saint-Évremonde (1614–1703), soldier, writer, and epicure; he lived in exile at the English court from 1661.

222 **double-edged account:** "Conversation de M. de Saint-Evremond avec le Duc de Candale," in "Portraits Divers," *Oeuvres de Saint-Evremond* (Paris, 1927), 3:288–307.

Les Côteaux: The most refined connoisseurs in the seventeenth century were facetiously called members of the "Ordre des Coteaux" because they could distinguish not only the best wines but the very slopes (*coteaux*) that they came from.

LE TEMPS JADIS: WALLET II

223 *A Lay . . . of the College:* Written in 1865, when Saintsbury was at Merton, by Reginald Copleston (afterward Bishop Metropolitan of India), a mock-heroic poem about a Guy Fawkes bonfire for which the entire college was "gated" for a week. The copy in the Merton library was a gift from Saintsbury (information from the Fellow Librarian, Merton College).

224 **Mr. Wilkins:** Henry Musgrave Wilkins (1823–87), Fellow of Merton, 1848–87, librarian and dean from 1851.

Creighton: Saintsbury's friend Mandell Creighton: see my note to p. 111.

225 **Enfield's *Speaker*:** William Enfield, *The Speaker, or Miscellaneous*

Pieces Selected from the Best English Writers (1774), a widely used text for elocution.

225 **Mr. Burke himself:** Edmund Burke (1729–97), the statesman, writer, and orator.

Randolph: John James Randolph, Fellow of Merton from 1840.

226 **Christopher in Pall Mall East:** Wine merchants at 43 Pall Mall, S.W. (later on Jermyn Street).

finest year of the century: "The best year of the decade," André Simon more modestly calls '65 (*Vintagewise* [London: Michael Joseph, 1945], p. 124). It was a '65 Krug that Saintsbury calls a "winy wine" (p. 91, above).

the song: One version goes thus:

> I saw Esau kissing Kate,
> The fact is we all three saw:
> For I saw him
> And he saw me
> And she saw I saw Esau.

Tanqueray: George Tanqueray and Co., wine merchants, 5 Pall Mall East.

227 **"Barton and Guestier":** Firm of wine merchants in Bordeaux, established in 1725 by Thomas Barton, an Irishman. The firm is now owned by Seagram's.

228 **Coningham of Regent Street:** Coningham and Son, 11 Regent Street.

Samuel Scott: Sir Samuel Scott (1772–1849), London banker, and his son Samuel (1807–69) after him were the ostensible owners of Château Lafite from 1821 to 1866; they were in fact acting for the owner, Mme. Lemaire, who did not wish to see the estate divided on her death but wanted it to pass intact to her son: the abolition of the law of primogeniture made this impossible, so a fictitious sale was arranged (Clive Coates, *Grands Vins* [Berkeley: University of California Press, 1995], p. 46). Scott is said to have raised the price of Lafite so high that only the English aristocracy could afford it (Edmund Penning-Rowsell, *The Wines of Bordeaux* [London: Michael

Joseph, 1969], p. 111). But he would have been acting under the instructions of the real owner, and, in any case, the estate was maintained to a high standard throughout the Scott years.

228 **Rothschilds:** Baron Nathaniel de Rothschild bought Château Mouton in 1853; Baron James de Rothschild bought Lafite in 1868.

Larose as 72s.!: "My good fellow, that claret, though it is a second growth, and I can afford no better, costs seventy-two shillings a dozen" (*The Adventures of Philip*, ch. 32; see my note to p. 112).

THE ORDER OF DRINKS

229 **"Te(a) *venient die*":** Virgil, *Georgics*, IV, 466: "[He sang] of thee as day drew nigh."

cocoa-*nib* infusion: The *OED* defines "cocoa-nib" as "the cotyledon of the cacao seed, being one of the states in which it is sold."

231 **"foaming grape of Eastern France":** Tennyson's elaborate way of saying "Champagne" (*In Memoriam*, cxxxi); the wine is being drunk at the wedding feast that closes the poem.

"would have gone anywhere": "Now, for lobster salad and champagne in an honourable manner, Miss Costigan [otherwise Miss Fotheringay] would have gone anywhere" (Thackeray, *Pendennis*, ch. 13).

233 **the four spirits:** I take it that these are whisky, gin, rum, and brandy.

THE QUALITIES OF WINE

234 **great translator:** Omar Khayam and Edward Fitzgerald's translation of the *Rubaiyat*. Such lines as these are meant: "But still a Ruby kindles in the vine" and "Wine! Wine! Wine! / Red Wine!— the Nightingale calls to the Rose / That sallow cheek of hers to incarnadine."

235 **an author:** That is, Saintsbury.

Dukes of Clarence out of Pussyfoot leaders: According to tradition, the Duke of Clarence was drowned in a butt of Malmsey.

235 **great novelist . . . pewter pot:** Not identified: George Meredith?

236 **Tom Brown the Elder:** Tom Brown (1663–1704), English hack writer, satirist, pamphleteer.

Sir Thomas Browne: Sir Thomas Browne (1605–82), the author of *Religio Medici* and *Hydriotaphia*.

Lockhart: John Gibson Lockhart (1794–1854), editor and critic, the son-in-law and biographer of Sir Walter Scott. I have not found his reference to Brown's poem.

Southey: Robert Southey (1774–1843), poet laureate and miscellaneous writer.

237 **it never seemed right to him:** See "The Order of Drinks," pp. 229–33.

THE CELLAR

239 **"Duque d'Alba":** The seventeenth Duque d'Alba (1878–1953), sportsman and Spanish ambassador to Great Britain, 1939–45, was descended from the Duke of Berwick, one of James II's illegitimate sons by Arabella Churchill, whose titles were attainted in 1695. Hernando Fitzjames-Stuart (1882–1936), fifteenth Duke of Penaranda, was the Duke of Alba's brother.

240 **Pendennis:** "The Marquis of Steyne . . . had ordered any quantity of his precious, his priceless Amontillado, that had been a present from King Ferdinand to the noble marquis, to be placed at the disposal of Mr. Arthur Pendennis. . . . The invalid was greatly invigorated by it" (*Pendennis*, ch. 53).

241 **never will:** The vineyards of Madeira, after being devastated by oidium and by phylloxera, were replanted mostly to inferior varieties: see pp. 59–62 and notes.

point of view: *Cimelia* means "treasure." I suppose Saintsbury means that only Edmund Burke, the champion of the old order, could adequately express the worth of what had been lost.

242 **Gautier:** Théophile Gautier. Saintsbury edited Gautier's *Scenes of Travel* (Oxford, 1886).

243 **"square-face":** As Hollands gin was called: see p. 114.

244 **with his name on it:** For Louis Roederer's refusal to sell dry Champagne, see p. 90.

Tantae molis erat: Virgil, *Aeneid,* I, 33.

No Thoroughfare: By Wilkie Collins and Charles Dickens (1867). I find no reference in the story to any "ghastly roof curtaining."

245 **F. L. Berry:** Of the long-established (1698) firm of wine merchants, Berry Brothers and Rudd, St. James's, London.

Joyous Gard: The Joyous Gard is Lancelot's castle in the Arthurian stories.

LE TEMPS JADIS; WALLET V., 90'S AND LATER

248 **Sala:** George Augustus Sala (1828-96), prominent Victorian journalist and editor. I have found no evidence of any connection between Sala and Saintsbury, but probably there was one.

"La Chenette": Not identified.

"Wine of Migraine": "This curiously named French (Burgundian) centre makes good red wine" (Oscar A. Mendelsohn, *The Dictionary of Drink and Drinking* [New York: Hawthorne Books, 1965]).

SELECTED LIST OF WORKS CITED

Allen, H. Warner. *Sherry and Port*. London: Constable, 1952.

——. *The Wines of Portugal*. London: George Rainbird in association with Michael Joseph, 1963.

Ayto, John. *The Diner's Dictionary*. Oxford: Oxford University Press, 1993.

Barnard, Alfred. *The Whisky Distilleries of the United Kingdom*. London: Harper's Weekly Gazette, 1887.

Bickerdyke, John [pseud. Charles Henry Cook]. *The Curiosities of Ale and Beer*. London: Swan Sonnenschein, 1889.

Blakemore, Trevor. "London Restaurants of Fifty Years Ago." *Wine and Food*, no. 65 (Spring 1950).

Bradford, Sarah. *The Englishman's Wine*. London: Macmillan, 1969.

Broadbent, Michael. *The Great Vintage Wine Book*. New York: Knopf, 1980.

Campbell, Ian Maxwell. *Reminiscences of a Vintner*. London: Chapman and Hall, 1950.

——. *Wayward Tendrils of the Vine*. London: Chapman and Hall, 1948.

Cherrington, Ernest Hurst, ed. *Standard Encyclopedia of the Alcohol Problem*. 6 vols. Westerville, OH: American Issue Publishing, 1925–30.

Coates, Clive. *Grands Vins: The Finest Châteaux of Bordeaux and Their Wines*. Berkeley: University of California Press, 1995.

Dallas, E. S. *Kettner's Book of the Table*. 1877. Reprint, London: Centaur Press, 1968.

Dickens, Cedric. *Drinking with Dickens.* Goring-on-Thames: Elvedon, 1983.

Faith, Nicholas. *The Story of Champagne.* London: Hamish Hamilton, 1988.

Fielden, Christopher. *Is This the Wine You Ordered, Sir?* London: Croom Helm, 1989.

Fletcher, Wyndham. *Port: An Introduction to Its History and Delights.* London: Sotheby, Parke Bernet, 1978.

Forbes, Patrick. *Champagne: The Wine, the Land, and the People.* New York: Reynal and Co., [1967].

Fougner, G. Selmer. *Along the Wine Trail, II: Distilled Liquors.* New York: The Sun, 1934.

Francis, A. D. *The Wine Trade.* New York: Barnes and Noble, 1973.

Gabler, James M. *Passions: The Wines and Travels of Thomas Jefferson.* Baltimore: Bacchus Press, 1995.

———. *Wine into Words: A History and Bibliography of Wine Books in the English Language.* 2nd ed. Baltimore: Bacchus Press, 2004.

Gold, Alec, ed. *Wines and Spirits of the World.* London: Virtue, 1968.

Gourvish, T. R., and R. G. Wilson. *The British Brewing Industry, 1830–1980.* Cambridge: Cambridge University Press, 1994.

Grossman, Harold J. *Grossman's Guide to Wines, Spirits, and Beers.* 5th ed. New York: Scribner's, 1974.

Hallgarten, Peter. *Spirits and Liqueurs.* London: Faber, 1979.

Hannum, Hurst, and Robert S. Blumberg. *Brandies and Liqueurs of the World.* Garden City, NY: Doubleday and Co., 1976.

Hayward, Abraham. *The Art of Dining.* Ed. Charles Sayle. 1836. Reprint, New York: G. P. Putnam's Sons, 1899.

Johnson, Hugh. *Vintage: The Story of Wine.* New York: Simon and Schuster, 1989.

Jones, Dorothy. *King of Critics: George Saintsbury, 1845–1933, Critic, Journalist, Historian, Professor.* Ann Arbor: University of Michigan Press, 1992.

Jullien, André. *Topographie de tous les vignobles connus.* 5th ed. Paris: Librarie d'Agriculture et d'Horticulture, 1866.

Kinross, Lord. *The Kindred Spirit: A History of Gin and of the House of Booth.* London: Newman Neame, 1959.

Leuba, Walter. *George Saintsbury.* New York: Twayne, 1967.

Lichine, Alexis. *Alexis Lichine's Encyclopedia of Wines and Spirits.* 5th ed. 1967. Reprint, New York: Knopf, 1987.

Lockhart, Sir Robert Bruce. *Scotch: The Whisky of Scotland in Fact and Story.* London: Putnam and Co., 1951.

Mayberry, Robert W. *Wines of the Rhone Valley. A Guide to Origins.* Totowa, NJ: Rowman and Littlefield, 1987.

Mendelsohn, Oscar A. *The Dictionary of Drink and Drinking.* New York: Hawthorne Books, 1965.

Mew, James, and John Ashton. *Drinks of the World.* New York: Scribner's, 1892.

OED: The Oxford English Dictionary. 2nd ed. Oxford: Clarendon Press, 1989.

Penning-Rowsell, Edmund. *The Wines of Bordeaux.* London: Michael Joseph, 1969.

Ray, Cyril. *Bollinger: Tradition of a Champagne Family,* 2nd ed. London: Heinemann/Peter Davies, 1982.

———. *In a Glass Lightly.* London: Methuen, 1967.

———. *Lafite.* London: Peter Davies, 1968.

Read, Jan. *Sherry and the Sherry Bodegas.* London: Sotheby's Publications, 1988.

———. *The Wines of Portugal.* Rev. ed. London: Faber and Faber, 1987.

———. *The Wines of Spain and Portugal.* London: Faber and Faber, 1973.

Robinson, Jancis, ed. *The Oxford Companion to Wine.* 2nd ed. Oxford: Oxford University Press, 1999.

Saintsbury, George. *A History of the French Novel.* 2 vols. London: Macmillan, 1917–19.

———. *A Last Scrap Book.* London: Macmillan, 1924.

———. *A Last Vintage: Essays and Papers by George Saintsbury.* London: Methuen, 1950.

———. *Miscellaneous Essays.* New York: Scribner's, 1892.

———. *A Scrap Book.* London: Macmillan, 1922.

———. *A Second Scrap Book.* London: Macmillan, 1923.

Schoonmaker, Frank. *Encyclopedia of Wine.* 6th ed. New York: Hastings House, 1975.

Sellers, Charles. *Oporto Old and New.* London: H. E. Harper, 1899.

Simon, André. *A Concise Encyclopedia of Gastronomy.* London: Collins, 1952.

———. *A Dictionary of Wine.* London: Cassell, 1935.

———. *Notes on the Late J. Pierpont Morgan's Cellar Book, 1906*. London: Curwen Press, privately printed, 1944.

———. *Port*. London: Constable, 1934.

———. *Vintagewise: A Postscript to Saintsbury's Notes on a Cellar-Book*. London: Michael Joseph, 1945.

Spencer, Edward. *The Flowing Bowl*. London: Stanley Paul, 1925.

Thomas, Wynford Vaughan. "The Rise and Fall of Welsh Whisky." *Wine and Food* (Summer 1962): 80–83.

Vizetelly, Henry. *Facts about Champagne*. London: Ward, Lock, and Co., 1879.

Webster, A. Blyth. "A Biographical Memoir." In *George Saintsbury: The Memorial Volume: A New Collection of His Essays and Papers*. London: Methuen and Co., 1945.

Weir, R. B. *The History of the Distillers Company, 1877–1939*. Oxford: Clarendon Press, 1995.

Younger, William. *Gods, Men, and Wine*. Cleveland: World Publishing, 1966.

INDEX

Note: An asterisk * indicates a quotation or direct allusion; an *italic* number indicates an illustration.

TEXT
10/14 Janson
DISPLAY
Janson
COMPOSITOR
Integrated Composition Systems
PRINTER AND BINDER
Maple-Vail Manufacturing Group